Rocky Mountain Horticulture

The Maroon Bells, near Aspen, Colorado, at sunrise

BEAUTY

Beauty is where we find it.
  Sure it may be in sunset glow,
Or it may be in flowers or birds or trees.
  We'll find it wherever we go.

Some see it only in human form,
  In hair or cheek or eye;
While others may find it in shells on a beach,
  Or stars in a cloudless sky.

Some strive to put it on canvas or page,
  Or chisel it out of stone.
Still others will see it in building tall,
  Or churches, or gilded throne.

There's beauty for many in organ or voice,
  Or a baby's laugh of glee
Beauty is where we find it—now—
  In sky, on land or sea.

Beauty is here for everyone,
  We need not hunt afar.
If we will open our eyes and look,
  We'll find it where we are.

We may hunt for it on the mountain top,
  In countries far we may roam;
But if we're not able to travel afar
  We'll find it right around home.

We all need beauty is some form or other,
  If barber or banker or wife.
It's just as important as clothes or bread
  It's part of our very life.

If we can't have orchids or furs or gems
  We may still have beauty galore
By looking around us through microscope,
  In weeds or common ore.

Beauty is where we find it.
  Let's look for it where we go.
And not for the crime and hate and grime.
  There's plenty of that we know.

GEORGE W. KELLY.

George Kelly's New Garden Book . . .

How to Have Good Gardens

in the Sunshine States

❦

A Landscape Architecture to Fit This Area

Plants that Will Thrive under Arid Conditions

Cultural Methods to Keep the Plants Happy

❦

By **GEORGE W. KELLY**

PRUETT PUBLISHING CO.
Boulder, Colorado

ISBN No.: 0-87108-014-1
Copyright 1958 by George W. Kelly
Revised 1967 by George W. Kelly
Printed in U.S.A. by Pruett Press, Inc.

Foreword

GEORGE W. KELLY

THIS book grew as the author grew; it resulted from his desire for down-to-earth knowledge and from his willingness to dig it out from any available source, testing it in hard experience.

It is the first, and so far, the only publication to give the gardener of our Rocky Mountain region solid, dependable information that can be used without having to make allowances for differences in climate, soil and conditions.

It illustrates an old story. Early Americans first depended on Mother England for garden knowledge, finding it inadequate for the new country; then they worked out their own. New England and Virginia then became the source of garden information for the rest of the United States; again modifications were needed. Particularly was there a big gap between the conditions of the arid and mountainous regions of the West and those of previously developed garden regions. This book is new source material for that "new country."

Trite as it may sound, it is most timely; George Kelly is the "natural", almost ordained person to write it.

With his rich background and love for the Great Outdoors, horticulture became both his vocation and his avocation. His practical nursery experience gave him close contact with growing plants in this unusual combination of conditions. His many years as editor of the Green Thumb, official magazine of the Colorado Forestry and Horticulture Association, gave him the opportunity to spread the new knowledge with his zeal and enthusiasm which placed it on a high level among American horticultural publications. His work with the newly established Denver Botanic Garden added to this combination of the practical and the educational.

In recognition for his achievements he was awarded an Honorable Citation by the American Horticultural Council in 1957, "for opening the way to successful gardening in a section of the country where growing conditions are adverse."

In 1955 he was given the Johnny Appleseed award by the Men's Garden Clubs. He is known over the country as horticultural expert for the Rocky Mountain region, the "land in the sun."

George Kelly is a pioneer in horticulture in his field just as much as Liberty Hyde Bailey, Frederick Law Olmsted and others are in their fields. Like them, he is a personality in his own right.

This volume brings together information that some of us have had to garner from many sources, but it is more: it is the tested garden guide for our land in the sun. I could not do without it.

M. WALTER PESMAN
Landscape architect and
author of *"Meet the Natives."*

Contents

Preface to First Book

(Rocky Mountain Horticulture is Different)

We now have hundreds of books and dozens of magazines written on the various phases of horticulture. Why do we need another? Principally because almost all of horticultural literature has been written for the older, more thickly populated parts of the United States, very little of which applies to the peculiar conditions found in the Rocky Mountain and Great Plains States.

Most of the cultivated plants grown in the Rocky Mountain area have been brought here from the East where there is more moisture and other favorable climatic conditions. Our greatest needs are two: learn how to better adjust our existing climatic conditions to the valuable plants that we bring into this country, and to discover and adapt plants which will tolerate Rocky Mountain and Great Plains conditions.

This little book will not attempt to duplicate all the fine things written by horticultural authorities of the East, West or South. It will simply try to supply information applicable to our horticultural conditions which is not given in other books. No attempt is made to make this a complete manual on gardening. Much of the material is written in generalities rather than details. Our aim is to help those gardeners who have come to our area without the knowledge of climatic differences or how to modify older garden practices to conform with the peculiarities of Rocky Mountain horticulture.

The material here contained is largely gleaned from personal experience, Our hope is that the reader will find it useful and it will make ornamental gardening a more profitable and enjoyable avocation.

Acknowledgments

To all those numberless people who have given encouragement, criticism and advise in this revision we are very thankful.

We especially appreciate the consent of the officers and directors of the Colorado Forestry and Horticulture Assn. for permission to use some material which was originally written for the "Green Thumb".

Claude Hansen has designed the cover of this new book.

All information in this book which is printed in the larger (10 pt.) type should be read in full by every gardener in the area.

That information printed in the smaller (8 pt.) type is intended as reference material. The "Contents" page will give you quickly a general idea where to find general information that you need. For specific information turn to the index in the back.

Introduction to Second Book

In 1951 we hastily put together various lists, stories and materials that we had been accumulating for many years and published it under the title of "Rocky Mountain Horticulture is Different". We had waited in vain many years for someone better qualified to publish a book to help the gardeners of the dry western part of the United States. Almost all the existing horticultural books and magazines failed to recognize this area as of sufficient importance horticulturally to warrant any special literature.

This work of assembling and editing was largely done at the insistence and with the help of Don Peach of KOA. Helen Fowler and Mrs. Churchill Owen assisted very materially with financing this venture.

We hope that this rough collection of necessary facts regarding gardening with little rainfall has been helpful to many and has allowed them to avoid much unnecessary work and expense through the elimination of mistaken information from older publications of the east.

We had hoped that this first crude attempt would stimulate some of the real authorities to compile a more complete and better written book, but as this has not happened we are again forced to attempt a revision and addition to the original book. The arrangement of this new book will be some different as we attempt to show "How to Make a Good Garden in the Sunshine States".

The general information and cultural practices given here applies to all that part of the Western United States where the precipitation is low, the winter sun hot and the soil alkaline. The majority of the plant lists apply to that area generally north of the Colorado-New Mexico line, but some lists of material are given for the south-west area. The accompanying map shows the five general divisions of the United States as to plant growth. This takes into consideration not only length of growing season, but these other vital conditions of precipitation and soil. These five general areas might be broken up into several sub-areas in each division, the principal ones being the northern rim which has a shorter season and the southern edge of the states along the gulf of Mexico where the climate is almost tropical. Local variations will be found in all areas depending on elevation, protecting hills, wind currents, soil or other factors, and these should be worked out with local authorities.

THIS THIRD BOOK

Little has been changed in this third edition but the title. Many things have happened since the last edition was written, so it would be a good idea to check with local authorities to learn of the new grasses, roses, insecticides, fungicides and weedicides which have been developed in the last ten years.

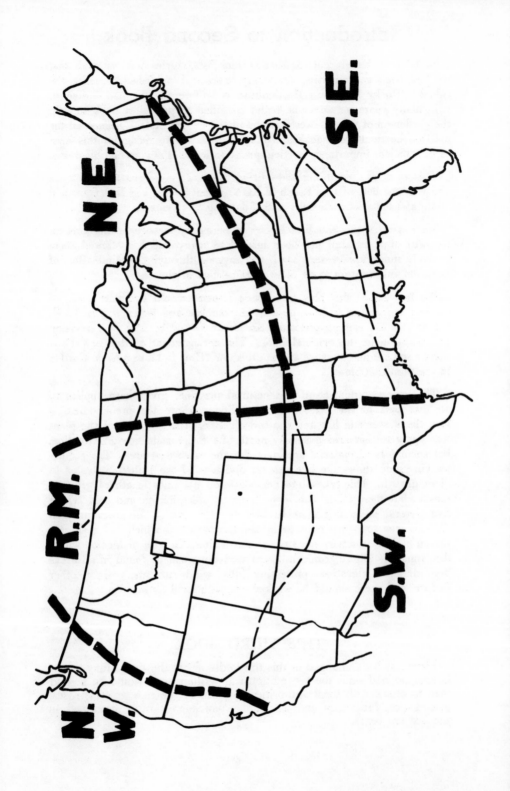

How Rocky Mountain Horticulture
Is Different

(If you read nothing else, study this chapter carefully.)

ONE-THIRD of the United States, including eight Rocky Mountain states and parts of four Great Plains and Pacific Northwest states, are included in this Plant Growth Zone. While this area is rather thinly populated and much of the land is unsuitable for horticultural development, it does include several million people who are rapidly awakening to the desirability of developing their horticultural possibilities. Denver, Colorado, located in the heart of this Plant Growth Zone, probably has the finest lawns of any city in the world, but there have been many disappointments in attempting to grow in the Rocky Mountain country familiar plants of the East. Let us then consider what are the peculiarities of climate which make Rocky Mountain gardening different—difficult though it is—but not impossible.

Most of our problems stem from lack of sufficient precipitation. Much of the area where the larger communities have developed has an average of only eight to fifteen inches annual precipitation. Significant, too, is the fact that much of this precipitation comes at times or in quantities which do not give optimum benefit to the growing plants. With less rain and snow, there are many more sunny days, which creates a dry, arid, atmosphere. It is from this drying effect of the hot winter sun that most of the causes of "winter kill" are derived. Erratic spring and fall weather with its unseasonably mild temperatures for several days and then sudden severe periods of cold, as well as severe changes in temperature between day and night, has a disheartening effect on the plants. It isn't uncommon to have tender growth nipped by freezing weather two or three times during a season.

The generally alkaline condition of the soil is another very important factor to be considered. Restricted rainfall in the Rocky Mountain region isn't sufficient to carry off the excess mineral salts and, because of small rainfall, fewer plants are growing to naturally use up these minerals, including the alkalies. The lack of humus from decaying tops and roots of plants does not provide the acidifying materials found in areas of greater rainfall. Many plants commonly grown in the more moist climates cannot tolerate our alkaline soil. The general lack of humus in our soil also affects the physical, as well as the chemical quality, making it impervious to water and difficult to cultivate.

A great majority of our population is located in the comparatively level areas at the foot of the mountains. Here the season is long enough to grow most common plants and snow from the mountains provides supplementary irrigation water. These are the areas where the soil is still more or less alkaline and the rainfall limited. As we go higher in the mountains, we get more rainfall and the soil becomes acid, but with these improvements, the length of the season becomes rapidly shorter, so that only a few plants can be successfully grown. In a few places at the foot of the mountains, such as the Boulder, Colorado, and the Florence-

11

Canon City, Colorado, areas, the favorable conditions from both the lower and the higher areas meet and, in these conditions, a great variety of plants can be grown.

While this whole western area is set apart, horticulturally, by these general conditions within this area, there is also a great variety of individual peculiarities calling for special solution. Roughly, three divisions can be made: One, the rich and level irrigated areas at the foot of the mountains; two, the high plains areas with level land but very little rainfall; three, the higher mountain areas of greater rainfall but shorter seasons.

Our problem, then, is to recognize these conditions and devise methods of adapting our practices to them. First we will need to revise our ideas on watering. The reason Denver has the finest lawns in the world is that the gardeners do not depend on natural rainfall at all, but plan on regular watering. On the other hand, many of the shade trees are in deplorable condition because the owners do not understand that there is practically no natural subsoil moisture and that they must water the trees thoroughly and deeply. One rule on watering is applicable in a majority of cases: WATER LESS OFTEN AND MORE THOROLY.

We are now learning that many plants, especially shade trees, which we had previously discarded as too tender, may be successfully grown if some protection from the sun and wind is given for a few years, or until they become established. Wrapping, shading with lath or burlap, and wind breaks are devices which will permit many otherwise tender plants to become established. This is demonstrated by the fact that border-line plants will often grow well after plantings of hardier plants have first become established.

We must, in every way possible, supply the humus which our soil lacks naturally. We must learn to cultivate and mulch properly. We need more and more research to introduce and breed plants which will tolerate these difficult conditions.

Because of our restricted rainfall, hot winter sun, and other conditions, including lack of natural controls, the insect pest control program requires special attention. We need much research to develop methods of combating insect, disease and weed pests which have developed in unexpected ways because of our climate. Our landscape architects should lead the way in developing distinctive types of design which will fit our peculiar conditions.

THREE PARTS OF A GOOD GARDEN

"What Makes a Good Garden?" is a good question. When we analyze thousands of good gardens, those that give pleasure and satisfaction to their owners, we find that all the desirable features can be separated into three main divisions: 1. The DESIGN, or *plan*, 2. The proper MATERIALS (plants and inanimate things) used to create the effects called for in the plan, and 3. Proper MAINTENANCE, that care which is necessary to keep these materials in effective use.

These three parts of a good garden will be the three main divisions of this book.

Why Have Gardens?

It is well for us to try to analyze just why we risk sprained backs, blistered hands, and depleted pocketbooks to have gardens. Generations back we all lived more in the open, among the beauties of Nature, under the trees, surrounded with flowers in season, with rocks and water and good brown earth and blue skies. Instinctively we feel a need for these things around us even though we have lived in crowded cities for many generations. Whether we recognize it or not these things bring us closer to the great power behind life from which we all sprang. Though we may try to ignore it we all have a craving for beauty in some form or other, and find it just as important as the more common things necessary for the bare maintenance of life such as food, clothing, heat and housing.

Gardening not only brings us closer to Nature and supplies part of our craving for beauty but it brings us health of mind and body through the fresh air, sunshine and exercise incidental to caring for a garden. After a frustrating day trying to get along with hordes of unreasonable people, nothing calms one more than an hour in the garden, where every plant's growth is governed by laws not made by man—where no plant can be talked into something not good for it by a high-pressure salesman —where none of them talks back to you or argues. If you give your plant charges the proper environment they grow and bloom, if any essentials are missing they do not develop properly, and no talking can make them do otherwise. Those who learn their lessons from the garden are the calmest, wisest, and healthiest of all people.

Plant life is fundamental. There were plants here on earth for a long time before animal life developed, for all animal life and most all energy depends on plant life—on that mysterious manufacture of energy-giving starches and sugars by the action of the sun on the green chlorophlyll in the leaves. Our food comes from plants either directly or after being transformed by being eaten by animals, which we later eat. Much of our clothing and housing material, and energy for power and heat comes from this material that plants have manufactured.

Most people have an instinctive love of plants, and some develop this to such a degree that we say that they have a "green thumb." This is simply an instinct, natural or developed, which lets these persons know when a plant needs water, when it is "happy" and when it is "miserable," when it needs something and when it should be left alone.

Some may get the greatest benefit from studying and enjoying the native flowers and trees, others may enjoy more the cultivation of flowers or vegetables around their homes, and others, lacking these, find great satisfaction in a few plants in their window. In what ever way we associate with them, the living plants of Nature will do us all good and will renew our health and our confidence in the rightness of everything.

These are some of the reasons why we think that it is worthwhile to help people of all ages and circumstances to know and appreciate plant life.

Landscape Planning

PERHAPS you have a new home with a house standing on an area of bare rough ground, or you have an old place which has never been properly planned or has been neglected for many years. You realize that the first step is a carefully worked out plan, but you are not sure how to go about it. Of course, you might go to a professional landscape architect or one of the local nurseymen who maintain a landscape planning service and turn the problem over to him, but for lack of finances (you are always broke when the house is completed) or because you want the fun of personally doing the work, you would like to make your own plan.

Here are given the logical steps which you should take, in properly developing your plan. This procedure would work equally well if you needed to plan the landscape development of a home, a park, a commercial or public grounds.

SURVEY OF NEEDS

First you should make a survey of the things desired in the finished grounds. To accomplish this you must consider the habits and customs of the people (you and your family) who will use these grounds. Do you spend much time at home? Do you entertain much and like to eat out doors? Do you love flowers? Do you like to work outdoors? Do the children or the dog need a playground? Do some members of the family have gardening or outdoor hobbies that should be provided for? Better give this careful thought and put the results down on paper so that you can refer to it later.

The list might include a rose garden, a dog yard, a shady nook with platform where the peas could be shelled and tea served, a pool, a snowball bush, a birch tree, a dry wall and a long border for the iris collection.

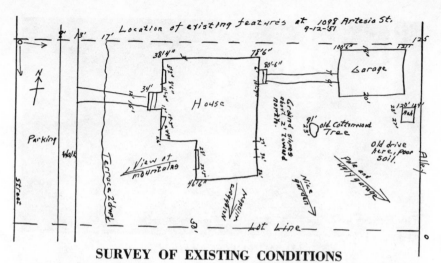

SURVEY OF EXISTING CONDITIONS

The next step would be to make a careful survey of what you have to work with. How big is your lot? What kind of soil do you have? What is the slope of the land? How much of this area will receive too much or not enough sun or wind? What are the immediate surroundings and what are the distant views?

Right here make a plan showing the existing conditions and draw it to scale on paper of some sort. Draw in the house, the boundary lines, any walks, drives, ashpits, phone poles, neighbors' fences or other features that are present and must be worked with or around.

A simple way to get the data necessary for making this first basic plan is to start at one corner with a tape line and measure the length and width of the lot marking the distance from this corner called "0" to the point opposite each feature necessary to include. At 6' you might be opposite the first side of the house, at 10' the first edge of the front porch, at 20' a telephone pole in the parking, at 35' the edge of a terrace and at 50' the lot line. Pick out a scale to use which will allow the greatest dimension of your grounds to fit on the size of paper available. For instance if your lot is 135' overall and your paper is 20" long you could use a scale of 1" equals 8'. This would make your drawing 16⅞" long allowing for margin on a 20" paper. If you can get graph paper the squares will be already marked off and will eliminate some measuring and figuring.

COLOR

Careful planning for color, form and texture will make a satisfying garden. Of these color is the most conspicious feature. Color effects may be obtained by using carefully thought out non-living things such as stone, brick and wood, but by far the most effective combinations are created by the use of appropriate plant materials. Some gardens may be splashes of bright color in the spring but really good gardens are planned to have interesting color effects all the year around. Trees, shrubs, evergreens, perennials, bulbs and annuals can all contribute to this show.

15

DOMINATING THEME

After you have these two sets of facts—what you want and what you have—then you can begin to pare down or fit the first list to the second. Before doing any work on this fitting in of desirable features, it might be well to decide what will be the dominating theme or character of the whole development. Will it be most appropriate to make it ultramodern, naturalistic, formal; or be influenced by some foreign or ancient design? Look around you as you drive home tonight and notice that the most satisfying plantings are those which conform to one scheme throughout with all the parts fitting together in unity. Landscape architecture is an art comparable to others like painting, sculpture, music or architecture, but landscape architects work with living plants and the pictures created are living pictures which must have continual care to remain as originally created. All the basic rules of other forms of art apply here, such as unity, balance, simplicity, scale, lines, proportion, rhythm, texture and color. The best result is obtained when everything is arranged for the greatest amount of beauty at the same time retaining maximum utility.

**These gardens have been designed
for living, keeping in mind one
general theme throughout.**

What It Takes to Make a Good Garden
in the Sunshine States

W E RECOGNIZE that the things that go in to making a good garden
in this area, all may be classified under three general heads: (1.)
Good Design, (2.) Suitable Material and (3.) Proper Maintenance. The
second and third divisions are treated in following sections of this book,
but here we would like to draw attention to the various elements that
contribute to the planning of a good garden. The satisfaction in the final
result depends on the good judgment and "feeling" of the planner, but
this need not always be entirely instinctive; it can be developed by studying the elements that go into making a good garden and then fitting
these various features to the particular problem.

CONTRIBUTING INFLUENCES FROM OUTSIDE

The design of existing gardens has been influenced by the pleasing
features of older gardens, and these satisfactory features are slowly changing with modern ways of living and changes in climate and environment
as pioneers move into new areas. There are two chief sources of most
of our details of garden design: both coming from European areas
where, at one time, there was prosperity and peace for a large enough
length of time to allow great pleasure gardens to be built. These two
original influences might be called the English and the Spanish. The
English with much humidity, their open lawns, walled gardens and shade
trees, and the Spanish with their dry climate, patios, pavements and effective use of water. These basic things have been filtered and modified
through the eastern states, with their colonial gardens, and through California with distinctive areas of indoor-outdoor living. Our Rocky Mountain arid area is the meeting place for these two influences, and our
good garden design will result from taking the best from each of these
sources and modifying it further to more exactly fit our particular conditions of climate, environment and culture. Let us, then, consider some
of the features that go to make up a distinctive Landscape Architecture for
this great Western Arid Area.

CONTRIBUTING INFLUENCES FROM INSIDE

IT MIGHT be well to review and list the existing influences that tend to modify these imported traditions of design. First of all, the thing that sets this area apart from all other sections of our country, is the small amount of precipitation which we receive. This results in little subsoil moisture; in very low humidity of the air, which is especially damaging to woody plants in winter; in clear skies with hot sun in day time most of the year; in cool nights in summer and occasional low temperatures in winter; in unpredictable and unseasonable periods of weather, especially in spring and fall; and a generally alkaline soil. Then, there are the bigness, ruggedness and freshness of our dominating mountains which automatically influence our actions here. The rocks of the mountains, the evergreens covering their slopes and everywhere the inspiring views, tend to influence garden design. We probably have more days, here, when it is pleasant to be out-of-doors than there are in California.

We must learn to select the best and most appropriate from all of these influences and not blindly copy those things that may be good in other areas.

Cactus—beauty from the desert.

The Magnolia that "Just don't grow here."

Primitive Nature sculptures many interesting forms. The "bear" from soft sandstone and "penguin" from wood.

On every hand we see the milling crowds that rave about old art, or modernistic art, or antiques, or some political theory, or some mode of dressing, or garden design—not because it is beautiful or practical, but simply because "everybody is doing it." How many play bridge or golf or smoke or take a drink or go to the opera because they really like it? Too many just do these things or others like this just because it is easier to follow the crowd. The world surely needs more independent thinkers.

19

Colorful Wildflowers

Rugged Timberline

Weather Sculptured Wood

Water, Sky and Bright Foliage

Ancient Eroded Rocks

Mountain Lakes

Natural features that influence landscape design in the Sunshine States.

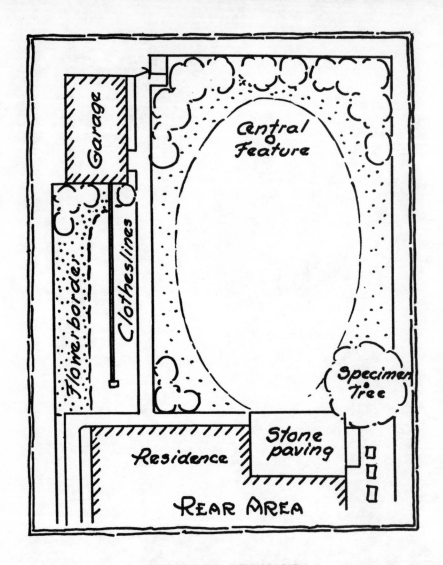

PRINCIPAL DIVISIONS

The next move after the general idea of the development has been determined will be to roughly lay out the grounds into the principal divisions as to their use. In most cases there will be three—the public area, that between the street and the house, once called the "front yard"; the service area, including drives, clothes yards, ashpits and such; and the garden area, which may be developed to suit the requirements and pleasure of the family. In the more modern designing of homes, there is increasingly more attention paid to arranging the rooms of the house and the outdoor "rooms" to fit together as to their uses; that is, the service area and entrances adjoining the kitchen and the garden area easily entered from the living rooms. In many modern developments the "front" room and "front" yard are not adjoining the street at all, but face the most desirable view. Likewise, the "front" and "back" doors may

22

both be on the same side of the house, adjoining the street, leaving undisturbed a larger garden area on the opposite side.

When these principal areas have been roughed in, the next move would be to locate the drives, walks and definite outline of areas. This would immediately give an idea of the restrictions and boundaries of spaces available and enable you to proceed with rather definite plans for the various features wanted.

A CHECK LIST OF MAIN LANDSCAPE FEATURES

Consider:

SHADE—For the house, on the southwest, for the garden area.
With trees, shrubs, vines and lattice.

BACKGROUND—Behind the house and garden.
With trees, tall shrubs and trellises.

FOREGROUND—In front of the house, in the center of the garden.
With lawns, gravel, walks, ground covers, water.

FRAME VIEWS—In and out, mountains, parks, other good gardens.
With trees, tall shrubs, evergreens.

HIDE OBJECTIONABLE VIEWS—Ash pits, weed patches, ugly buildings.
With screens of shrubs, vines on fences, trellises, hedges.

SOFTEN SEVERE LINES—Of foundation, property lines, drives.
With foundation plantings, shrub and flower borders.

ADD BEAUTY—All around the house and grounds.
With trees, shrubs, perennials, annuals, bulbs, furniture.

UTILITY—Of walks, drives, clothes lines, incinerators.
Efficiently arranged and screened from garden.

YEAR-ROUND COLOR—In trees, shrubs and evergreens.
By colored bark, fall color, berries.

WINDBREAKS—Usually on northwest.
With evergreens, tall trees, hedges, shrubs, fences.

ATTRACTING BIRDS—For their beauty, interest and control of insects.
With shrubs and trees, having edible berries, and shelters.

MARKING BOUNDARIES—Of property or garden and service areas.
With hedges, fences, shrub borders.

SECLUSION—In pleasure garden and by windows.
With shrub screens, lattice, vines and fences.

HOBBIES—For every member of the family.
With specialty gardens, pools, rockeries, seats, shelters, platforms.

Recommended Reading:

GARDENS ARE FOR PEOPLE, Thos. D. Church, Pub. by Reinhold.

LANDSCAPING YOUR OWN HOME, Alice L. Dustan, Pub. by Macmillan Co.

LANDSCAPE FOR LIVING, Garrett Eckbo, Pub. by F. W. Dodge Corp.

READING THE LANDSCAPE, May Theilgaard Watts, Pub. by Macmillan.

How Do I Start?

13 GARDEN STEPS

LET'S suppose that you are moving into a new home in November, and that nothing has been done to the grounds around the house since the builders left. Let's plan together what we would do to get the landscaping started. Here are 13 logical steps that can be taken between November and the next June.

1. Since all your garden success for the next 20 years or so depends very largely on the quality of the soil that it is planted in, let's see first what kind of soil has been left for us to begin with. I would first of all, take a shovel and "prospect" all over the place, at least every 10 feet, and see what is found. I would dig down a foot at least, and in a few typical places I would dig two or three feet deep and see what kind of subsoil was present. If there were spots where dirt had been filled in or other places where it had been scraped off I would make a note of that. If I found buried rubbish, especially plaster and cement, I would remove it entirely, even though it might run deep into my garden budget. If necessary I would replace poor soil removed with good top soil. (Where to get it is your problem.)

2. Next I would do (or have done) the rough grading, getting the level down to within a couple of inches of the final grade wanted. I would consider making a slope away from the house of at least 1 inch in 3 feet or a little more if possible. I would plan to eliminate steep slopes where it would be difficult to start or mow a lawn. I would take advantage of any natural changes in grade to establish terraces, sunken gardens or raised areas which might add character to the garden. A carpenter's or surveyor's level might have to be borrowed to work out accurate grades.

3. Then I would do the most important thing in all gardening. I would work humus into the soil. I would, if at all possible, spread about an inch or two of manure, compost, mixture of peat and manure or some such material on the surface and rototill or disk it in thoroughly. This would probably go 4 to 6 inches. Then I would turn this under with spade or plow, which should put it down about 8 inches or more. Then I would put on another dressing of humus and disk or rototill that in thoroughly. This would give a bed of loose, rich soil deep enough to give all plants a good start, at least. I would leave the surface a little rough over winter so that any rain or snow would be caught and soak in. If no moisture came soon I would slowly

and carefully soak, so that the soil was wet to a foot or more deep. The above could be done in the fair days until the ground froze up for winter.

4. During the stormy days I would begin to plan the general features that I wanted in a garden and home grounds. Unless your memory is better than mine it would be well to put these ideas on paper. Decide what use you want to make of your grounds. Do you have room for a playground for the kids, a dog yard, a rock garden, a pool, a platform to sit on while shelling the peas and distributing gossip? I would, especially at this stage, plan where the necessary service features such as walks, drives, fences, garages, incinerators or steps would have to go. Much of the further planning would depend on the location of these necessary service features.

5. Next I would plan, at least roughly, where the shrub plantings would go; such things as shrub screens, foundation plantings, hedges. I would take a tape measure and garden hose and lay out the outlines of these plantings. I would put in a few stakes that would last until spring or scratch rather deep lines with the shovel so that these areas would not have to be laid out again.

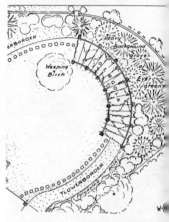

6. I would carefully locate the necessary trees, considering each thoughtfuly, carefully as to its purpose, its ultimate size and character, and its hardiness. I would put in stakes where I thought these should go, and as I lived with them over winter I would try to imagine that they were really trees of the sort needed and then I would move the stakes a little one way or another to make the location of the ultimate tree most effective. It is much easier to move a tree on paper than to actually move it after it is well established. I would consider their location for the benefit of their shade over the house (this would be largely on the southwest corner), for their framing (at the front corners), and their background effect (in the rear of the house). I would consider the possible need for shade over a platform or playground in the rear. I would consider their ultimate size in relation to existing overhead wires, buildings or other trees. I would plant no more trees of any kind than there was a real need for.

25

7. With the shrub borders, trees and fences located I would see if I could still get any of the fall bulbs and plant them in place in front of the ultimate shrub borders or in relation to the other final features, I would move in any of the perennials that were needed and that could still be obtained. Most of the perennials should be rather well dormant by this time and could be moved in, with a shovel of dirt around their roots if possible.

8. If the weather continues open I would attempt to move in a few of the hardier shrubs. Lilacs and some other of the hardy shrubs move well in fall if they are thoroughly dormant (have dropped their leaves), are handled carefully and promptly, watered in thoroughly and carefully thinned or cut back. If my nurseryman wanted to assume the risk of winter damage I would move in many more things.

9. By this time it would be getting into winter and I would spend any fair days that happened along in constructing the inanimate features such as fences, walls, walks, gates, platforms, clothes lines and steps. These should be carefully planned in advance so that they would fit in the area allowed for them.

10. Between the time of open fall weather and the thaws of spring I would study garden books, visit good gardens, nurseries and parks, talk to good gardeners and then plan the balance of my grounds in detail. I would make a list of plants and other materials needed and I would put this all down on paper, preferably on a plan of the place drawn up to scale. I would place definite orders for any nursery stock needed, dealing, wherever possible, with established firms who could advise me from experience (in this area) what are suitable plants to use.

11.   When the frost was out of the ground (which might be any time from Feb. 1 to Mar. 30) the real fun would begin. I would plant the balance of the things I needed as fast as I could work the soil. (There are a few things like Birch trees and some of the slow growing woody plants that should wait until May.) Whenever I could get plants dug freshly from the soil I would see to it that they were dug carefully with lots of roots, and I would make every effort to get them back into the soil promptly with no chance of the sun or wind drying their roots.

12.   At this stage I would consider doing the thing that possibly most new home owners would want to start with—I would put in the necessary lawn areas. The soil should be well enough settled by now so that I need only till the top few inches to get enough loose soil to rake down for a good seed bed. This would eliminate the necessity of using a heavy roller at any time and make the lawn much easier to water and give the new grass a good start. I would fiinish the seeding with a light top dressing of humus and water carefully.

13.   By this time it might be getting along about the season when it is safe to plant the annuals (June 1) and I would fill in between all the shrubs and perennials with selected annuals to give a first year effect. Then would begin the summer's routine of water-weed-spray which is another story.

I may prefer to spend my evenings working in my garden, while my neighbor plays pool. I may climb mountains in week-ends while others play golf. I may enjoy corned beef while others must have their cocktails. I may like to get up early and and go to bed early while others put off both things as long as they can. Who can say that one set of habits is better than the other.

You May Modify Your Climate

MANY of us enjoy going up into the mountains or out on the barren desert and learning to make ourselves comfortable with the extremes of heat, cold, wind and weather as we find it. This is a real challenge, and we may make a game of it and learn to enjoy beating raw Nature at her own game.

Around our own homes, we prefer to modify these extremes of climate, so that we are as comfortable as possible. While we think that the climate is naturally more pleasant in this area than in many of the older sections, still we find that by taking steps to ameliorate some of the extremes, we can have still more pleasant living. Our special problems may include hot sun, low humidity, wind, dust, noise, traffic and abrupt changes in weather.

Because our climate is "Different" one of the first things to consider in planning a good garden is to include ways to enjoy the nice features of our climate and then, so modify the less agreeable things that our outdoor living is made more pleasant.

Some of the desirable modifications may be obtained by careful planning in the construction of our houses, considering ventilation, insulation, reflection and shading, but much more can be done by proper planning of the landscaping around our homes. It is very important to have a plan carefully worked out in advance to take advantage of the modifying influence of shade trees, shrubs, hedges, vines, walls or lattice.

Most people recognize the importance of trees for the shade which they cast on our houses and grounds in summer, but not everyone appreciates the fact that all trees must be planted for a particular effect, and that it may be just as bad to have too many trees or improperly placed trees as to not have them where they are needed. Each tree should be selected to perform a specific job and should be of a variety that will grow to the size and shape necessary to give the maximum benefit.

Vines and tall shrubs also may be planted to shade certain walls of the house or important spots in the garden. The shade of pergolas, lath houses or fences may subdue the sunlight in some places where growing plants might not be suitable. Platforms may be planned which will store heat and make an area comfortable, when wanted in winter, and adjoining trees or lattice might keep the same area pleasantly cool in summer.

The gardens here shown all show good planning for shade when and where needed , with sun coming through when warmth is wanted.

While most of our states are not subject to severe or unpleasant winds, some areas on the open plains and in mountain country do need protection. We can do much to break the cold winds in winter and encourage cool breezes in summer by properly located windbreaks and lanes of trees or shrubs to direct the breezes where they are wanted. A study of the prevailing direction of the winds at different seasons of the year is necessary.

The average humidity of the air around our homes may be increased by the use of water in some form, such as, in pools, running streams, the sprinklers that water our lawns, or the natural evaporation from trees and lawns. We are fortunate, here, that extremes of heat and cold are not amplified as in areas of greater humidity; in fact, our problem is the reverse—to increase the humidity rather than decrease it.

We should consider the influence of reflected sun. Sometimes, stepping stones replacing solid concrete walks may effectively reduce heat from reflection. Where much of the ground surface in an outdoor living area is pavement, it is especially important to plan shade from deciduous trees to keep the area pleasant over the greatest part of the year.

Light and heat may be encouraged to enter our rooms in winter, when we need it, and be kept out in summer, when it is not wanted, through the carefully planned "solar overhang". Awnings, verandas, patio umbrellas or trees may be arranged to give much the same effect.

In winter, when plants are dormant, it is especially important that lines and proportions have been considered. The outline of a walk, or platform or fountain, when designed by a skillful landscape architect, may be very beautiful, even when partly covered with snow. Satisfying, year-'round gardens don't just happen, they are planned.

Dust, noise and moving traffic can be screened out, to a great degree, by planting hedges of appropriate height and density between our homes and highways or other undesirable features. Of course, walls and fences will do the same thing, but may not be as attractive.

Glass panels can, sometimes, be used to break severe wind and still leave a desirable view, when it happens that both come from the same direction. Glass has been used for many years to protect tender plants, as in a greenhouse. A screen of lath may sometimes give just enough modification to make an area pleasant for human use or growth of some of the nicer plants. Screening out insects may make an outdoor area livable, though now very effective insecticides are available for this purpose.

In addition to making the climate around our homes more agreeable for human use, we often would like to modify the natural climate to accommodate the preferences of desirable imported plants. For these, we may often create "climatic pockets" where sunshine, heat, cold, humidity or other conditions are more to the liking of the plants. For most of the nice plants that we would like to bring in from other areas, this usually indicates a spot on the north or east of our homes. Our severe winter sun is the cause of most "winterkill". Sometimes, similar conditions can be made behind a tree, shrub or fence.

Whenever possible the house should be placed with a corner rather than a side facing the south. This will eliminate the two greatest planting problems around a conventionally placed house: the too-shady north side and the too-hot south side. With this diagonal placing of the house, there will be a little sunshine on every side and not too much on any, thus allowing a much better selection of ornamental plants.

The color of walls, roofs and floors or platforms will often make quite a difference in their temperature. Black or dark colors hold heat and white or light colors reflect it.

The design of homes, in warmer areas such as California or Arizona, has shown a greater and greater tendency towards bringing the indoors and outdoors closer together. In some modern designs, the walls, windows, roofs, doorways and screens have been so designed that it is difficult to tell, exactly, when one is indoors, and when out. Here, we cannot go quite as far in that direction, but we can gain much comfort and pleasure in our own home design by giving more consideration to this idea.

All of these things mentioned are important to the pleasure to be had from one's home and garden. Money is well spent to secure the advice of a competent landscape architect and plantsman in the planning, to incorporate all these desirable features into the plan to fit one's particular needs and circumstances.

The above and two following pictures show the patio and garden of Mr. and Mrs. Frank McLister as planned by Mrs. Persis Owen.

Outdoor Living

OFTEN, the heart of the whole garden design will be a patio of some sort. This will usually be attached to the house and may be most effective if placed on the south side of the house and shaded by a large deciduous tree, so that the sun comes through to warm the area in winter and it is shaded to keep pleasantly cool in summer.

An essential part of this design will be the easy and gradual transition from indoors to outdoors so that it is made convenient to use the outdoor living areas.

There should be provisions for all appropriate civilized activities in the well-planned garden: eating, with fireplaces, barbecues and platforms; resting, with seats, benches and comfortable places to lie down; places arranged where one may sit and read, shell the peas or entertain guests; equipment and space for games for the children and adults; allowances for the various hobbies and vocational projects of the members of the family, such as, growing roses, practicing golf, collecting rocks, raising goldfish or dogs.

The garden or outdoor living room should be designed to have a feeling of enclosure, similar to the rooms in the house. This is done by planning for a ground surface of grass, gravel or pavement, walls of shrubs, vines, masonry, wood or small trees and a partial roof of overhanging trees. This enclosed outdoor area should then have features planned which would entertain, amuse, stimulate and relax the occupants as would a well planned living room.

If suitable lighting is installed, it will extend the hours of usefulness and emphasize the most interesting features.

Scene in the Brooder Garden, showing appropriate use of native flagstone and water

The mountains have been and still are the dominating influence in planning our gardens. They influence our climate, supply us with the necessary water for irrigation and give us our inspiration. Most of our population lives near the foot of the mountains, where there are level areas but it is close to the supply of water.

"FRONT" AND "BACK" YARDS

It would be well to revise our traditional thinking of "front" and "back" yards. If appropriate and necessary, there is no reason why we should not plant and use what was once the useless "front" yard dedicated only to the public and arranged simply to set off the house.

These grounds pictured have no definite "Front" and "back" but have entrances where needed and the balance of the grounds are garden.

VIEWS

Any garden may be made more enjoyable by a careful consideration of the interesting views. The views from the principal windows to the outside should be carefully planned, by screening out distracting or objectionable things, and if it is not possible to have a good distant view, to make an attractive close-up feature which is worth seeing. Meaningless "picture windows" which look out only on the neighbor's ashpit are poor design.

Views into the house and garden from all sides are equally important. From the front or street side, it is important to have the 45 degree angle from each side and the straight front view carefully considered, so that it is open where needed and framed by trees or screened by shrubs to draw attention to the entrance or any other attractive feature of the house. While the pleasure of a garden may depend a great deal on its privacy, still good distant views should not be unnecessarily blocked out.

A SETTING FOR THE HOUSE

Much of the landscape planning in the past has been concerned chiefly, with developing a suitable setting for the house by foreground lawns, background trees and "foundation" plantings of shrubs and flowers. This procedure was developed at the time that many architects did not seriously consider the appearance of a house from the outside, and left ugly concrete foundations and drab, blank walls, which, it became the landscape architect's job to hide or beautify. Considering setting for a house is still an important item, but not as essential with the lower foundationless houses as it once was, for the modern well-designed house does not have to be hidden by shrubbery, but simply needs a carrying out of the good design of the house in the plant material surrounding it.

One reason that we like to work with horses and dogs is that they are not civilized enough to be dishonest. If they like you they show it and if they don't like you, you are likely to be bitten or kicked.

Brick and flagstone.   *Gravel*

GROUND PATTERNS

Planned ground patterns may make a garden interesting at all seasons of the year. ALL level or open areas need not be in a mowed lawn, but we may learn from the Spanish to include appropriate areas of gravel, pavements, ground cover plants or water areas.

Bluegrass lawns should be planned primarily to walk or sit on and areas where this is not practical or desirable may often be just as effective and easier to maintain when covered with other materials. Some of the common mat-forming weeds which worry the overly neat gardener may often make just as effective and useful ground cover as the perfect bluegrass lawn, which takes too large a proportion of the owner's time to properly maintain.

Some of these other materials may serve as effectively for foreground effects, be much easier of maintenance and, if carefully done, actually add much interest, especially in winter when plants are dormant. A carefully worked out proportion of lawn and other ground covers can be most effective, for often, it is just as wrong to plan all lawn as to have no lawn at all. Lawn areas do help to modify our overly dry atmosphere and as such should not be ignored.

Water   *Kinnikinnick*

Changes in elevation even of a few inches will give interest to an otherwise mediocre area. Walls, steps, planters, terraces or rock gardens, if planned to fit the general theme, will often add much to the attractiveness of a garden.

PROPER USE OF TREES

Trees may be the first thing considered by the average homeowner when thinking of landscaping a new home, and this is good, for they are the backbone of the whole planting plan. The common mistake is to assume that because trees are desirable, any kind of tree planted in any place is good. A tree out of place may be just as bad as no tree at all. Each tree should be planted for a specific effect on the house or grounds, and when these needs are satisfied, it is well to plant no more trees. This gives a crowded, too-shady effect.

The meaningless, crowded and jumbled "parking" plantings should be a thing of the past, for they complemented neither the street nor the residences. Each effect needs to be carefully planned and appropriately planted.

The native Aspen (above) and Goldenraintree (below) are good small trees for the right place.

When settlers first came to this area, they brought some of the familiar trees from their old homes and planted them here. Many did not grow or thrive, so soon only the hardiest were used. Now, we are learning how to treat the better trees, and find that most of them make good specimens. They will continue to become more attractive with the years rather than deteriorate quickly as do the fast-growing ones. To fit the new, low houses and the modern street layout, we are also learning to plant more of the small scale trees, which will not become overgrown, so soon. Flowering trees are increasing in favor.

Oaks can be grown here if given extra care.

Cane Cactus

Chokecherry

USE ADAPTED MATERIAL

We must learn to plant more of the materials, both living and inanimate which are better adapted to use here. We have, up to now, practically ignored the plants that grew here naturally, and have became adapted to our peculiarities of climate. Our list of ornamental plants is still 90 per cent those that we have used in other areas of a very different climate. We are just learning to select not only the appropriate natives, but to use plants from other arid areas of the earth.

We may effectively use many more of the natural inanimate materials, such as rocks, and massive timbers to match the feeling in the mountains. We can use water in ways copied after the natural effects in the mountains, but reduced in scale and "civilized" to fit our small garden areas.

We may learn to plant more suitable areas in the native grasses, which may be a little coarser than the bluegrass but require only a fraction of the time, in water or mowing, as do the more conventional lawns.

Flowering Currant

Wild Plum

BEAUTY EVERYWHERE

With all the various details to be considered in planning for the ornamentation and use of grounds, we should not forget that one of the prime considerations is still beauty, and we must always keep in mind the proper use of the green foliage of plants, large and small, and the effects to be had from flowers, not only in their masses of color, but in their perfume and texture. We need to so plan this use of growing plants that it will be effective from the first crocus of spring to the last red leaf of fall. We need to consider special locations, such as the shady north side and the overly hot south side, so that no spots are left bare and ugly.

BALANCED PLANTINGS

A proper balance in our plantings will add much to their beauty and effectiveness. This balance should be seen in the right proportion of evergreens to deciduous plants. Seldom are all evergreen or all deciduous plantings fully effective.

The proper balance may be worked out in the planning for trees, shrubs, perennials, annuals, vines and bulbs, and for the effect of plants, at all seasons. Year 'round beauty and interest may be had from the early bulbs, the plants with gray or red foliage in summer, plants with good fall color or bright, persistent berries, or colored winter twigs, as well as the usual green foliage and flowers.

A good place to plan a proper balance is also in the proportion of plants of known hardiness and those of questionable ability to withstand our climate.

It is also well to plan for a proper balance between the plant material and the inanimate or architectural features.

To some this balance in all things may be instinctive, but it may be cultivated by anyone.

ARCHITECTURAL FEATURES

The architectural features of a garden may add much to its general effectiveness. These things may include garden houses or shelters, pergolas, fences, gates, fountains, walls and planters. These permanent, inanimate things, if suitably designed, may help to tie the house to the garden.

GARDEN FURNISHINGS

Garden furniture or furnishings might be distinguished from the architectural features by being movable rather than constructed in a fixed spot. Included might be chairs, benches, tables, portable barbecues, statuary, sundials and gazing globes, with many other articles which might be useful in an "outdoor living room."

GOOD DESIGN

In the individual designing of these features and in their association with each other it should be constantly kept in mind that there should be definite rules for their proportion, scale, texture, lines, masses, colors and balance. These are some of the things that make a planting satisfying if they are properly considered. The same features may be arranged in the same yard so that they all contribute to a satisfying picture or they may be just so many independent features like canned goods on a store shelf.

✦ ✦ ✦

Above and on the following pages are illustrations of well designed home grounds in six drawings by Nancy Sotoodeh. The first two are of the garden of Dr. & Mrs. Edward J. Swets, 1420 E. Cornell, and the following four are of the new home of Mr. & Mrs. J. V. Petersen at 909 Ridge Road. In these we see the satisfying development of a small intimate garden with practically no outside view and the development in the real Rocky Mountain feeling of the grounds on a steep hill with a wonderful view. These grounds have been carefully designed to fit the situation and have made practical application of all the principles of good design.

The Art in Landscape Architecture

LANDSCAPE architecture is a combination of beauty and utility. Some contend that, if something is designed for utility, it is automatically beautiful. We do not agree with this theory, but still strive to combine the greatest amount of beauty with the maximum utility for the greatest satisfaction.

The same principles apply to the creating of beauty in landscapes as in any other of the arts, such as painting, sculpture, music or architecture. It is true that many beautiful things are created with no conscious knowledge of the principles of art by the creator. This seems to be done by instinct, but it is well for most people to know what are the basic principles of good art.

The Petes
909 Ridge Road

BALANCE is one of the first considerations, but this does not need to be symmetrical balance, where each side is exactly like the other. A symmetrical balance may be had by different objects and effects, if the final feeling is pleasant. A small, bright or very interesting spot may easily balance a large simple mass. We instinctively get our feeling for balance from Nature all around us, for a man or a tree falls over when it is not balanced.

Symmetry, repetition, rhythm, simplicity, interest, harmony and other principles may all be considered (possibly unconsciously) in designing the grounds around a home or business.

UNITY is another thing that should be thought of in all plans. Do the various parts of the plan fit together, and is there one dominating idea or motiff throughout, rather than a conglomeration of unrelated ideas and materials? SUITABILITY might be another consideration. Does the design and plan fit the people who are going to use and enjoy it? Are all members of the family (and pets) considered?

In considering the use of these principles of art in our landscape designs, we will be dealing largely with masses, textures and colors.

We are gradually getting away from the ancient idea that all design must be either formal (man-made) or informal (made by Nature). We are learning that some of both ideas may be used if it is appropriate and fits the needs of owners.

Garrett Eckbo in his excellent book, "Landscape for Living" says, "We don't solve the practical problems first and then beautify them; we develop beautiful solutions for the practical problems." In other words, we should not first build the house, install the drives and fences and then try to cover up the architectural mistakes by plantings, but plan all these necessities to be complete units, as beautiful as possible, without reducing their usefulness. Mr. Eckbo also argues that it is not necessary to destroy all of Nature's beauty to create ugly cities to live in, but that we may plan our homes and businesses so that they lose none of their efficiency and still retain satisfying beauty.

*Appropriate use of native stone and naturally finished wood at
the Cottonwood Garden Shop, Littleton, Colorado.*

Much of landscape design is in creating pictures, pictures with living material rather than paints or ink, pictures that are not static but ever-changing and requiring frequent redoing, pictures made of the necessary utilities even, but beautiful pictures just the same.

Again, we must always keep in mind that Landscape Architecture is the art of designing grounds for human use AND enjoyment, including the greatest amount of beauty possible and still retaining the maximum utility.

MATERIALS TO USE

Up to now you have been concerned with effects wanted. Now, you should begin to consider more the materials to create these effects. The trees, ever-greens, shrubs, perennials, annuals, bulbs, grasses, and articles of stone, wood and metal.

Some trees are the backbone of any planting, so consider them first. Their first use might be for shade—shade for the house from the heat of the sun in the southwest and shade for the recreation area in the garden. Then, there should be considered the importance of properly located trees, to

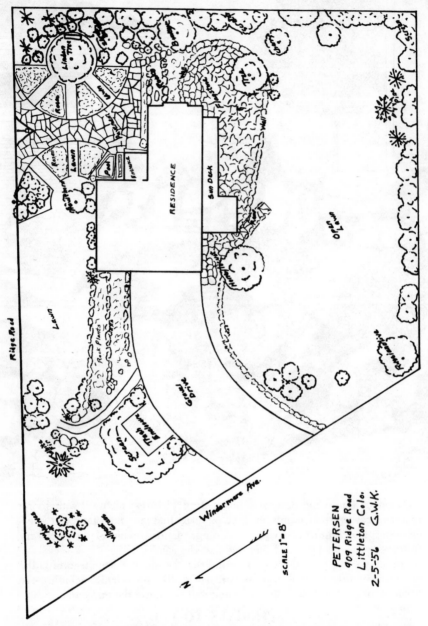

give background to the house and grounds, and trees to frame it from the important (approach) view.

If trees are the backbone of a planting then shrubs would be the flesh and muscle. Their uses are many and varied. The first consideration might be their use as screens for objectionable views—the alley, the neighbor's clothesline or kitchen window, the vacant lot next door or your own ashpit. Then, they might be used to mark boundaries of areas, to soften severe architectural lines, especially as a foundation planting. They might be used to secure seclusion for certain parts of the garden or to supply fruit for the birds or just for their own beauty of flowers, fruit or leaf.

Then the perennials, annuals and bulbs would put the covering skin on the whole picture and supply many of the finishing touches of beauty. The lawn would supply the foreground carpet or a background for flower beds and other small features.

Special forms of plants should be considered for appropriate places—hedges, espalier trees, tall slim trees, vines or ground covers. The inanimate materials should be considered for their part in the whole picture—stone for walls, platforms, rockeries, walks, steps and fireplaces, and brick for these same uses or the construction of garden house or pergola. There might be many places where wood would be used—for fences, gates, trellises, seats or screens. Water might be used to create reflection pools, lily and fish pools, fountains and naturalistic streamways. Beds of specialized plants such as roses, iris, cacti or tulips might fit in the general scheme. Gardens may be judged roughly for the excellence of three qualities—the design, the materials used to carry out this design and the later maintenance. If the plan calls for a tall slim tree to screen a phone pole, then the tree which most nearly does this and fills other requirements of size, color, life, health and beauty should be selected. If a wall is needed it should be determined whether brick, wood, stone or metal would fit best in the design, be most economical and provide the greatest beauty. The kind of lawn grass should be selected which would best tolerate the particular amount of use, water and sunshine that it would be likely to receive. If a low shrub is appropriate for growing under a window, the kind should be chosen which will most nearly grow to the required size. Here is where you must either learn the habits of plants and qualities of other materials or depend on some dealer to advise you. To help you select the right plant for each situation, you will find in section II of this book lists of all kinds of plants for every possible use.

LANDSCAPING DOESN'T COST—IT PAYS

It seems that when a new house is built, we, the proud owners, are always broke. There are always those unexpected costs. Thus, the lady of the house must wheedle us out of a few dollars to fix up the yard. Of course, we like to have nice trees and flowers and lawns around our homes. But there are those who consider this just an extra expense, perhaps just to please the women folks.

Most property deteriorates with age, but properly selected plants increase in value as they grow older.

In a recent survey, ninety-nine per cent of the real estate men in an eastern community reported that landscaping increased the value of property an average of thirteen per cent. This would indicate that landscaping has more than aesthetic value; that it pays in actual cash value. Perhaps time and money spent for good landscaping will increase the value of your property more than any other single thing.

THE PLAN ON PAPER

With all the little details pretty well worked out in your mind it is time to begin to put them down on paper.

THERE is no magic in the beautiful landscape plan which a professional Landscape Architect delivers to his client. It is simply the good ideas of a man who is experienced in landscape design and materials, put down on paper so that anyone may properly execute it.

The real plan is that which is in the head of the planner, and if this same person carried out his ideas at once, no drawing might be needed on paper. Because this is seldom the case, it is well for most home owners to have a plan and to consider the reasons for making it.

One reason for an accurate plan, on paper, is, that it is not often that all parts of a design can be carried out at one time, and so, it is necessary to have a detailed plan, so that all parts will properly fit together when they are all completed. Another reason is to enable some one, other than the planner, to carry out parts or all of the work so that the ultimate results are achieved. Each individual section of the grounds to be planned might be designed properly from one viewpoint, but the only way that ALL the parts can be visualized at once and their proper relation to each other be seen, is on a flat plan that has no corners to see around. Unity in a design requires a plan so that all parts can be compared and fitted together. Finally, a plan, accurately drawn, may prove valuable in later years when renewals or repairs may be necessary. The plan gives permanence to the plantings.

HOW TO MAKE A LANDSCAPE PLAN

While the creating of a landscape plan in one's head requires considerable knowledge of design, plants and other materials, its execution on paper is largely a modified mechanical drawing job. Plans may be very elaborately drawn and colored or they may be very simply done, but there are a few essentials which it is necessary to consider if any style of plan is to be useful.

Every finished plan should show at least these six things: 1. Name of the owner. 2. Location of the property. 3. Date. 4. Compass directions. 5. Scale of the map. 6. Name of the one making the map.

Measurements and details of drawings need not be as absolutely accurate as those of an architectural drawing, as the sizes of plants vary considerably, but, in general, details should be accurate within a foot. If distances

---

GOOD LANDSCAPE DESIGN

Anyone may plant quantities of bright flowers around his home and make a big display in the summer. When the flowers are gone, however, there comes a time when good planning and design must have been used if the satisfying effect is maintained. We must live in our homes twelve months out of the year and with careful planning there is no reason why a garden cannot be beautiful and interesting the year around.

are measured with a tape, they may be recorded right down to the inch, but for a simple plan, often accurately paced distances will be close enough to carry out the ideas wanted.

The first procedure in making a plan would be to locate all existing features, boundary lines, and existing or proposed buildings. Next, would be the compiling of the list of desirable features to be located on the grounds, and finally, there would be the fitting together on the plan of the needed features that the limits of the grounds would permit.

A drawing board or table where the drawing paper may be fastened down with thumb tacks makes the further drawing operations much simpler. With this arrangement, a T-square and triangle will allow the making of accurate parallel and right angle lines. Simple arithmetic will allow one to figure what scale to use to allow the extreme dimensions of the plat to be drawn on the size of paper available. Many landscape plans are drawn up at the scale of 1 inch equals 4 feet, or one inch equals 8 feet. A draftsman's scale rule will save a lot of mental arithmetic. Pencil may be used for preliminary drawing, for there may be many erasures before you are finally satisfied with it. You will find that a tree, improperly placed is much easier to move on paper than on the ground (and that gives another good reason for making the plan, first, on paper). After all details are located to the best of your ability, you will probably want to ink in the final drawing or fasten a piece of transparent paper over it and draw up neatly just the final and approved parts of the plan.

Symbols used to represent trees, shrubs, hedges, fences or other features may vary with each individual landscape architect. Look at some plan that you like and follow those symbols. Blue prints or B&W (black and white) prints may be made of the final drawing, if it is made on tracing paper or tracing cloth, then these prints may be used by various sub-contractors with no damage to the original drawing.

To make a good landscape architect, might require a lifetime of study and experience, so we will not attempt to do that here, but just give enough pointers so that anyone can know what it is all about.

In planning we attempt to bring out the reasons why we do certain things, while in the balance of this book we attempt to tell HOW to do the things necessary to have a good garden.

MINIATURE GARDENS

You do not need a plot of ground to be able to enjoy growing and creating beautiful effects with plants. Some people have tiny gardens maintained with loving care in a teacup, a dish, or a fish bowl. On a scale that can be handled in small apartments, they can give much of the joy of working with plants. To be sure, there is a definite technique in making these little gardens. The plants grown must be those which will survive under difficult conditions. Especially adaptable are the succulents like cactus.

Truly, there is much benefit in handling living plants of any size, from the largest to the tiniest. And so it is in Nature that there is interesting life in a drop of water or a pinch of soil, as well as in the vast expanse of the sky.

THE PLAN ON THE GROUND

Now you are ready to order the necessary materials and begin to put them into place when the proper season arrives. This can be a very interesting job. Before starting the actual planting or construction you should lay out the location of all necessary features on the ground to correspond with the specifications on the plan. Here you may use named and numbered stakes, outlines scratched on the soil or, if necessary, grade stakes. Some minor adjustments may be made at this time, but it is best to stick rather close to the accepted and previously worked out plan. As most contractors leave the grounds about a new building rather rough you should carefully work out grades and level the soil where needed, then prospect to discover any unsuitable soil, or litter. The soil should be improved by the addition of some form of humus or fertilizer and carefully cultivated before anything is planted. Remember that a penny saved here may cost you many dollars in later work, fertilizer and poor growth of plants, for most grounds will not be disturbed, except for the surface, for many years to come.

PLANTING AND CONSTRUCTION

Now you are ready to plant and this is a subject worthy of a separate story which will be found later. Much of the effectiveness of the whole plan depends on getting the plants back into the ground in good healthy condition so that they may immediately begin to grow vigorously.

WEEDS

To every real gardener a weed is simply "a plant out of place." The same plant which may be a garden pest when it crowds out our vegetables and flowers may be very beautiful and desirable in another place. Plants like the sweet clover which for generations was considered a weed may suddenly develop into a valuable crop when its full potentialities are recognized. Some of the native grasses are very beautiful along the roadside and vacant lots, though they are considered quite troublesome in lawns and gardens. The common sunflower is often called a weed, but it is a bright and cheerful thing in vacant places. A species of dock (Rumex) has been introduced along some of our railroad embankments where it grows quite happily under conditions which would support few other plants, and performs a useful purpose. In still other places, the beautiful blue spiderwort, despised in the gardens and lawns, grows in masses along the roads. In our parks and mountains, we enjoy many flowers and trees which, by name and in our gardens, are considered weeds.

Even plants which do not have all of the desirable properties and may be dry and unsightly at some season cover the barren ground with a carpet of green and are to be much appreciated at certain times of the year. These wild green things seemingly try their best to cover up the ugliness which we humans carelessly leave.

Yes, weeds are not always pests. Let's also look for their beauty. They, like the poor, are always with us; so we had just as well learn to love them.

Landscape Materials

Plants to Fit the Climate

DESIGN of a good garden in Boston or Santa Fe may be surprisingly similar, since the principles of good arrangement apply the world over. However, the plants and other materials necessary to properly carry out these arrangements may vary considerably because of climate. Our greatest need at the present time is the correct information on plants suitable for growing in the Rocky Mountain area to create the effects indicated on any good garden plan.

It should be kept in mind that in the Rocky Mountain area three general classes of conditions can be found: namely, the dry, windy, alkaline conditions of the plains; the short season, cold conditions of the mountains; and the alkaline conditions of the irrigated areas. In the lists of plants that follow we will indicate plants which are especially adapted to each of these special conditions.

Perennial flowers and bulbs are generally less affected by our difficult climate than many other kinds of plants for the obvious reason that they die to the ground every winter. Thus, their limitations are largely a matter of short season, drought, alkaline soil and difficulty of propagation.

It is in the list of woody plants such as trees, evergreens, shrubs and vines that our chief adjustment to climatic conditions must be made. Woody plants may suffer from alkaline soil, erratic spring and fall weather and low temperatures. However, their chief damage comes from the hot sun and dry air common here during the winter. It should be noted that most of these fine woody plants come from places where they have naturally more moisture in the soil and air, more snow on the ground and more clouds in the sky to modify the climate.

Through selection and breeding, gardeners may hope to gradually increase the following lists of suitable plants for the Rocky Mountain area.

How to Select the Right Plant for Each Situation

FIRST the general plan should be worked out and all the features and effects definitely planned. Then, plants and material should be selected which will most nearly give the effects desired under the circumstances that must be worked with. It must be continually kept in mind that growing conditions here are vastly different from those in the older populated centers of the east where most of the horticultural literature is written.

More attention should be given to selecting plants which will grow to a size and of a character which will give the desired effect for the greatest length of time; yet it must be remembered that plants are living things and so are continually changing — either growing larger or becoming mature or damaged and dying. Sometimes a certain plant may only be expected to give ten or twenty years of service and then should be replaced with a new plant, while some slow growing things may be placed where they may grow and become better each year of their life.

Trees which grow rapidly and eventually become large should not be placed so close together or to buildings or wires that they soon conflict and must be seriously damaged by cutting back. Shrubs may be selected which will soon get to the desired height but will never get too large.

Let us suppose a few typical situations and see how we would go about selecting the right plant. First we will need two parking trees, let us say. We have 75 feet front and no wires so two trees which eventually grow large would be suitable. In the list of tall trees for street use we will find the best trees listed. If we have good soil and take care of them we may select from the better but more difficult ones such as Red Oak, Schwedler Maple, or American Linden; but if our soil is poor or alkaline or we know we will have difficulty in watering them we will select from the hardier ones such as Hackberry, Honeylocust or Ash.

Let us suppose then that we need some shrubs for the north side of the house to make a screen between our place and the neighbor's kitchen window. We will select from those in the "tall" list that also are in the list of those that will tolerate shade. Here we will find some of the Mock-oranges, Honeysuckles and Viburnums. If a variety of bloom and fall effects are wanted select one or several from each of these groups.

Another situation might be a vine to cover a trellis built to screen the ashpit. We need a hardy vine and one that will grow quickly and will give a screening effect for the greater part of the year. When the list of available vines is studied it will be found the Hall's Japanese Honey-suckle, Virgin's Bower Clematis or Silverlace Vine will come close to filling all these requirements.

Let us suppose that all the various situations called for in the landscape plan are filled this way and one area is left where the soil is good, the sunlight sufficient and the facilities for watering are adequate. Here we may play with some of the borderline, new or questionable things that are advertised in the beautiful catalogs of other areas. If they grow, possibly we will have discovered a new plant and we can crow to all our gardener friends, and if they do not grow, we can charge it to experience and tell no one about it.

Whenever it is possible, the prospective gardener should arrange trips around to good gardens and parks with some one who knows the plant materials and can point out the good and bad qualities of each. Learning plant material this way will save many disappointments.

CONIFEROUS vs. DECIDUOUS PLANTS

One of the joys of deciduous plants is their characteristic of changing with the seasons. There is the thrill of delicate new leaves, the grand splurge of their blooming season, the varying tones of green in their summer foliage, and their brilliant fall colors. There is even interesting character in the bare winter stems.

A carefully considered combination of both coniferous and deciduous plants makes the most effective plan.

Evergreens, for Year 'Round Beauty

A GOOD proportion of suitable evergreens is needed in every good plan. Since many of the familiar evergreens of the East are not hardy here we must learn those kinds which will grow well and create the effects wanted.

We need evergreens in the Rocky Mountain area for their year-around effect. Most of our native timber is composed of the coniferous evergreens including several species of Pine, Spruce, Fir and Juniper. Of these, the larger types of Pine, Spruce and Fir are seldom adapted to use on small home grounds. Evergreens which get too large and shut off important views should be avoided by the average home gardener. The Colorado Cedar *(Juniperus scopulorum)* has become our most useful native evergreen. It is slow growing and may be sheared to keep it even smaller.

We are just beginning to find use for the more bushy types of native juniper: the One Seed and the Utah. The native Pinyon Pine is in the same middle height class and is coming to be more appreciated. All three are especially useful in dry and alkaline soil. The one low native evergreen *(Juniperus communis saxatilis)* is hardy and quite appealing in summer but is inclined to winter-burn and turn brown. White Fir, Douglasfir and Alpine Fir are all subject to winter-burn in their smaller stages, when planted in exposed places in lower altitudes.

Many fine evergreens from other parts of the world have been introduced to the Rocky Mountain area. The Austrian and Scotch Pines seem to be as hardy as any natives. The Black Hills and some other Spruce varieties do rather well, and the Eastern Red Cedar has been planted frequently and some grafts made from select specimens have been very successful. The latter tends to winter-burn more than our native *Juniperus scopulorum* and is less tolerant of drought. As a low evergreen the Pfitzer Juniper is unexcelled. Occasionally the Sabin variety is still used and others are subjects for experimentation. Mugho Pine is being generally used in the low height class. Also for low effects, the *Juniper sabina tamariscifolia* is very effective, growing slowly and retaining good winter color.

For ground covers the Andorra and *Juniperus procumbens* have been successfully used. Of the introduced evergreens, the White Pines, Yews and various Arborvitaes have been most difficult. A few, however, have for some reason or other managed to survive.

Recommended reading:

THE FRIENDLY EVERGREENS, L. L. Kumlien, Pub. by D-Hill Nursery, Dundee, Ill.

COLORADO EVERGREENS, Robert E. More, Pub. by Denver Museum of Natural History.

EVERGREENS FOR COLORADO LANDSCAPING, Robert E. More, Pub. by Author.

CULTIVATED EVERGREENS, L. H. Bailey, Pub. by Macmillan.

The older civilization grows, the smarter, and smarter man must become, to keep ahead of the results of his meddling with Nature that he began long ago.

Evergreens Listed by Size

I—Indicates usefulness in irrigated areas.   M—In mountains.   P—On the plains.

TALL—20 to 60 FEET

Abies concolor, WHITE FIR, IM—Our most beautiful native tree. Of much the color and habit of Blue Spruce, but softer effect. Subject to winterburn when small.

Abies lasiocarpa, ALPINE FIR, M—Tall erect tree, native to the high mountains. Seldom used in ornamental plantings.

Picea densata, BLACK HILLS WHITE SPRUCE, I—Short needles and dense habit of growth. May be kept small by pinching the candles.

Picea englemanni, ENGLEMANN SPRUCE, M—A native of high altitudes. Seldom as good in color or shape as the Colorado.

Picea pungens, COLORADO SPRUCE, IM—Seedlings may vary from green to blue and silver. A stiff, symmetrical tree. Eventually becomes very large.

Pinus aristata, BRISTLECONE PINE, IMP—Native, 5-needle pine. Naturally slow, and irregularly branched, which habit may be encouraged by yearly pinching.

Pinus contorta latifolia, LODGEPOLE PINE, IM—A tall, slim native, with yellow-green needles. Makes a good specimen tree when it is given room.

Pinus flexilis, LIMBER PINE, IMP—Our native White Pine. Slow, irregular growth. Should be used more.

Pinus nigra, AUSTRIAN PINE, IMP—Similar in size and habit to the Ponderosa Pine, but darker and denser.

Pinus ponderosa scopulorum, ROCKY MOUNTAIN PONDEROSA PINE, IMP—A coarse, irregular, native tree. Suitable for informal use where there is plenty of room. Drouth resistant.

Pinus strobus, WHITE PINE, I—Graceful habit of growth and soft green needles. Subject to winterburn when young.

Pinus sylvestris, SCOTCH PINE, IP—The most rapidly growing of all pines for this area. Grows in tall open effect, not as beautiful as either Austrian or Ponderosa Pine.

Pseudotsuga taxifolia, DOUGLASFIR, M—The Christmas tree of this area. Similar in habit to Spruce but of softer effect. Should not be planted with Spruce because of insect damage.

MEDIUM—6 to 25 FEET

Juniperus scopulorum, ROCKY MOUNTAIN JUNIPER, IMP—Native on the eastern slope of the Continental Divide. Usually tall and symmetrical. Varies in character from seedlings. Named grafts are becoming most popular.

Juniperus monosperma and *utahensis,* ONESEED and UTAH JUNIPERS, IMP—Similar in habit. Often irregular and many stemmed. Generally round in character. Tolerates dry, hot conditions.

It requires careful planning to keep a garden full of color all through the season, especially during the hot days of August. With the best of planning we must depend a great deal on the annuals to take us through this difficult period. In the perennials the Phlox is probably the most valuable hot weather bloomer. Shasta Daisies, Delphinium and Day Lilies will often help. Tamarisk, Elderberry, Mallow Marvel, Desmodium and Leadplant are shrubs that usually bloom at this time. The Sweet Autumn Clematis, Silverlace Vine and some of the Honeysuckles will contribute their bit to the summer color.

Juniperus virginiana, REDCEDAR, IP—The eastern, native Juniper which generally is poorer in Colorado than our Rocky Mountain native. Some good grafts have been introduced.

Pinus cembroides edulis, COLORADO PINYON PINE, IP—Irregularly round in habit. Likes a dry warm place. May be trained to stay small indefinitely.

LOW—2 to 6 FEET

Juniperus chinensis pfitzeriana, PFITZER JUNIPER, IMP—The best all around evergreen of this size. Rapid, feathery growth, virtually pest free. May be sheared into any shape. There is also a "compact" and a "golden" form.

Juniperus chinensis hetzi glauca, HETZ JUNIPER—Similar in habit to the familiar Pfitzer, but of a very attractive "blue" color.

Juniperus communis saxitalis, MOUNTAIN COMMON JUNIPER, M—A hardy native. Variable, but generally beautiful except towards spring when they are often brown.

Juniperus sabina, SAVIN JUNIPER, I—Well-known but not as good as the Pfitzer as it becomes bare and leggy with age.

Juniperus sabina tamariscifolia, TAMARIX JUNIPER, I—Dense, mounded habit of growth, fine winter color. The best of its size, seldom growing over 3 feet tall.

Juniperus sabina vonehron, VONEHRON SAVIN JUNIPER, I—Very rapid growth, somewhat similar to the Pfitzer.

Picea glauca albertiana, DWARF ALBERTA SPRUCE, I—If planted on the north or east side of the residence, is hardy and furnishes a specimen plant in miniature that is distinctive and unusual.

Pinus mugo mughus, MUGHO PINE, I—Seedlings from various sources may vary 2 feet to 10 feet high at maturity. May be clipped to keep them dwarf and dense. Tolerant to heat but not shade.

CREEPERS—6 INCHES to 2 FEET

Juniperus horizontalis, TRAILING JUNIPERS, IM—Very low creeping junipers of varying habit and hardiness. The following all have desirable qualities and are generally hardy: *Juniperus admirabilis*; *Juniperus pulchelius*; BLACK HILLS CREEPING JUNIPER; RUSSIAN SAVIN JUNIPER; GLENMORE CREEPING JUNIPER.

Juniperus procumbens, CHINESE CREEPING JUNIPER, I—Spreading, under a foot high. Hardy and good, green winter color.

Juniperus procumbens nana, DWARF JAPGARDEN JUNIPER, I—Dense, very dwarf, contorted growth. Good green winter color.

Juniperus horizontalis plumosa, ANDORRA JUNIPER, I—Irregularly spreading. Turns purple in winter.

Broadleaf Evergreens

ONE of the most conspicuous differences in plant material suitable for use in this area is the lack of broadleaf evergreens, which constitute a goodly proportion of the shrubs available in more moist climates. Obviously our hot, dry winters will burn these plants which retain their broad leaves over winter. Thus there are only a very few of these things which can safely be used, even under protected conditions.

The Oregon Holly Grape, *Mahonia aquifolium*, will provide a nice effect, if given partial shade, and the winter-burned leaves are cut off in the spring. Several of the vining Euonymus will hold their foliage rather late if planted on the north side of buildings or walls. They have been known to occasionally grow well, even on the south side of the house. These include the common Wintercreeper *Euonymus fortunei radicans*. The big-leaf Wintercreeper, *Euonymus fortunei vegetus*, as well as the purple-leafed variety and the Kew, or Baby type, Kewensis, or Minimus. The Euonymus patens has been used successfully in nearby States, but can only be grown with good protection in this area. Several upright forms of the Euonymus radicans or vegetus have recently been introduced and appear to have good possibilities. One true vine will hold evergreen leaves here, if planted on the north. It is called the English Ivy, or *Hedera helix*.

Pyracantha, though it is hardly a true evergreen, has been tried by many gardeners, but seldom survives, unless planted in a protected place on the north or east side of a building. Two other native plants are broadleaf evergreens, the Mountain Balm, *Ceanothus velutinus*, and Mountain Lover, *Pachistima myrsinites*. Both plants, however, require more acid soil and better drainage than we can ordinarily offer. Other tolerant broadleaf evergreens may be discovered later, but due to our peculiar climatic conditions, we can never expect to have many of them.

Trees, the Backbone of the Planting

IN THE early pioneer days of this western arid area, trees were planted with little thought as to their eventual growth or usefulness. Most of the early newcomers came from areas where trees grew naturally and they missed them here. As they brought in some of the trees that they were familiar with in the East and tried to grow them here they were disappointed, for they had not learned that most of their nicer trees from the East required special care if they were to grow here. Because of this failure to adjust growing conditions to the introduced trees only a few very hardy kinds were planted and these were placed with little thought of their eventual effect. Now we are learning to give special care in planting, watering, fertilizing and trimming so we can grow many of the nicer and longer-lived trees, and with the lower height of the modern dwelling we are also learning to plant more of the smaller-scale trees which will not overpower the house in a few years.

Trees are the backbone of most landscape plantings. They should be carefully located on any plan before filling in with shrubs, vines, and flowers. Trees are the largest of the plants used in the garden, they take a long time to develop, and live the longest of all plants used. Not so many years ago two or three trees were planted in a fifty-foot space and they were the kind of trees which naturally grew large. Now in the older parts of any city or town, parking trees which have been grown with interlocking limbs and are too crowded to be very beautiful can be seen. These crowded trees also have crowded roots and the cost of proper care is sometimes excessive. Crowded trees break easily in storms and appear to be half starved most of the time.

These trees were often planted under light and phone wires and so have had to be headed back to keep them in bounds. The damage to both trees and wires has often been considerable. Yet it is possible to avoid this conflict if varieties are planted to fit the space available.

We are learning to plant trees for a definite reason, and so are being more careful as to the exact location of each tree and the kind of tree to give each special effect. Landscape Architect, M. Walter Pesman, has divided the uses of trees into four general classes: parking, shade, framing and ornamental. Formerly everyone planted several trees in the parking strip in front of their home, usually just because everyone else did so. The result was a conglomeration of trees of various sizes and kinds which did not improve either the landscaping of the home or the street. Now we are learning that parking trees, if needed at all, should be for the effect on the street, and so should be planted of uniform species and sizes in each block, at least. Parking trees, as they are grown on city property, should properly be planted and maintained by the city or town.

Trees for shade are the first thought of the average home owner. To be effective, trees primarily for shade must be planted to the south or southwest of the area to be shaded whether this be the house itself, a play area, or some other place. Too much shade is just as bad as none at all. Often a high headed tree is called for which will furnish an umbrella over the area to be shaded without seriously interferring with important views.

Framing trees may be of various character and size to give the effects needed and fit the size and style of house. In general, taller trees as background in the rear are proper, while often a small, low-headed tree in the front will be more effective. Often a properly placed tree will serve for framing and shade at the same time.

Other than these three obvious uses for trees many may well be planned primarily for their beauty. This often is for the flowers of such trees as the flowering crabs, hawthorns, goldenrain or catalpa, or it may be for the ornamental fruits of Catalpa, Goldenrain or Dolgo crab. Just the beautiful green leaves of some trees justify their use and the restrained use of trees with colored foliage such as Russianolive, Schwedler Maple or Purple Plum, may be very effective. Some trees have attractive bark or twigs such as the willows, or poplars.

Trees of unusual or distinctive shape may be used effectively in certain places. Upright and slim trees, weeping trees and globe-headed trees all have their place. There are few places where the elaborately sheared "Topiary" trees so popular once in Europe are effective here.

LAWN FERTILIZER

What is it we see when the first warm day of spring comes along? No, not the crocus or the robin. We see the fertilizer man going from door to door.

"Fertilize your lawn, lady? Three yards of good fertilizer for $6. Everybody is doing it." So, you tell him to go ahead, and he dumps a few bushel baskets of something on the lawn, collects his money and is gone. You go in feeling quite proud of yourself that you have done right by your lawn for the season.

Do you have any idea what you are getting? It may be fresh scrapings from some dairy yard, or it might be half dirt from scraping a little too deep, it may be almost anything that looks and smells a little like manure. Do you know what a yard of fertilizer should look like? (That's 27 cubic feet, you know). Did the man leave his name, address and phone number?

These itinerant fertilizer men "work" the city every spring, and their "take" runs into the thousands of dollars. Do you get your money's worth? Sometimes, but more often not.

What can you do about it? Plenty. Learn a little about what good fertilizer should look and smell like. Learn how big a pile a yard of fertilizer should make. Go out and measure his truck and figure up the cubic feet yourself. Demand his name and phone number.

Will you do this? No. All right, then there is one other way. Order your fertilizer from some reputable landscape gardener or nurseryman. If he expects to remain in business he will at least try to give you something for your money.

Three Trees to Be Used More in This Area

Oaks

THE ABSENCE of oak trees in this area is noticed by most people who come from other places. While a great part of our foothills are covered with the native scrub oak, these shrubs are very difficult to transplant, do not thrive in the alkaline soil of lower elevations and at best are only occasionally tree-like. Several species of oaks will grow here if they are given extra care in transplanting, reasonably good soil and proper watering and fertilization.

The Bur Oak is the hardiest-of-all over most of our area. While it does not have the attractive fall color of other oaks it makes a beautiful, sturdy, long-lived tree. The Red and Pin Oak come next in hardiness, with the English Oak close. Occasionally other species are found growing under very favorable conditions.

Oaks often become chlorotic because of our alkaline soil, but this condition can usually be corrected by the addition of one of the iron preparations like iron sulphate or sequestrene or by some acidifying agent like sulphur or aluminum sulphate.

Anyone may plant quantities of bright flowers around their home and make a big display in summer; but when the flowers are gone and the leaves are off there comes the time when satisfying effects are only maintained if there has been good planning, and good design has been used. We must live in our home 12 months of the year and with careful planning there is no reason why home grounds can not be beautiful and interesting the whole year around.

71

Hawthorns

Every year the houses are being built lower and we need to use more small-scale trees to fit them. Many of the Hawthorns are suitable for they all have attractive flowers and fruit and do not grow too large. The different species have a variety of shapes and habits of growth. The Downy is usually a singlestem, small tree with wide spreading branches and large red fruit that hang on for several weeks in fall. The English Haw has refined leaves, a compact, rather tall habit of growth and small red fruit that hang on all winter. The sport from this with double red or pink flowers is called the Paul's Scarlet Hawthorn. Both of these are a little fussy as to location but are quite worth the risk. The Washington Hawthorn has the most attractive fruit, which remains bright red all winter, and looks like holly berries. The Cockspur Thorn forms a low, widely spreading, small tree with many berries, almost black, that hang on all winter. Several species of Native Hawthorns may be grown here that have attractive flowers, fruit and winter stems.

The Hawthorns are all slow growing and rather difficult to transplant which accounts for their scarcity in most plantings.

Hopa Crabs in bloom in Civic Center, Denver, Colo.

Flowering Crabapples

Not all of the beautiful flowering crabs of the East will do well here because of our alkaline soil, their susceptibility to fire blight or other reasons. Most of the kinds that do best are related to the Red-vein Crab of Siberia. These include the very popular Hopa, Red-silver, Eley and many newly introduced kinds. These all have rose-red bloom and the wood shows the characteristic red strain. Of the white flowering kinds the Dolgo is the most popular. The dwarf Bechtel and its recent improvements, such as Klehm, are still popular, for they make a grand display with their large light pink flowers, even though they do have a "morning after" appearance the next week. Because so few trees of this character thrive here we should plant more of those that we know are good.

OUR SHADE TREES DESERVE BETTER CARE

The planting and appreciation of shade trees and other ornamental plants goes hand in hand with the aging and permanency of a community. When people feel that they want to settle down and really live in a community they soon begin to improve their private and public grounds with suitable plantings.

In our own Rocky Mountain Plains area, for many years, trees and other ornamental plants were simply planted out, watered occasionally and otherwise left to their own devices to grow or at least survive. Most of these trees were brought in from older communities where the climatic conditions were favorable for their growth. We could supply the water that they required through irrigation, but we did little to correct the many other differences in growing conditions that we had here. Our soil was alkaline, our air was dry, our winter sun hot, our spring weather very erratic and few of the natural controls of pests and diseases were found here. After a few years, various pests appeared here and found little to stop their rapid spread. Scale insects, especially, seriously damaged our Elm, Ash and Maple. Still, we left "Nature to take care of them" as it would have done in their native habitat, and did little to control these serious pests as they were getting started. We found when we did begin to study a little about these things that most plant diseases spread less readily here, but that many insects spread much more rapidly than they did in the East. We were compelled to devise new controls to fit our different climatic conditions. Too few professional men gave any thought or study to this problem until the problem became serious, and then there were not enough trained men to handle it.

Many trees are now in serious condition. First we have not learned to soak the soil deep around trees as they grew. We are just beginning to realize that many of our trees were planted in soil which did not give them the proper nourishment and that we must develop a regular program of fertilizing. Spraying to control many insect pests has become a real necessity if trees are to be kept beautiful enough to justify the space they occupy. Careful and scientific trimming has been found to be absolute necessary both to train properly small trees and maintain older ones.

Trees are gradually coming to be recognized as important and worthy of more attention and expense than has been given them in the past.

List of Trees, with Good and Bad Qualities

Per cent number after each name indicates our comparative rating of each tree, in relation to a perfect tree or other trees. Advantages given first and disadvantages second. I. indicates usefulness in irrigated areas. It. also for irrigated areas, but partly tender. M. for the higher altitudes. P. for the plains.

MOST USEFUL LARGE TREES

Acer Platanoides, NORWAY MAPLE, It—60%. Beautiful at all seasons, permanent.—Subject to sunscald when young, slow growing.

Acer platanoides, Cl., SCHWEDLER MAPLE, It—60%. Red leaves in Spring, permanent, good shape.—Subject to sunscald when young, slow growing.

Acer saccharinum, SOFT MAPLE, IMP—80%. Nice clean tree, medium rate of growth, tolerant of Colorado climate.—Sensitive to alkaline soils, subject to chlorosis, shallow rooted.

Acer saccharinum, cl., CUTLEAF WEEPING MAPLE, It—70%. A light, graceful tree.—A little more difficult to grow than common soft maple.

Acer saccharum, SUGAR MAPLE, It—60%. Beautiful, permanent, fall color.—Subject to sunscald when young, hard to start, slow growing.

Aesculus hippocastanum, COMMON HORSECHESTNUT, It—60%. Very attractive bloom, symmetrical shape.—Deep rooted and hard to transplant, slow growing.

Aesculus octandra, YELLOW BUCKEYE, It—60%. Symmetrical shape, large flower heads, no serious pests.—Slow growing, hard to transplant, deep roots, not generally known.

Catalpa speciosa, WESTERN CATALPA, IP—70%. Beautiful and picturesque leaves, seed pods and flowers, no pests.—Young trees sometimes kill back and larger trees sunburn, drops pods and withered flowers.

Soft Maple   **Green Ash**

Celtis occidentalis, COMMON HACKBERRY, IMP—80%. Good shape, drought resistant, no serious pests.—Hard to transplant, nipple galls sometimes on leaves.

Fraxinus pennsylvanica lanceolata, GREEN ASH, IMP—80%. Hardy, drought resistant, few serious pests.—Slow growing, irregular in form unless grown rapidly.

Gleditsia triacanthus inermis, THORNLESS HONEYLOCUST, IMP—80%. Hardy and drought resistant, picturesque shape and pods.—Slow growing, drops leaves and pods, serious borer threat.

Gymnocladus dioicus, KENTUCKY COFFEETREE, IP—70%. Nice shaped tree, hardy and nearly pest free.—Slow growing, hard to transplant.

Juglans nigra, EASTERN BLACK WALNUT, IP—60%. Bold, rugged tree, edible nuts, few pests.—Deep rooted, slow growing and hard to transplant.

Populus acuminata, SMOOTHBARK POPLAR, IMP—70%. Neat and clean, rather upright in growth, hardy.—Rapid and rank growing, shallow rooted.

Populus sargenti, WESTERN BROADLEAF COTTONWOOD, IMP—70%. Very hardy and pest free, grows in difficult places.—Needs plenty of room and water to grow well, female trees produce cotton.

Quercus falcata, RED OAK, It—50%. Long-lived, sturdy tree, good fall color.—Slow growing and hard to transplant, subject to chlorosis.

Quercus macrocarpa, BUR OAK, IP—70%. A bold sturdy tree, tolerates our alkaline soil better.—No fall color, slow-growing and difficult to transplant.

Quercus robur, ENGLISH OAK, It—50%. Good form and sturdy.—Slow growing and particular as to soil.

Tilia americana, AMERICAN LINDEN, IP—80%. Beautiful, symmetrical shape, medium-fast growth.—Bark tender and subject to sunburn when young.

Tilia europea, EUROPEAN LINDEN, It—80%. Usually more symmetrical and dense than American.—A little more difficult to establish.

Ulmus americana, AMERICAN ELM, IP—60%. Good shape and grows anywhere.—Must be sprayed frequently to control scale and aphids.

Ulmus, sp., AUGUSTINE ASCENDING ELM, IP—70%. Tall, narrow growth, resistant to diseases.—Subject to some insect pests.

Honeylocust Pods   **Catalpa**

There seems to be some confusion in people's minds as to what constitutes "shade." To some it seems to mean a plant or structure to keep the setting sun out of their eyes, but to most it means a spreading tree or roof to the southwest of the area to be used so that it will temper the heat of the sun at its hottest time.

LESS USEFUL LARGE TREES

Acer negundo, BOXELDER MP—20%. Will grow where nothing else will, attractive when young.—With age becomes ragged and full of galls, harbors bugs.

Acer pseudoplatanus, PLANETREE MAPLE, It—40%. Beautiful shape and leaves. —Difficult to establish.

Betula papyrifera, PAPER BIRCH, It—50%. Clean, white bark and graceful effect. —A little difficult to transplant, subject to beetle and drought damage.

Betula populifolia, GRAY BIRCH, It—60%. White bark, light effect.—Subject to beetle and drought damage.

Betula pendula, *Cl.*, CUTLEAF WEEPING BIRCH, I—60%. A most beautiful tree, with white bark and light effect.—Subject to beetle damage, hard to transplant.

Fraxinus americana, WHITE ASH, IP—40%. Sturdy, hardy tree, drought resistant. —Slow growing and sometimes of irregular shape.

Juglans cinerea, BUTTERNUT, It—30%. Good tree when established.—Very difficult to grow.

Larix sp., LARCH, It—40%. Beautiful, light effect, especially in spring.—Hard to get established (a deciduous conifer).

Morus alba tatarica and *rubra*, RUSSIAN and RED MULBERRY, ItP—50%. Attractive foliage and fruit, fruit edible by birds and man.—Often partly winterkills, fruit may become a nuisance.

Platanus occidentalis, SYCAMORE, ItP—40%. Clean tree with interesting bark and fruit.—Subject to chlorosis and other diseases, hard to grow.

Populus alba, *Cl.*, BOLEANA POPLAR, I—20%. Narrow upright growth, clean appearance, smooth green bark.—Rank feeder and shallow roots, subject to several serious pests.

Populus alba, SILVER POPLAR, MP—20%. Quick growing, drought resistant, makes a large tree.—Often sends out suckers in lawn, rank feeder.

Populus angustifolia, NARROWLEAF POPLAR, M—50%. Chiefly valuable for high altitudes where other trees will not grow.—Has most of the faults of all poplars.

Populus deltoides missouriensis, BALSAM POPLAR, M—30%. Size is smaller than cottonwood.—Chiefly for high altitude use.

Populus canadensis eugenei, CAROLINA POPLAR—20%. Grows fast, easy to propagate and transplant.—Soon becomes overgrown, subject to storm and insect damage.

Populus nigra, LOMBARDY POPLAR, IP—20%. Attractive, narrow, upright shape, very useful.—Rank feeder, subject to attacks of canker and scale.

Populus simoni, CHINESE POPLAR, I—20%. Upright shape but broader than Bolleana or Lombardy.—Still has most faults common to poplars.

Prunus serotina, BLACK CHERRY, It—40%. Large, clean tree with attractive flowers and fruit.—Bark subject to sunscald, difficult root system to transplant.

Quercus alba, WHITE OAK, It—30%. Beautiful, sturdy tree.—Slow and difficult to grow in our soil.

Quercus coccinea, SCARLET OAK, It—30%. Beautiful, especially in fall color.— Prefers a more acid soil than that usually found in Colorado.

Quercus palustris, PIN OAK, It—50%. Beautiful shape and fall color.—Dislikes our alkaline soil, hard to transplant.

Salix, WILLOWS, IMP—20%. Some, especially the golden weeping, are beautiful trees when in the proper situation.—All rank feeders and must have water and lots of room, short lived and easily broken, clog sewers.

Ulmus procera, ENGLISH ELM, IP—50%. Good shape, corky bark.—Subject to scale, aphids and sometimes suckers from roots.

There always has been and probably always will be plenty of water on this earth. Our problem is just a matter of arranging to have it where and when we need it.

Ulmus pumila, SIBERIAN ELM, MP—50%. Nice shape, quick growing and easy to plant, grows well under dry conditions.—Short lived and easily broken in storms, shallow roots.

USEFUL SMALL TREES

Aesculus glabra, OHIO BUCKEYE, It—60%. Beautiful, symmetrical shape, attractive flowers, fruit and leaves.—Deep rooted and hard to transplant, slow growing.

Ailanthus altissima, TREEOFHEAVEN AILANTHUS, IP—40%. Will grow under difficult city conditions of smoke and poor soil, attractive foliage and fruit.— Suckers from the roots, disagreeable odor, weedy habit of growth.

Catalpa ovata, CHINESE CATALPA, I—80%. Smaller scale tree and fruit than Western Catalpa.—Slow growing and subject to some winter-kill, unknown by many.

Cercis canadensis, EASTERN REDBUD, It—40%. Very early pink flowers.—Partly winter-tender.

Crataegus coloradensis, COLORADO HAWTHORN, IM—60%. A small tree attractive in flower and fruit.—Slow growing, difficult to transplant, irregular in shape.

Crataegus crusgalli, COCKSPUR HAWTHORN, I—70%. Distinctive, low, round-headed shape, fruit hangs on late.—Low headed and slow growing, difficult to transplant.

Crataegus mollis, DOWNY HAWTHORN, I—70%. Small tree of attractive shape, good flowers and fruit.—Slow growing and difficult to transplant.

Fruit of Aesculus.

Crataegus oxycantha and *monogyna*, ENGLISH HAWTHORNS, It—60%. Beautiful cut-leaves, white flowers and red fruits.—Subject to fireblight, hard to transplant.

Crataegus oxycantha, *Cl.*, PAUL'S SCARLET THORN, It—50%. Beautiful double red flowers.—More tender than the English.

Crataegus phaenopyrum, WASHINGTON HAWTHORN, I—70%. Attractive shape, bright red fruits hang on late.—Slow growing and hard to transplant.

Elaeagnus angustifolia, RUSSIANOLIVE, IMP—80%. Picturesque, informal habit of growth, drought resistant and pest free, narrow silvery leaves.—Gets scraggly with age, drops leaves, twigs and fruit.

Juglans rupestris, TEXAS BLACK WALNUT, I—60%. More hardy and rapid growing than Eastern Black Walnut.—Very small nuts, deep-rooted and hard to transplant, generally unknown.

Koelreuteria paniculata, PANICLED GOLDENRAINTREE, It—70%. Beautiful flowers and interesting persistent fruit, tolerates alkaline soil.—Slow growing and often kills part way back.

Malus, sp., DOLGO CRABAPPLE, IMP—80%. White flowers and bright red fruits, good to see or eat, blight resistant.—Slow growing and may be damaged by boys gathering fruit.

Malus, sp., HOPA CRABAPPLE, IMP—80%. Rose-red flowers, fruit very small, resistant to blight.—Slow growing.

Malus Pumila, *Cl.*, NIEDZWETSKYANA CRABAPPLE (Redvein), I—60%. Attractive rose-red bloom, usually hardy and vigorous.—Loose, irregular shape.

Malus purpurea, ELEY CRABAPPLE, IMP—80%. Rose-red bloom.—Spreading habit of growth.

Malus ionensis, *Cl.*, BECHTEL CRABAPPLE, IP—60%. Covered in spring with large, double pink flowers, no fruit.—Petals hang on after fading, subject to fireblight.

Malus, sp., REDSILVER CRABAPPLE, I—80%. Rose-red flowers, leaves green above and silvery-red beneath.—Slow growing.

Prunus cerasus, SOUR CHERRIES, I—70%. Of good shape, flower and fruit.—Subject to vandalism when on street.

Prunus americana, *Cl.*, NEWPORT PLUM, IP—60%. Red leaves all summer, fair flowers and fruit.—Normally a tall shrub.

Russianolive

Sophora japonica, JAPANESE PAGODA TREE, It—60%. Attractive foliage and flowers.—Only a few have grown here.

Sorbus americana, MOUNTAINASH, I—70%. Beautiful orange fruits.—Subject to sunscald and blight.

Sorbus aucuparia, EUROPEAN MOUNTAINASH, I—70%. Erect habit of growth, attractive orange fruits in fall, few serious pests.—Bark of lower trunk subject to sunscald when young, sometimes has fireblight.

Sorbus hybrida, OAKLEAF MOUNTAINASH, I—70%. Attractive orange fruit, oak-like leaf.—Not as hardy or attractive as the European.

Syringa japonica, JAPANESE TREE LILAC, IP—70%. Clean, neat habit of growth, attractive white flowers, hardy and few pests.—Slow growing and must be trimmed in tree form.

Tilia cordata, LITTLELEAF LINDEN, It—80%. A clean looking tree with dense, symmetrical growth.—Subject to sunscald when young, slow growing.

LESS USEFUL SMALL TREES

Acer campestre, HEDGE MAPLE, It—30%. Beautiful small tree.—A little hard to transplant.

Alnus glutinosa, EUROPEAN ALDER, It—20%. Beautiful and interesting tree.—Very few have survived in Colorado.

Carpinus betulus, EUROPEAN HORNBEAM, It—20%. Slow growing, clean tree.—Difficult to start, needs well drained soil.

Carya sp., HICKORY, It—20%. Very interesting and sturdy.—Difficult to start here.

Catalpa bignonioides, UMBRELLA CATALPA, It—20%. Small, formal shape.—Very often winterkills here.

Cladrastus lutea, AMERICAN YELLOWWOOD, It—30%. Smooth bark, interesting flowers and fruit.—Requires some protection to become established.

Crataegus punctata, DOTTED HAWTHORN, I—50%. Good flowers and fruit.—Hard to transplant, slow.

Fagus sylvatica, EUROPEAN BEECH, It—10%. Makes a beautiful large tree where it will grow.—Usually does not survive in our soil and climate.

Linden seeds, like miniature airplane wings.

80

Ginkgo biloba, GINKGO (Maidenhair Tree), It—20%. Unusual fan-shaped leaves, large size if it grows, and an ancient tree.—Difficult to get to grow here when small.

Liriodendron tulipifera, TULIPTREE, It—20%. Tall clean tree with tulip-like flowers, distinctive leaves.—Difficult to grow except in good soil and must have protection.

Malus, CRABAPPLE, It—20% (Including Arnold, Carmine, Parkman, Tea, Aldenham, Scheidecker and other similar species and varieties). Beautiful flowers and interesting fruits.—Winterkill and blight.

Malus baccata, SIBERIAN CRABAPPLE, It—40%. White flowers and attractive edible fruit, fast growing.—Very subject to fireblight.

Malus floribunda, JAPANESE FLOWERING CRABAPPLE, It—20%. Very beautiful pink flowers.—Subject to fireblight damage.

Morus alba, Cl., WEEPING MULBERRY, It—40%. Interesting "upsidedown" tree. —Frequently winterkills back.

Populus tremuloides, QUAKING ASPEN, ItM—40%. Beautiful white bark and interesting leaves.—Hard to transplant, very subject to damage by scale.

Prunus sibirica, SIBERIAN APRICOT, It—40%. Attractive foliage, flowers and sometimes fruit.—Blooms so early that fruit is often killed.

Robinia neomexicana, NEW MEXICAN LOCUST, IM—20%. Attractive pink flowers, quite hardy and easy to grow.—Soon damaged by locust borers.

Salix pentandra, LAUREL WILLOW, IM—20%. Attractive glossy leaves.—All the faults of willows.

Xanthoceras sorbifolium, CHINESE CHESTNUT YELLOWHORN, It.—50%. Attractive flowers and interesting fruit, hardy.—Loose sumac-like growth, difficult to propagate.

Tuliptree

81

USUALLY SHRUB-LIKE, but may be trimmed into small trees

Acer ginnala, AMUR MAPLE, IP—80%. Finest fall color, small tree, slow growing.
—Soon becomes open and scraggly in form.

Acer glabrum and *tataricum*, ROCKY MOUNTAIN and TATARIAN MAPLES, IM
—60%. Neat appearance, dwarf, yellow fall color.—Normally tall shrubs, particular as to soil, slow.

Alnus tenuifolia, MOUNTAIN ALDER, IM—60%. Hardy, beautiful early bloom, may
be trained as a tree.—Usually of shrub form.

Aralia spinosa, HERCULES CLUB, It—40%. Very large doubly compound leaves,
large prickly stems.—Only partly hardy, seldom gets large, suckers from ground.

Betula fontinalis, WATER BIRCH, IM—40%. Clean, cherry-like bark, slim twigs,
dwarf.—Does not have white bark.

Caragana arborescens, SIBERIAN PEASHRUB, IMP—40%. Fine foliage and small
yellow flowers, very drought resistant.—Gets coarse with age.

Euonymus europeus, EUROPEAN EUONYMUS, I—40%. Attractive "bittersweet"
berries, good fall color.—May grow as a tree.

Prunus pennsylvanica, PIN CHERRY, IM—40%. Good white flowers and red fruit,
attractive to birds.—Normally shrub-like, suckers from ground.

Rhamnus cathartica, COMMON BUCKTHORN, IP—40%. Very hardy, black fruit.
—Thorny, slow growing.

Rhus typhina, STAGHORN SUMAC, IP—40%. Good fall color, easily trained as a
small tree.—Shallow rooted, suckers, short lived.

Salix discolor, PUSSY WILLOW, IP—20%. Early "pussies," may be trained as small
tree.—Frequently killed away back by blight.

Syringa villosa, LATE LILAC, IP—40%. Good bloom, as it does not sucker it may
be trained as a small tree.—Slow growth, subject to attack by borers.

Native Alder Catkins

Plants with bright colored bark will carry the interest in a garden
through the winter. Some of the Willows and Poplars have attractive
bark, and the Birch is loved by all. You probably know that the Redtwig
Dogwood is so called because of its "loud" bark. Even the gray and
brown barks are often attractive in winter.

Good Blooming Trees

Crabapples
Catalpa
Cherries
Apricots
Hawthorns
Mountain Ash
Plums
Goldenraintree
Japanese Tree Lilac
New Mexican Locust

Informal Shaped Trees

Catalpa
Apricot
Mountain Alder
Russianolive
Amur Maple
Redvein Crabapple
Goldenraintree
Japanese Tree Lilac
Japanese Pagoda
Tree

Heavy Shade Trees

Catalpa
Linden
Poplars

Spreading Trees

Honeylocust
Plains Cottonwood
Russianolive
American Elm
Willows
Cockspur Thorn
Kentucky Coffeetree
Redvein Crab
Japanese Pagoda
Tree

Narrow Trees

Mountain Ash
English Hawthorn
Hopa Crab
Chinese Catalpa
Smoothbark Poplar

Formal Shaped Trees

Buckeye
Mountain Ash
Horsechestnut
Bechtel Crabapple
Linden
Washington Thorn

Light Shade Trees

Honeylocust
Birch
Willows

Horsechestnut Tree

83

Kinnikinnick in bloom.

Shrubs

S HRUBS are distinguished from trees by the fact that they are generally lower, that they are generally many stemmed and that they usually are branched to the ground.

Shrubs are the most useful class of plants for ornamental planting. They may be used for foundation planting, for screens, for borders, hedges and informal groups. They may be had in tall or low, spreading or erect form and in a great assortment of colors of bloom, types of fruit and character of leaf. Some will tolerate considerable shade and others will enjoy a hot, dry location.

To select a shrub to fill a particular situation first consult the accompanying list which classifies them as to size, then of those of suitable size select some that will grow well in the location, such as shade or alkali. Then turn to the general list and find the detailed description of each to select a variety of bloom, color of twig or fruit effect as wanted.

Shrubs are not as slow growing as trees in general, but most of them will continue to be effective for many years.

Descriptive List of Useful Shrubs

THE following lists of shrubs are arranged to help all gardeners select the right kind for each requirement. Select them for size, shape; season of blooming, type of soil or location. These have all been tried in Colorado and are here rated for their good and bad qualities.

T—following name indicates a tall shrub, over 6 feet; M—medium height, 3 to 6 feet; and L—low, under 3 feet.

Acanthopanax spinosus, FIVELEAF ARALIA, M
Erect spiny shrub. Usually hardy.

Acer ginnala, AMUR or GINNALA MAPLE, T
The leaves are very attractive and in the fall turn to a brilliant red.

GINNALA MAPLE ⅓

MAPLE TARTARIAN ⅓

MOUNTAIN ALDER ⅓

Acer glabrum, ROCKY MOUNTAIN MAPLE, T
More dense and bushy than the Ginnala Maple. Leaf-stems and winter buds are bright red. A good native shrub.

Acer tataricum, TARTARIAN MAPLE, T
A large shrub similar to Ginnala Maple. Leaves not deeply lobed. Yellow fall color.

Alnus tenuifolia, THINLEAF or MOUNTAIN ALDER, T
Native tree-like shrub, useful for tall backgrounds. Smooth grey bark, beautiful early spring catkins and interesting seed cones.

Amelanchier sp., SERVICEBERRY, T
There are several native species adapted for cultivation here. Slow growing. White flowers and edible fruit.

Amorpha canescens, LEADPLANT AMORPHA, L
A low shrub with silvery-white foliage and heads of violet blue flowers throughout late summer. Very hardy and drought resistant.

Amorpha fruticosa, INDIGOBUSH AMORPHA, M
A native shrub of loose growth. Purple flowers in June. Good for dry places.

Amorpha nana, DWARFINDIGO AMORPHA, L
Hardy and drough resistant. Fern-like leaves and spikes of purple flowers in summer.

Leadplant   *Serviceberry*

Aralia spinosa, DEVILS-WALKING STICK, T
Also called ANGELICA TREE and HERCULES CLUB.
Large prickly stems, and very large, compound tropical-
looking leaves. Unusual, half hardy shrub.

Arctostaphylos uva-ursi, BEARBERRY KINNIKINNICK, L
Evergreen, trailing native. Useful for ground cover on
very well-drained slopes. Difficult to transplant.

Berberis koreana, KOREAN BARBERRY, M
A barberry with large, leathery leaves and long clusters
of small yellow flowers in spring followed by bright red
berries and brilliant red leaves in fall. Resistant to
wheat rust.

Berberis thunbergi, JAPANESE BARBERRY, M
A good dwarf shrub for low informal hedges or specimens. Thorny stems and attractive red berries in fall and
winter. Prefers a rich clay soil.

Berberis thunbergi atropurpurea, REDLEAF JAPANESE
BARBERRY, M
Leaves remain red all summer. Very attractive, but not
as hardy or vigorous as greenleaf variety.

Berberis thunbergi, Cl., TRUEHEDGE COLUMNBERRY, M
The new dense, upright form of Japanese Barberry.
Makes good hedges with very little trimming. Hardy
and reliable here.

Betula fontinalis, WATER or ROCKY MOUNTAIN
BIRCH, T
A native, tree-like shrub found growing in moist places
in company with Mountain Alder. Branchlets slender
and graceful and the bark is beautiful cherry-brown.

Buddleia alternifolia, FOUNTAIN BUTTERFLYBUSH, T
Does not kill back in winter. Tall, loose habit. Long
arching stems of lavender flowers.

Buddleia sp., BUTTERFLYBUSH, M
Large purple, blue, red or white spike-like flowers in
summer. They are very fragrant and attract butterflies.
Should be treated as a perennial as it dies to the ground
each winter.

Caragana arborescens, SIBERIAN PEASHRUB, T
Of narrow upright growth, useful for tall hedges or
specimens. Neat foliage and small yellow flowers in
spring. Very hardy and drought resistant.

Caragana aurantiaca, DWARF PEASHRUB, L, and

Caragana pygmaea, PYGMY PEASHRUB, L
These very dwarf shrubs have small green leaves and
small orange flowers. Drought resistant.

Caryopteris incana, COMMON BLUEBEARD, M
Also called Blue Spirea and Sage Orchid. Blooms in
summer. Usually winter kills partly back.

Ceanothus velutinus, SNOWBRUSH CEANOTHUS, or
MOUNTAIN BALM, L
A native, broadleafed evergreen, most common on the
Western Slope. Very difficult to transplant.

Cercis canadensis, EASTERN REDBUD, T
Sometimes hardy here in protected places. Distinctive
reddish-purple flowers in very early spring.

Cercocarpus montanus, MOUNTAINMAHOGANY, M
An interesting native shrub of dry hillsides. Covered in
fall with peculiar, twisted, fuzzy-tailed seeds.

ROCKY
MOUNT-
AIN
BIRCH
⅓

SIBERIAN
PEA
⅓

BLADDER
SENNA ⅓

Chaenomeles japonica, JAPANESE FLOWERING
QUINCE, M
>The common form has brilliant red flowers in spring.
Other varieties in shades of pink and white. Slow grow-
ing.

Chionanthus virginicus, FRINGETREE or
WHITE FRINGE, M
>Nice shaped shrub with feathery, white bloom. Only
occasionally hardy here.

Colutea arborescens, COMMON BLADDERSENNA, T
>Foliage and flowers similar to Siberian Peashrub, but of
more spreading habit and not as hardy. The silvery in-
flated seed pods hang on throughout winter.

Cornus racemosa, GRAY DOGWOOD, T
>Of very neat upright habit similar to Nannyberry. Flow-
ers and fruit small.

Cornus stolonifera coloradensis, COLORADO REDOSIER
DOGWOOD, T
>One of the most useful native shrubs. Graceful and
symmetrical habit of growth. Stems are bright red all
winter, making an interesting spot of color especially
good in association with evergreens.

Cornus alba sibirica, YELLOWEDGE or VARIEGATED
DOGWOOD, M
>White-edged leaves. Grows slower than the common
kind, but makes a striking effect.

Cornus stolonifera flaviramea, YELLOWTWIG REDOSIER
DOGWOOD, M
>Similar in habit to the Red Dogwood, but stems are
golden yellow and it is not as hardy.

Corylus cornuta, BEAKED FILBERT or HAZELNUT, T
>Very slow growing native. Likes a moist north slope.

Cotinus coggygria, COMMON SMOKETREE or PURPLE
FRINGE, T
>An interesting, half hardy shrub covered with clouds of
feathery bloom in fall.

Cotoneaster acutifolia, PEKING COTONEASTER, M
>A clean, nicely shaped shrub, with slender spreading
branches, bearing small glossy, dark green leaves. Small
bloom, but the attractive black berries hang on all
winter.

Cotoneaster integerrima, EUROPEAN COTONEASTER, M
>Slender, spreading and arching branches. Persistent red
fruit. Tolerates alkaline soil.

Crataegus crusgalli, COCKSPUR HAWTHORN, T
>Low, round-headed shrub or tree. Very long thorns and
dark red fruits persisting all winter.

Crataegus intricata, THICKET HAWTHORN, T
>Large leaves which are brilliantly colored in fall. White
flowers in spring and red fruits in fall.

Crataegus oxyacantha, Cl., PAUL'S SCARLET THORN, T
>Has clusters of beautiful, double, red flowers in favorable
years. Similar to the English but not as hardy.

Crataegus saligna, WILLOW HAWTHORN, T
>Native shrub of irregular habit. Willow-like leaves and
small black fruits.

Deutzia, sp.
>Several species of Deutzia have survived here in pro-
tected places. They would not be hardy in the open.

THICKET HAWTHORN

BRILLIANT HAWTHORN

COLO. HAWTHORN

COCKSPUR THORN

DOWNY HAWTHORN

ENGLISH HAWTHORN

PAUL'S SCARLET
HAWTHORN

87

½

½

KOREAN FORSYTHIA

Elaeagnus angustifolia, RUSSIANOLIVE, T
Very hardy and drought resistant shrub with silvery-gray leaves. May be grown as a large shrub, small tree or trimmed as a hedge.

Euonymus alatus, WINGED EUONYMUS, M
Rose-red and green corky bark. Red-orange and rose-red leaves in fall. One of the best.

Euonymus atropurpureus, EASTERN WAHOO, T
Somewhat similar to the European Burningbush, but of slower growth, larger leaves and much richer fall color. Attractive red and orange fruit hanging on till late.

Euonymus europeaus, EUROPEAN EUONYMUS, T
Also called Burningbush or Spindle Tree. A large shrub with dark green leaves and stems, and upright habit of growth. Rose-red fall leaves and red-orange fruit in fall and winter.

Exochorda racemosa, COMMON PEARLBUSH, T
A nice half-hardy shrub. Small white flowers which resemble a string of pearls when in bud.

Fallugia paradoxa, APACHEPLUME, M
A native shrub of dry alkaline places. Bears small, white, rose-like flowers followed by fuzzy, clematis-like seed heads.

Forestiera neomexicana, NEW MEXICAN FORESTIERA or MOUNTAIN PRIVET, T
A native shrub similar to privet. Hardy and useful for specimens or hedge.

Forsythia intermedia spectabilis, Cl., SHOWY FORSYTHIA, T
The familiar early-blooming Goldenbells. Flowers large and profuse (when not killed by a late frost). Quick growing and of upright habit.
Several new varieties have been introduced recently which have superior habits of growth and color of flower. Their ancestry is obscure. These include:
Spring Glory, light yellow
Lynwood Gold, dark yellow

Forsythia suspensa, WEEPING FORSYTHIA, or GOLDENBELLS, M
Covered with golden bells in very early spring before the leaves appear. Drooping habit useful above walls or on banks. Stands partial shade. Variety Fortunei is more erect in habit of growth.

Hibiscus palustris, COMMON ROSEMALLOW, M
Kills back each fall like a perennial, otherwise considered as a shrub. Beautiful large hollyhock-like flowers in colors from white to red.

Hibiscus syriacus, SHRUBALTHEA, T
Large hollyhock-like flowers on a tall slim shrub. Only hardy here in a protected place.

Hippophae rhamnoides, COMMON SEABUCKTHORN, T
A small tree or large shrub with silvery leaves similar to the Russianolive. Orange berries in fall.

½

SEA-BUCKTHORN

EUROPEAN EUONYMUS ¼
¼

WINGED ¼

WAHOO or BURNING BUSH ¼

YEDDO EUONYMUS ¼

PEARL BUSH ⅓
⅓

FONTANESIA ⅓

MOUNTAIN PRIVET

Holodiscus dumosus, BUSH ROCKSPIREA, M
  A valuable slow-growing native shrub, closely related to
  the familiar spireas. Its dense regular growth and its
  ability to withstand drought make it very useful. Covered in summer with large heads of white flowers.

Hydrangea paniculata, Cl., PEEGEE HYDRANGEA, M
  Large panicles of flowers in summer. Usually kills to
  ground each winter, but, in protected place, will bloom
  each year.

Hydrangea arborescens grandiflora, HYDRANGEA A. G.
  Usually kills to the ground each winter, but as it
  blooms in fall will often make a nice showing when
  planted on the north.

½

ROCK SPIREA

Hypericum sp. ST. JOHNSWORT M
  The variety "hidcote" seems to be hardier and will
  sometimes survive when planted in a very protected
  place.

Jamesia americana, CLIFF JAMESIA, M
  Sometimes called Wax Flower or Wild Hydrangea. Delicate waxy-white flowers. One of our nicest natives, but
  requires a very well-drained location and prefers partial
  shade.

Jasmidum nudiflorum, WINTER JASMINE, L
  Arching green stems. Yellow flowers at same time as
  Forsythia. Hardy only in a protected place.

Kolkwitzia amabilis, BEAUTYBUSH, T
  Nice arching habit of growth and neat leaves. Covered
  in spring with pink bell-shaped flowers.

Laburnum vossi, GOLDEN CHAIN, M
  Half-hardy shrub similar to Caragana.

Lespedeza thunbergi, THUNBERG LESPEDEZA, M
  Also called Desmodium or Purple Bush Clover. Drooping stems loaded with rose-purple pea-like flowers in
  fall. Dies to the ground each winter.

½

BEAUTY BUSH

Ligustrum obtusifolium regelianum, REGELS BORDER
PRIVET, M
  Loosely arranged horizontal branches. More valuable as
  a specimen shrub than for hedges. Heads of fragrant
  white flowers and jet black berries.

Ligustrum vulgare, EUROPEAN PRIVET, T
  The best privet in our climate. Makes a dense hedge
  when properly trimmed. Foliage a dark glossy green and
  retained well into the winter. Attractive flowers and
  fruit when not trimmed. Varieties called Thompsons,
  Swedish and Polish are improvements of this type.

Ligustrum vulgare, Cl., LODENSE PRIVET, L
  A dwarf type suitable for making a low hedge as a sub-
  stitute for boxwood. Holds its dark-green leaves until
  Christmas.

½

REGEL PRIVET

Lonicera compacta nana, CLAVEY'S DWARF HONEY-
SUCKLE, M
  A stemmy, dwarf honeysuckle in the size class of the
  snowberries.

Lonicera involucrata, BEARBERRY HONEYSUCKLE, L
  A native shrub found in moist places. Conspicuous red
  involucres enclosing two black berries.

Lonicera korolkowi, BLUELEAF HONEYSUCKLE, T
  Of spreading informal habit with blue-gray foliage covered in spring with clouds of apple-blossom-pink flowers.

Lonicera maacki, Cl., AMUR or LATE HONEYSUCKLE, T
Large dark green leaves and attractive fragrant, white flowers followed by persistent red fruit. The most rapid growing and the latest flowering of the bush honeysuckles.

Lonicera maximowiczi, sachalinensis, SAKHALIN HONEYSUCKLE, M
A new species of bush honeysuckle of much promise. Of dwarf habit and dense growth. Numerous small rose-red flowers and crinkly green leaves.

Lonicera morrowi, MORROW HONEYSUCKLE, T
Wide spreading branches with leaves dark green above and grayish beneath. Creamy-white flowers in May and yellow or red fruits from August to late fall.

Lonicera spinosa alberti, THORN HONEYSUCKLE, M
Dense, spreading shrub with fragrant lilac flowers in spring.

Lonicera syringantha, LILAC HONEYSUCKLE, M
Fragrant lilac flowers in May. A spreading, slender branched shrub with many small gray-green leaves.

Lonicera tatarica, TATARIAN HONEYSUCKLE, T
Upright branches with deep pink flowers in May and June and attractive red berries in fall. Has been our most popular large shrub.

Lonicera zabeli, TRUE RED HONEYSUCKLE, T
Flowers small but numerous and of a darker red than other honeysuckles. Very attractive.

Lycium halimifolium, MATRIMONY VINE, M
Very hardy and drought resistant. Becomes unkempt when neglected but may be trained in many interesting ways as a vine or shrub. Good for covering dry banks.

Mahonia repens, CREEPING MAHONIA or OREGON-GRAPE, L
A very attractive, native ground cover, lower than the Eastern species. Suckers freely from the roots. Requires a very well-drained location.

Philadelphus coronarius, BIG SWEET MOCKORANGE, T
Hardy, fast growing, erect shrub that will stand some shade. Large white fragrant blossoms in June.

Philadelphus lemoinei, LEMOINE MOCKORANGE, M
A neat dense, symmetrical shrub covered with small white flowers in spring. Several hybrids such as Avalanche and Mont Blanc have been used where well protected.

Philadelphus sp., MOCKORANGE, T and M
Several hybrids and sports of mockorange have been introduced recently. Some of these combine larger flowers and more fragrance with partial hardiness. Some of the better kinds include Bouquet Blanc, Sylvia, Minnesota Snowflake, Frosty Morn and Atlas.

Philadelphus virginalis, VIRGINALIS MOCKORANGE, T
Semi-double, fragrant, white flowers in June and throughout summer. Slow growing and rather tender but worthwhile in a partly protected location.

Physocarpus monogynus, MOUNTAIN NINEBARK, L
A native low spreading shrub of the north slopes. Covered in spring with masses of white flowers.

Physocarpus ramaleyi, RAMALEY NINEBARK, M
This native shrub is intermediate between the common Ninebark and the native P. monogynus. It should fill a valuable place.

½
COLORADO LOW NINEBARK

⅓
WHITE BELLE HONEYSUCKLE

⅓
BEARBERRY HONEYSUCKLE

⅓
SAKHALIN HONEYSUCKLE

⅓
LATE HONEYSUCKLE

⅓
MORROW HONEYSUCKLE

⅓
LILAC HONEYSUCKLE

⅓
RED BUSH HONEYSUCKLE

⅓
TRUE RED HONEYSUCKLE

Physocarpus opulifolius, COMMON NINEBARK, T
Large spreading shrub, having clusters of creamy-white
flowers, followed by interesting brownish seed pods.

Physocarpus opulifolius, Cl., DWARF NINEBARK, M
Similar to bridalwreath spirea, but lower and less spreading. Covered with white flowers in spring and attractive
red-brown seed pods in summer. Good fall color.

Potentilla fruticosa, BUSH CINQUEFOIL, L
A native dwarf shrub with spreading stems. Loose clusters of small, rose-like yellow flowers throughout the
summer. It will grow in dry or wet, shady or sunny
locations. The variety Gold Drop is much denser flori-
ferous and vigorous.

Potentilla fruticosa veitchi, VEITCH BUSH
CINQUEFOIL, L
Similar to above but has white flowers and is less dam-
aged by spider mites.

Prunus americana, AMERICAN WILD PLUM, T
Our native wild plum, useful for a tall, hardy background. Beautiful when in bloom and frequently produces good plums.

Prunus americana, Cl. Newport, PURPLELEAF PLUM, T
Similar to Prunus cistena in color but more upright in
habit of growth.

Prunus besseyi, BESSEY CHERRY or WESTERN
SANDCHERRY, M
White flowers in spring and small black edible plums in
fall. A native of spreading habit, useful for covering
banks. The variety called Hansen Bushcherry has better
quality fruit and better habit of growth.

Prunus cistena, HANSEN PURPLE PLUM, M
Leaves remain purple-red all summer. Useful for an
accent point among green foliage. Flower and fruit
unimportant.

½

COMMON
NINEBARK

½

DWARF
NINEBARK

½

PURPLE LEAF PLUM

The Wild Plum is beautiful in bloom.

91

Fernbush

Shrub Maple

Squaw Apple

Silver Buffaloberry

Yucca

Western Thimbleberry

Useful Native Shrubs

Prunus glandulosa, Cl., DOUBLEWHITE FLOWERING
ALMOND, M

An attractive shrub of early spring. Should be used more.

Prunus glandulosa, Cl., DOUBLEPINK FLOWERING
ALMOND, M

One of the most popular shrubs of early spring because
of its masses of beautiful pink flowers.

Prunus padus, EUROPEAN BIRDCHERRY or
MAYDAYTREE, T

Bloom and fruit like our native Chokecherry but this
plant does not sucker from the roots and so is more
useful. Not as hardy as our native Chokecherry.

Prunus pennsylvanica, PIN or BIRD CHERRY, T

A neat and attractive shrub which is adaptable for
planting in groups or in tall backgrounds. It has a profusion of white blossoms in spring and tiny bright red
berries in summer.

Prunus tenella (nana), RUSSIAN ALMOND, L

Beautiful red buds and pink flowers in early spring.
Very slow growing.

Prunus tomentosa, MANCHU or NANKING CHERRY, T

Large attractive shrub having beautiful pink blossoms
and red edible fruit, will be more commonly planted
when it is better known.

Prunus triloba, multiplex, DOUBLE-FLOWERING
PLUM, T

Covered with beautiful double pink flowers in early
spring, often mistaken for a large flowering almond.

Prunus virginiana demissa, WESTERN CHOKE-
CHERRY, T

The familiar native shrub with clusters of white flowers
and black edible fruit. Useful for tall thickets. Hardy
and slow-growing.

½

BIRD CHERRY

½

NANKING CHERRY

½

DOUBLE-
FLOWERING PLUM

Common Native Chokecherry

93

Ptelea trifoliata, COMMON HOPTREE or
WAFER ASH, T
> A partly hardy shrub with inconspicuous flowers but large showy clusters of silvery, hop-like fruit which remain attractive through winter.

Purshia tridentata, ANTELOPE BITTERBRUSH, M
> Low native shrub on dry hillsides. Very fragrant yellow flowers each spring, difficult to transplant.

Rhamnus cathartica, COMMON BUCKTHORN, T
> A large drought-resistant shrub often used for tall hedges, but usually as a background shrub. Clusters of black berries remain through winter.

Rhamnus frangula, GLOSSY BUCKTHORN, T
> An upright shrub, with lustrous green leaves, interesting spotted bark and berries which turn from red to black in September.

Rhodotypos scandens, BLACK JETBEAD, L
> White, raspberry-like flowers and shiny black berries. Neat habit of growth. Needs a protected location.

Rhus glabra, SMOOTH SUMAC, M
> Smooth bark, and more compact dwarf growth than Staghorn Sumac. Leaves turn to a beautiful deep red in fall and ornamental red seed heads hang on all winter.

Rhus glabra cismontana, ROCKY MOUNTAIN SMOOTH SUMAC, L
> Valuable for its brilliant fall color. A native of dwarf habit making it useful where a large sumac would get too tall.

Rhus glabra laciniata, CUTLEAF SMOOTH SUMAC, M
> Very attractive leaves with red stems. Of dwarf habit and attractive fall color.

Rhus trilobata, SKUNKBUSH SUMAC, M
> Also called Lemonade, Aromatic or Three-Leaf Sumac. An informal, slow-growing, aromatic native shrub that can stand much drought and abuse.

Rhus typhina, STAGHORN SUMAC, T
> Loose picturesque tree-like shrub with velvety stems and large tropical-looking leaves. Makes a grand display of red fall color and the red seed heads persist all winter.

Rhus typhina laciniata, CUTLEAF STAGHORN SUMAC, M
> Of sprawly habit but attractive foliage. The fall color is golden yellow and pink.

Ribes alpinus, ALPINE CURRANT, L
> A neat shrub of slow dense growth. Can be trimmed for a low hedge. Will grow in partial shade.

Ribes aureum, GOLDEN CURRANT, M
> Spicy-fragrant bright yellow flowers in May. Edible black or yellow berries. A useful native shrub for thickets and to attract birds.

Ribes cereum, WAX or SQUAW CURRANT, M
> Dense, slow-growing native shrub of attractive shape. Thrives in dry places. Small pink flowers in June and scarlet currants in summer.

Ribes inerme, WHITESTEM GOOSEBERRY, M
> Low-growing thorny native shrub with graceful habit and neat foliage. Good for covering banks and rocks. Valuable edible berries.

CUTLEAF
SMOOTH SUMAC ⅙

⅙ SMOKE TREE

THREE-LEAF SUMAC

Yellow Flowering Currant.

Robinia hispida, ROSEACACIA LOCUST, M
  Of loose spreading habit similar to dwarf sumac. Beautiful large heads of pink pea-like flowers. Spreads from suckers.

Rosa blanda, MEADOW ROSE, M
  Bright red upright stems, mostly thornless. Small pink flowers and persistent red fruit.

Rosa, FLORIBUNDA ROSES, L
  These should be used more. They come in a good range of colors, and bloom all summer.

Rosa foetida bicolor, AUSTRIAN COPPER ROSE, M
  Also known as the Denver University Rose. Covered in June with large single flowers of a coppery flame color, or sometimes distinct red and yellow petals. Probably the most striking bloom of any of our shrubs. Makes a bush of attractive shape and is hardy here.

Rosa foetida persiana, PERSIAN YELLOW ROSE, M
  Double yellow June-flowering rose. Flowers more double than Harison and darker than either Harison or Hugonis. Shrub of rather irregular shape.

Rosa harisoni, HARISON YELLOW ROSE, M
  A double yellow spring-flowering rose, similar to Persian but more hardy and free flowering.

Rosa rubrifolia, REDLEAF ROSE, T
  Leaves and stem are dark red all summer. Very small pink flowers and persistent red fruit.

Rosa sayi, NATIVE RED STEM ROSE, L
  Low-growing spreading shrub, similar to Meadow Rose but more dwarf. Useful for naturalistic plantings and covering banks. Effective in combination with Snowberries or Thimbleberries.

Rosa setigera, PRAIRIE ROSE, M
  Small pink flowers and persistent red fruits. Of spreading habit, useful for ground cover and covering banks.

MOUNTAIN CURRANT

AMERICAN BLACK CURRANT

SLENDER GOLDEN CURRANT

ROCKY MOUNTAIN GOOSEBERRY

Shrub Roses

Native Thimbleberry or Boulder Raspberry.

Rubus deliciosus, THIMBLEBERRY or BOULDER
RASPBERRY, M
    One of the most valuable of our native shrubs. Gracefully
arching thornless branches with attractive foliage. Large
white rose-like flowers in May and June. Very hardy
and easily grown.

Rubus idaeus strigosus, AMERICAN RED RASPBERRY, L
    A native growing in loose, well-drained soil. Edible fruit.

Rubus parviflorus, WESTERN THIMBLEBERRY or
SALMONBERRY, L
    A native of higher altitudes. White flowers and red fruit.
Very large leaves.

Salix discolor, PUSSYWILLOW, T
    The common pussywillow of old gardens. Usually has
some blighted limbs but produces large "pussys" each
spring.

Salix irrorata, BLUESTEM WILLOW, T

The silvery-blue stems of this rapid-growing native willow are especially attractive in winter. Small gray pussies burst out from their jet-black buds in early spring. Not as large buds as the pussy willow, but it seems to be resistant to the blight which damages the pussy willow. Several other species of shrub willows of various colors are native here and useful for planting.

Salix purpurea, DWARF WILLOW, M

A plant from arctic regions. Very slender twigs and delicate blue-green leaves. Suitable for specimen or clipped hedge under difficult conditions. Blights.

Sambucus canadensis, AMERICAN ELDER, T

A rapid growing shrub with attractive white flowers in summer and black edible fruit. There is also a cutleaf and golden variety which are useful.

Sambucus microbotrys, BUNCHBERRY ELDER, M

White flowers and beautiful red fruit. A native in high altitudes.

Shepherdia argentea, SILVER BUFFALOBERRY, T

A native shrub with narrow gray foliage similar to Russianolive and bright red, edible berries. Spreads from suckers.

Shepherdia canadensis, RUSSET BUFFALOBERRY, M

A low shrub growing under pines in high altitudes of our mountains. Bright red fruit and interesting russet leaves. Difficult to grow in alkaline soils.

Sorbaria arborea glabrata, SMOOTH TREE FALSESPIREA, M

Large neater blooms and later than the Ashleaf Spirea.

Sorbaria sorbifolia, URAL FALSESPIREA or ASHLEAF SPIREA, M

Large panicles of small white flowers in summer. Spreads from root suckers and looks ragged at times.

Sorbus scopulina, GREENES MOUNTAINASH, T

An uncommon native shrub which bears heads of white flowers and showy orange fruit similar to the European tree species. Very slow growing.

BLUESTEM WILLOW ½

DWARF WILLOW ½

ELDER ⅙

SILVER BUFFALO BERRY ⅙

FALSE SPIREA ⅙

WESTERN MOUNTAIN ASH ⅙

Native, red-fruited Bunchberry Elder.

97

Spirea arguta, GARLAND SPIREA, M
Completely covered with masses of small white flowers in earliest spring. Hardy in most situations. Should be clipped back each year after blooming.

Spirea bumalda, Cl., FROEBEL SPIREA, L
Of dwarf growth, sometimes winterkilling, but always producing enough new growth by blooming time in the fall. Flat heads of magenta flowers which are difficult to harmonize with other flowers, but, as it blooms in summer when there are few other things, it is very valuable.

Spirea prunifolia, DOUBLE BRIDALWREATH SPIREA, M
Masses of small double white flowers in spring. A shrub of irregular growth and often full of dead wood.

Spirea thunbergi, THUNBERG SPIREA, M
A shrub of neat shape and feathery light-green foliage. Similar to Garland Spirea but not as desirable.

Spirea trichocarpa, KOREAN SPIREA, M
Flowers similar to Vanhoutte but about a week later. A shrub of irregular spreading habit, but one of the most beautiful.

Spirea vanhouttei, VANHOUTTE or BRIDALWREATH SPIREA, M
The most popular of all shrubs. Neat arching form, nice foliage and a grand display of white flowers.

Symphoricarpos chenaulti, CHENAULT CORALBERRY, L
A valuable introduction with neat leaves and gracefully arching stems. Small red berries dotted with white.

Symphoricarpos mollis, SPREADING SNOWBERRY, L
Low spreading growth. Snow-white berries in winter.

Symphoricarpos occidentalis, WESTERN SNOWBERRY, L
A coarse native shrub forming dense masses on moist slopes.

Symphoricarpos oreophilus, MOUNTAIN SNOWBERRY, L
A superior species of native snowberry of graceful arching habit. Nice pink flowers.

Symphoricarpos albus, COMMON SNOWBERRY, M
White berries in winter. Will grow in sun or shade. Spreads from root suckers.

Symphoricarpos orbiculatus, INDIANCURRANT CORALBERRY, L
Also known as Missouri Buckbrush. The persistent red berries on arching stems are very ornamental. Grows in shade.

Syringa amurensis japonica, JAPANESE TREE LILAC, T
May be trimmed as a small tree. Cherry-like bark and large panicles of creamy-white flowers a few weeks after the common lilacs.

Syringa pekinensis, CHINESE TREE LILAC, I T
Similar to Japanese Tree Lilac, but grows larger and more tree-like.

Syringa persica integrifolia, PERSIAN LILAC, T
Smaller leaves and stems than the common lilac. Bears large heads of fragrant flowers. May be sheared for a hedge.

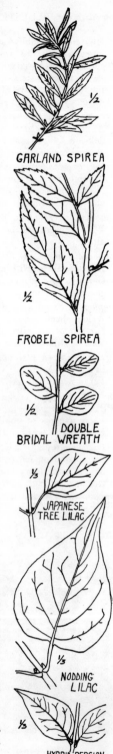

½
GARLAND SPIREA

½
FROBEL SPIREA

½
DOUBLE BRIDAL WREATH

⅓
JAPANESE TREE LILAC

⅓
NODDING LILAC

⅓
HYBRID PERSIAN LILAC

Syringa vulgaris, COMMON PURPLE LILAC, T

Known by everyone. Useful for specimen, screen or hedge. May also be had in white and in a great variety of colors and characters known as the French hybrids. The one flowering shrub that will grow almost everywhere in the state where people live. Some of the most popular French hybrids include:

Blue Hyacinth, S, blue
Charles Joly, D, deep purple
Charles Tenth, S red
Congo, S, deep red
Clarke's Giant, S, large gentian-blue
Decaisne, S, clear azure-blue
Esther Staley, S, pure pink
Katherine Havemeyer, D, pink
Ludwig Spaeth, S, purplish-red
Lucie Baltet, S, pink
Mme. Lemoine, D, white
Mme. Antoine Buchner, D, pink
Mme. Florent Stepman, S, pure white
Mme. Chas Souchet, S, sky-blue
Mme. F. Morel, S, rosy-lilac
Pres. Grevy, D, soft-blue
Pres. Lincoln, S, soft-blue
Purple Glory, S, dark purple
Thunberg, D, mauve-purple
Volcan, S, ruby-purple.

HUNGARIAN & LATE LILAC   1/3

COMMON LILAC   1/3

Syringa villosa, LATE LILAC, T

Very fragrant pinkish-lilac flowers in large clusters a week or two after the common lilacs have bloomed. Does not root-sucker so may be trained as a small tree. The species josikea is very similar to this. There are several new hybrids with the late lilacs which retain all the advantages of these with the added feature of a greater range of color. Some good named varieties include:

Aladdin, S, deep-pink
Evangeline, D, deep-lilac
Isabella, S, violet
Miranda, S, light-purple
Nocturne, D, hazy-blue
Pocahontas, S, deep-purple
Royalty, S, clear purple-violet.

ARROWWOOD   1/4

WAYFARING TREE   1/4

Tamarix hispida, KASHGAR TAMARISK, T

Feathery, juniper-like foliage and large pink plumes of tiny flowers throughout the summer. Very drought and alkali resistant.

Viburnum burkwoodi, BURKWOOD VIBURNUM, T

Viburnum carlesi, KOREANSPICE VIBURNUM, T

Very beautiful but tender new viburnums. Should only be planted in protected place on the north or east.

Viburnum dentatum, ARROWWOOD VIBURNUM, T

Slim graceful stems with white flowers in June followed by heads of black fruit. Will grow in shade.

Viburnum lantana, WAYFARINGTREE VIBURNUM, T

A distinctive, slow-growing shrub. Has flat heads of white flowers followed by fruit which gradually turns from green through yellow, orange and red to black. Thickish crinkled gray-green leaves.

99

Nannyberry Viburnum   *"Chinese Chestnut"*

Viburnum lentago, NANNYBERRY VIBURNUM, T
A tall, slim shrub of neat habit for backgrounds or specimen. Has flat heads of white flowers and edible black fruit.

Viburnum opulis, Cl., COMMON SNOWBALL, T
The old familiar shrub of Grandmother's garden. Usually damaged by aphids in early spring but still useful.

Viburnum pauciflorum, MOOSEBERRY VIBURNUM, M
of thin growth. Found in moist, shady places in our mountains.

Viburnum prunifolium, BLACKHAW VIBURNUM, T
Similar to Nannyberry but stiffer in habit and more difficult to grow here. White flowers and black edible fruit.

Viburnum trilobum, AMERICAN CRANBERRYBUSH VIBURNUM, T
Leaf like the common snowball but of looser habit and bears flat heads of white flowers which are followed by persistent red berries. Tolerates shade. Species opulis is similar.

Vitex macrophylla, CHASTE TREE, M
Small, light blue flowers in fall. Kills back similar to Butterfly Bush.

Weigelia sp., M
Several species have been hardy here with extra care. Not for open places.

Xanthoceras sorbifolium, YELLOWHORN or CHINESE CHESTNUT, T
A very interesting shrub with some characteristics of sumac and chestnut. Quite hardy. Beautiful in bloom.

Recommended reading:

THE BOOK OF SHRUBS, by Alfred Hottes, Pub. by DeLaMare.

GARDENING WITH SHRUBS AND SMALL FLOWERING TREES, Mary D. Lamson.

The Best Shrub for Any Situation

To help new home owners select the most suitable shrub to fill each need we have made lists of shrubs in many classifications which should include almost every condition where shrubs could appropriately be used. By consulting these lists a shrub can be selected which will fill the requirements for ultimate size, character, bloom, hardiness or ability to take shearing.

Shrubs for a Tall, Informal Screen (6 to 8 feet).

FIRST CHOICE

Gray Dogwood
Privet
Euonymus
Serviceberry
Manchu Cherry
Hoptree
Nannyberry
Shrub Willow
Bush Honeysuckle
Redleaf Plum
Highbush Cranberry
Snowball
Redtwig Dogwood
Beautybush
Mock Orange
Buckthorn
Common Lilac
Chokecherry
Sumac
Arrowwood
Native Mountainash
Siberian Peashrub
Ninebark
Late Lilac
Tamarix
Hawthorn

SECOND CHOICE

Rocky Mountain Maple
Tatarian Maple
Thinleaf Alder
Devil's Walkingstick
Water Birch
Eastern Redbud
Smoketree
Mountain Privet
Showy Forsythia
Shrubalthea
Regal Privet
Blueleaf Honeysuckle
Amur Honeysuckle
Virginal Mockorange
Wild Plum
Pin Cherry
Elderberry
Silver Buffaloberry
Blackhaw
Goldenchain
Minn. Snowflake Mockorange
Frosty Morn Mockorange
Atlas Mockorange
Pussy Willow
Yellowhorn

Tall Shrubs to use as Specimens or in prominent places.

Ginnala Maple
Wahoo (Euonymus)
Wayfaringtree (Viburnum)
Thimbleberry
Paul's Scarlet Hawthorn
Blueleaf Honeysuckle
French Hybrid Lilac
Washington Hawthorn
Flowering Plum
Rose-acacia
Hardy Buddleia
Tree Lilac
Redleaf Rose

Medium height Shrubs (3 to 6 feet) used as an informal border.

FIRST CHOICE

Redtwig Dogwood
Shrub Roses
Thimbleberry
Alpine Currant
Flowering Almond
Flowering Quince
Golden Currant
Sorbaria
Rock Spirea
Mugho Pine
Cotoneaster
Spirea arguta
Gooseberry
Dwarf Ninebark
Spirea Vanhouttei
Lemoine Mock Orange
Pfitzer Juniper
Purple Plum

SECOND CHOICE

Fiveleaf Aralia
Indigobush
Mountain Mahogany
Bladder Senna
Yellowtwig Dogwood
Pearlbush
Peegee Hydrangea
Cliff Jamesia
Desmodium
Bearberry Honeysuckle
Sakhalin Honeysuckle
Matrimony Vine
Antelope Brush
Glossy Buckthorn
Jetbead
Smooth Sumac
Skunkbush Sumac
Cutleaf Sumac
Wax Currant
Dwarf Willow
Bunchberry
Russet Buffaloberry
Double Spirea
Thunberg Spirea
Burkwood Viburnum
Koreanspice Viburnum

Medium height shrubs for prominent places or specimens.

Winged Euonymus
Austrian Copper Rose
Lilac Honeysuckle
Hybrid Mock Orange
White Flowering Almond
Forsythia
Korean Barberry
Korean Spirea
Redleaf Rose
Apache Plume
Thimbleberry
European Cotoneaster

Shrubs for a low, informal boundary (under 3 feet).

Sandcherry
Lemoine Mockorange
Alpine Currant
Dwarf Peashrub
Coralberry
Frobell Spirea
Redleaf Barberry
Floribunda Rose

Leadplant
Russian Almond
Japanese Barberry
Bush Cinquefoil
Wild Rose
Wild Gooseberry
Snowberry
Tamarixleaf Juniper

Shrubs for Shady Places.

Forsythia
Elderberry
Viburnum carlesi
Ribes aureum
Privet
Snowberry
Honeysuckle
Winter Jasmine

Euonymus
Viburnum dentatum
Hydrangea
Currant
Dogwood
Coralberry
Mockorange
Jetbead

Shrubs for Hot, Dry or Alkaline Places (such as south of a house or on the plains).

Sumac
Buckthorn
Wild Plum
Chokecherry
Elderberry
Lilac
Buffaloberry
Cotoneaster
Matrimony Vine

Flowering Quince
Rock Spirea
Oldman Wormwood
Shrub Rose
Snowberry
Yucca
Coralberry
Bush Cinquefoil

Shrubs to use in the Mountains, at altitudes of 6,000 to 9,000 feet.

TALL

Chokecherry
Lilac
Hawthorn
Serviceberry
Nannyberry
Bush Honeysuckle
Highbush Cranberry
Shrub Willow
Siberian Peashrub
Redtwig Dogwood

Rocky Mountain Maple
Thinleaf Alder
Water Birch
Hazelnut
Mountain Privet
Wild Plum
Pin Cherry
Bluestem Willow
Shrub Mountainash

MEDIUM

Korean Spirea
Wax Currant
Thimbleberry
Shrub Rose
Golden Currant
Rock Spirea
Redtwig Dogwood

Cliff Jamesia
Bearberry Honeysuckle
Sandcherry
Antelope Brush
Alpine Currant
Bunchberry

LOW

Gooseberry
Snowberry
Low Ninebark
Bush Cinquefoil
Sandcherry
Alpine Currant

Mountain Balm
Oregon Grape
Rocky Mountain Sumac
Wild Rose
Wild Raspberry

Ornamental Plants which also furnish edible fruit for human use.

Crabapples
Thimbleberry
Currant
Grape
Mulberry
Elderberry
Gooseberry

Raspberry
Chokecherry
Plum
Buffaloberry
Nanking Cherry
Sandcherry
Flowering Quince

Shrubs having fruits to attract Birds and add color in Fall. All the above and the following:

Barberry
Euohymus
Juniper
Sumac
Cotoneaster
Honeysuckle
Russianolive
Buckthorn
Coralberry
Hercules Club
Forestiera

Wild Plum
Rose
Pincherry
Engelmann Ivy
Mountainash
Viburnum
Dogwood
Hackberry
Privet
Hawthorn
Snowberry

Shrubs to give Fall Color:

Sumac
Barberry
Cotoneaster
Euonymus

Ginnala Maple
Englemann Ivy
Shrub Rose
Viburnum

Shrubs for color of bloom:

YELLOW

Forsythia
Siberian Peashrub
Shrub Rose

Flowering Currant
Bush Cinquefoil

PINK AND RED

Flowering Almond
Nanking Cherry
Lilac
Honeysuckle
Beautybush

Flowering Quince
Apple
Rose
Rose-acacia
Althea

WHITE

Spirea
Cherry
Viburnum
Mock Orange
Sorbaria
Snowball
Plum

Ninebark
Mountainash
Privet
Thimbleberry
Elderberry
Hawthorn

Vines for All Purposes

VINES of various kinds may be made to fill a very important place in landscape planting. Each situation and exposure calls for a vine of particular characteristics to fit that place, and many of the commonly recommended vines used in the East are not happy here, so it is well to learn a little about the vines which can be expected to grow here and the environment they prefer.

There is little choice in vines to cling to a wall which is in the sun on the south or west. The common Engelmann Virginia Creeper and its refined relative the St. Paul Virginia Creeper are about the only suitable plants. The common Engelmann is rather coarse and too rapid growing but the St. Paul is slower growing and has more sticking disks to help cling to a wall.

On shady north walls and sometimes east walls there are several nice clinging vines, including the Boston Ivy, the English Ivy and the Wintercreeper Euonymus. These are all slow growing, neat in habit and the last two are evergreen.

In sunny locations where there is a fence or trellis to support them there are many good vines which will make a nice showing. Wistaria and Trumpet-vine are slow growing and frequently kill back in the winter when young but eventually form large plants with almost tree-like stems. The Trumpet-vine blooms freely but the Wistaria is temperamental in this respect, apparently only blooming when it gets good and ready.

The Bittersweet vine will grow under favorable conditions but is temperamental as to blooming. They do not readily self-pollenize, so there is greater assurance of bloom and fruit when two or more are planted close together.

Grapes, especially the hardy "Beta" hybrid, will quickly cover trellises and arbors and often also produce good fruit for juice and jelly. Climbing roses, of course, fill an important place in covering fences and arches. The oldtimers are, generally, hardier here: The Paul's Scarlet still leading the parade and such as American Beauty, Dorothy Perkins and American Pillar following. The climbing types of hybrid tea roses are generally not hardy here.

For a vine to grow over fences and arbors in full sun and poor soil probably nothing equals the Silverlace Vine.

For shady and partly shady locations we can rely on a great variety of Clematis and Honeysuckles. Everyone knows the Purple or Jackman Clematis which is a little hard to start but makes a wonderful display of bloom in summer. Few realize that there are other large flowered clematis which will grow here with proper care. The white Henry Clematis, the wine-colored Duchess of Albany, Mme. Andre and powder-blue Ramona are occasionally seen. There are several medium sized clematis which are very easily grown. The red C. texensis, the purple C. crispa and the yellow C. tangutica and orientalis adapt themselves to culture here readily. The small white stars of the Sweet Autumn clematis will make a beautiful and fragrant cloud over an otherwise drab fence. The native counterpart C. ligusticifolia is hardier, blooms earlier and is not fragrant. There are several non-climbing clematis which are grown as garden perennials. These include such as C. recta, white; and C. davidiana, blue. The best known of the honeysuckle vines are the Hall's Japanese with fragrant creamy white bloom and the Scarlet Trumpet with brilliant red bloom and no fragrance. Recently the "Goldflame" with red and orange bloom has become popular. There are several others that might be grown here with care. In general all the clematis and honeysuckles like a deep, moist and fairly rich soil with good drainage.

There are several annual vines which can be used temporarily and will give nice displays of colored bloom. These include the Morning Glory, the Flowering Bean and that very rapid grower the Wild Cucumber. The Hop vine is a perennial which grows rapidly every summer, covers a fence completely and dies down until the next spring.

For ground covers in the shade, the English Ivy and Hall's Honeysuckle are often used. Ground covers in sun would include the Engelmann Ivy and Hall's Honeysuckle.

A dainty little vine for covering rocks in a rockery is the Euonymus minimus.

There will be several other vines occasionally found but they need more trials before they can be generally recommended.

LIME

One of the most frequent pieces of misinformation Rocky Mountain horticulturists have to correct, is the use of lime on their soil. It is hardly possible to read two pages in any garden book or magazine without there being something about using lime to "sweeten" soil.

We must remember that we live in the Rocky Mountains and that most of the garden books and magazines are written in the East where the soil is inclined to be acid. THERE ISN'T ONE ROCKY MOUNTAIN GARDEN IN A THOUSAND WHICH NEEDS LIME. In fact, most of our soil has too much of the alkaline salts in it already.

In any region of restricted rainfall, the soil is inclined to be alkaline. The reason for this is that our small amounts of rainfall do not wash out the excess alkaline salts, and limited plant growth is not sufficient to counteract this alkaline tendency by falling back and decaying on the ground, as is done in other regions. Our soil needs more humus, which will improve its physical condition; and at the same time add a little nourishment and tend to counteract the excess alkalinity.

For the same reason that our soils are too alkaline already, those building new homes should be sure that no lime or plaster is left on the ground to be worked into the soil.

We should recognize that Rocky Mountain gardening IS different and remember that everything written about gardening doesn't necessarily apply here.

LIST OF VINES

M—For use in the mountains. P—For hot, dry, or plains use. I—Irrigated areas. It—Will grow in irrigated areas, but tender or unreliable. S—Will grow in partial shade.

Campsis radicans, COMMON TRUMPET CREEPER, It
Large trumpet shaped scarlet flowers in fall. Slow-growing and tender when young, but in age becomes large and woody.

Celastrus scandens, AMERICAN BITTERSWEET, It
Slow-growing with attractive red berries. Plant more than one for best fruiting.

Clematis crispa, CURLY CLEMATIS, It
A rather frail vine, but bears beautiful purple bells.

Clematis jackmani, JACKMAN CLEMATIS, It
The most popular large flowered clematis. Half-hardy but very much worthwhile. There are other colors in large flowered clematis which will bloom in protected places. Some of the other large-flowered clematis will often grow if given some protection and good soil. Henryi, large flat white; Mme. Andre, large wine-red and Ramona, powder-blue are popular.

Clematis ligusticifolia, WESTERN VIRGINSBOWER, IMP
A rapid growing native climber which is covered with small white flowers in summer and wooly white seed heads in fall. More hardy than the Sweet Autumn, but not scented.

Clematis orientalis, ORIENTAL CLEMATIS, IM
Very hardy, having naturalized itself near Idaho Springs. Small yellow flowers and attractive seed heads.

Clematis paniculata, SWEETAUTUMN CLEMATIS—I
Bears a profusion of fragrant white flowers in autumn.

Clematis tangutica obtusiuscula, GOLDEN CLEMATIS, I
Yellow flowers and fuzzy seed heads. Hardy.

Clematis texensis, SCARLET CLEMATIS, I
Small, bright, red and white, half-opened flowers. Tender but makes a good growth each year.

Euonymus fortunei radicans, COMMON WINTERCREEP-ER EUONYMUS, I
An evergreen vine, clinging to walls or trailing. Usually grows better in the shade. Attractive fruit.

Hedra helix, ENGLISH IVY, I
Dark-green evergreen leaves. Only hardy on the north side or in shade. Adapted types will cling to a rough wall. Makes a good low ground cover.

Lonicera heckrotti, EVERBLOOMING HONEYSUCKLE, I
Flame-red trumpets lined with gold. Rich green leaves which persist until late winter. Blooms almost continually. A selected variety is called Goldflame.

Lonicera japonica halliana, HALLS JAPANESE HONEY-SUCKLE, IP
Deep green foliage held well into winter. Fragrant white flowers. Useful for climbing on fences or as a ground cover.

Lonicera sempervirens, Cl, SCARLET TRUMPET HONEY-SUCKLE, I
Not as vigorous or fragrant as Halls, but the flowers are more attractive

105

WINTERCREEPER

JACKMAN CLEMATIS

SCARLET CLEMATIS

SWEET AUTUMN CLEMATIS

HALLS JAP. HONEYSUCKLE

SCARLET TRUMPET HONEYSUCKLE

Parthenocissus engelmanni, ENGELMANN VIRGINIA CREEPER, IMP
> The common vine which clings to a rough wall. Usually grows too rank and becomes a nuisance.

Parthenocissus saintpauli, ST. PAUL VIRGINIA CREEPER, I
> Slower growing and neater than Engelmann. About the only good vine which will cling to a south wall.

Parthenocissus tricuspidata, JAPANESE CREEPER or BOSTON IVY, I
> The neatest and slowest growing of the ivies. Only hardy on the north or shaded places. Fine fall color.

Polygonum auberti, SILVERVINE FLEECEFLOWER, IP
> A hardy quick-growing vine, hardy almost everywhere. Covered in summer with a cloud of small white flowers.

Rosa, Cl, CLIMBING ROSES, I
> A great variety of colors which may be trained on trellis or fence.

Vitis, Cl., BETA GRAPE, IMP
> This is a hybrid of Wild and Concord grapes. Grows vigorously and produces grapes good for jelly and juice, almost every year.

Wistaria frutescens, AMERICAN WISTARIA, It
> Slow growing and slow to bloom, but worth waiting for when it comes.

Boston Ivy

Clematis henyri

THE PERFUME OF PLANTS

One does not have to be blind to appreciate the perfume of plants. Of course everyone loves the fragrance of roses and violets, but there are many other flowers which give pleasure from their fragrance. The Flowering Tobacco (Nicotiana) will fill the air at sundown. Many of the mints and other herbs are interesting for their fragrance as they are stepped on or brushed by. The foliage of many evergreens, especially the Pinion Pine, are very fragrant, and several native shrubs have distinctive odors, such as the Aromatic Sumac and Mountain Spirea.

Rose, The Doctor

Roses Are Loved by Everyone

There are iris enthusiasts and growers of immense dahlias; there are gardeners who specialize in delphinium or peonies, and there are some who prefer the wildflowers, but EVERYONE likes roses. There are probably more named varieties of roses than any other cultivated, ornamental plant. "Standardized Plant Names" lists over 3500. The culture of roses goes away back into ancient history.

We are gradually learning to give roses the place that they well deserve in the list of suitable plants for the Rocky Mountain Plains area. While to many people "roses" mean simply the hybrid tea varieties which are grown for their individual blooms, there are several other classes of roses which also deserve consideration. There are many ways that these various types of roses may be used in a garden to add to its beauty. A good landscape plan is hardly complete without roses being used in several places.

The largest plants and the longest-lived class of roses are the shrubs. These are used along with other shrubs in borders, screens and foundation plantings. They generally are hardy to cold, but bloom just once, (usually in June). The good shrub roses include the flame colored Austrian Copper, the yellow Harison's, Hugonis and Persian, the Redleaf (R. rubrifolia) with its red leaves all summer and red fruit all winter, the Sweetbriar (R. rubiginosa) with its fragrant leaves and large red hips, the spreading prairie rose with its pink flowers, the red-stemmed Meadow rose, the Japanese multiflora so widely used for hedges and roadside planting, the rugosa (when planted in suitable soil) and the great variety of sizes and colors in the hardy wild roses.

Next in size and long life are the climbers. There are several of the hardy, old-fashioned kind that are still very popular. These bloom just once, usually, but will withstand most winters without seriously killing back. The list is topped with the popular Paul's Scarlet and includes the Blaze, which is supposed to be an everblooming Paul's Scarlet, the American Beauty, American Pillar and the Dorothy Perkins in pink and white. Slightly less hardy but more everblooming are the pale pink New Dawn, yellow High Noon and small flowered white City of York, pink Blossomtime or the new Golden Showers. Many of the hybrid tea roses also have climbing forms. They are very beautiful, but are no hardier than the regular types so must be hilled up, and even then will die back almost to the ground each winter.

The climbers are used to grow over fences, pergolas and gates; sprawl over a steep bank or even give the effect of a shrub rose with a little support and trimming.

Rapidly becoming the most useful roses are the small flowered, hardy kinds included in the polyanthas, floribundas and grandifloras. As these are largely hybrids, the line between the different classes and the regular hybrid teas is very vague. In general, the polyanthas are the smaller flowered and clustered kinds including such favorites as Improved Lafayette, the pink Else Poulsen and Poulsen's Bedder or the tiny pink Cecile Brunner and Pinkie. There are so many now included in the Floribundas

that it is difficult to select just a few of the most popular. Among the most popular reds should be included, Spartan, Red Pinocchio, Eutin, Frensham, Donald Prior, Floradora, Independence, Permanent Wave, World's Fair, Baby Blaze, Garnette, Red Ripples, Redcap and Red Favorite. Pinks include Betty Prior, Pink Bountiful and Rosenelfe.

Only one good yellow is generally known, Goldilocks.

Whites are, Dagmar Spath, Summer Snow, Irene of Denmark and the new White Boquet. In the blends are some of the nicest, including Fashion, Vogue, Ma Perkins, Masquerade, Pinocchio, Siren, Circus, Jiminy Cricket and Fanfare.

The floribundas can be mixed in with the perennials, used as borders in various places, planted in beds or masses and used as specimens.

The new class of grandifloras can be used either like the hybrid teas or the floribundas. Representative of this class are Buccaneer, Carrousel, Montezuma, Queen Elizabeth, Dean Collins and Roundelay.

The hybrid teas are generally planted in beds where they may be given the special care which they require. These beds should be planned to fit in with the general scheme of the grounds rather than be just an isolated spot in the middle of the yard. Other features such as low hedges, shrub or evergreen backgrounds, sculpture or walls may be incorporated in the plan for the rose garden and make of the whole, a spot of year-round beauty.

Hybrid tea roses would be divided into several general color classes. While it is hard to select just a few from the many that are available, the following would certainly be a good group to start with, and by the time a gardener wanted more than this he would have developed decided preferences of his own.

The reds should include Chrysler Imperial, Charlotte Armstrong, Crimson Glory, Tallyho, Heart's Desire, Mirandy, Nocturne, McGredy's Scarlet, New Yorker, Christopher Stone and Happiness.

The most popular pinks are probably The Doctor, Show Girl, Picture, Capistrano, First Love, Courtship and Ft. Vancover. There are not many good whites but K. A. Viktoria, Rex Anderson, Pedrables, McGredy's Ivory, Snowbird and Mme. Jules Bouche should be mentioned.

The true yellows should include Golden Masterpiece, Golden Scepter, Lowell Thomas, Eclipse, McGredy's Yellow, Burnaby, Soeur Therese, Mrs. P. S. DuPont, Joanna Hill and Golden Wings.

Poplar blends are, Condesa de Sastago, Duquesa de Penaranda, Tiffany, Helen Traubel, Mme. Henri Guillot, Sutter's Gold, Opera, Mission Bells, Pres. Herbert Hoover, Countess Vandal and Diamond Jubilee.

Classed as orange-blends are, Mojave, Fred Edmonds, Mme. Jos. Perraud, Horace McFarland and Centennial.

Peace is in a class by itself both as to color and vigor.

In the last few years there has been an increasing interest in the single hybrid teas. Dainty Bess leads the list and there are other good ones including White Wings, Isobel, Cecil, Golden Wings, and Innocence.

Tree roses are simply Hybrid teas grafted on a tall stem so that they are more nearly at eye level. As this "tree" stem is only as hardy as an ordinary hybrid tea, they must be dug, laid down and completely covered with soil if they are to survive the normal winter here. This is more bother than the average gardener cares to take.

The Miniatures are dainty little things just a few inches tall. Most of them are quite hardy and it is worth while to have a few in any garden.

In general the directions for planting and culture of shrubs apply also to roses, though they may become quite a specialized subject in some gardens. Roses prefer good soil and will thrive in a heavier soil than most plants. They will not tolerate large quantities of fertilizer near their roots but will thrive on heavy mulches of manure or small quantities of fertilizer spread occasionally on the soil surface.

General rules for watering will apply to roses. It should be recognized that roses are deep-rooted plants and prefer thorough and infrequent waterings. There should be just enough cultivation to keep the surface loose and free of weeds. A mulch of manure, leaf mold, or sawdust will largely take the place of cultivation.

DEEP CULTIVATION

We still see some gardeners spading around shrubbery, turning up the soil four to six inches deep and cutting a large proportion of the roots of adjoining plants. This is often done after a raking off of all fallen leaves and humus. Sure, this system will destroy some weeds and give your garden a cared-for appearance. But, how much better it would be to take a tip from Nature and leave this mulch to cover the ground.

The natural "duff" which accumulates on the ground in the forest helps to absorb water as it falls, and slows up evaporation. It helps keep the soil cool and loose, allowing plant roots to grow near the surface where they can get moisture, air and nourishment.

We are slowly learning these lessons from Nature and are doing less cultivation and more mulching.

It is a relatively simple job to prune roses in this area. Just cut off the extra-long shoots in the fall and cut back to live wood in the spring. If they have been properly hilled up over the winter, there will be just about the right amount of live wood left (about six to eight inches).

The practice of hilling up about six inches with soil in the late fall provides the best winter protection. Unless the roses are planted especially far apart, the dirt for this hilling should come from some other place and may be returned in the spring. Gardeners should be sure their roses go into the winter with thoroughly moist soil around them.

Some roses may be planted among other flowers in a border, but most gardeners prefer to grow the hybrid teas in beds, since they do require special care. They may be planted twelve to thirty inches apart, depending on the width of the bed. To assure the easiest care, four feet should be about the maximum width of a rose bed.

Most rose experts prefer plants grown in the northern states over those grown in the south, as they often are ripened better. Some gardeners prefer to order roses in the fall and heel them in over the winter, while others will plant a rose only in the spring. It is a fact, however, that all roses are dug in the fall and it is simply a matter of when, where, and how they are kept until spring. If they are hilled up, watered in thoroughly, and cut back, they may go through the winter as successfully in the open ground as in a cellar. When the roses are put in the ground, be sure to see that the roots are spread out in as natural position as possible. There is no need to cut back the roots unless they are dried up or damaged. The heel, or graft should be set so that it comes about an inch under the surface.

There are many insect pests and a few diseases of roses which will be treated in the chapter on insects and diseases. The best assurance of keeping roses healthy and vigorous is to watch the plants carefully for signs of damage. Often when there happen to be two gardeners in the family, one will take care of the roses and the other the rest of the garden.

Recommended reading:

ROSES FOR EVERY GARDEN, R. C. Allen, Pub. by Barrows.
ROSES OF THE WORLD IN COLOR, J. H. McFarland, Pub. by Houghton-Mifflin Co.

BLENDING ART AND SCIENCE

From the simplest garden to the most complicated problem of landscape architecture the arts and sciences work together. The apartment dweller with his window box must appreciate color, form and arrangement of his dozen or so flowers as well as have some understanding of soil, water and fertilization. The landscape architect with his drawing board must have a deep appreciation of the artistic principles underlying many associated arts as well as his own. He must have a full working knowledge of plant life, and a dozen or so applied sciences. It is in the garden where the eternal conflict between the artist and the engineer is blended—the artist who sees beauty with little regard for utility and the engineer who must have perfectly straight lines irrespective of how ugly they may be.

The Perennial Garden

TO MANY people, a garden simply means beds of perennials. As the name indicates, perennials do come up each year, though no perennial border stays put indefinitely. The more rapid growers like iris and shasta daisies must be divided or transplanted every few years to prevent them from completely smothering out some of the less vigorous varieties. There are many perennials which may be grown with a little extra care and protection, but for most gardens the old reliable varieties that will grow under almost any conditions are desirable. When planning a perennial border it is well to consider ultimate height of the plant, season of bloom, color of bloom, hardiness and preference for sun, soil or water. Heading the list of tall perennials is the Delphinium. Other tall perennials which fill a place and are quite hardy include Fall Aster, Goldenrod, Goldenglow, Blue Salvia and Hollyhocks. Most of the common perennials come in the medium height class and are represented by such plants as Peony, Perennial Phlox and Shasta Daisy. Also in the medium height class and of hardy nature are: Coreopsis, Columbine, Chrysanthemum, Painted Daisy, Oriental Poppy and Day Lily. There are not so many low perennials until we get into the trailing or rock garden things. Some of the taller low things suitable for the average garden would include dwarf Dianthus, Blue Flax, Trailing Phlox and Cushion " 'mums".

Bulbs are generally thought of as those plants with thickened underground parts ranging from tulips to dahlias. The fall planted, spring flowering bulbs are probably the most popular. These include the Tulip, Narcissus, Hyacinth, Crocus and such. Tulips do very well over much of the Rocky Mountain area if planted where they may have protection from excessive drouth and sun. They should be set in the ground a little deeper than usual directions indicate. Some of the Narcissus seem to be hardy enough but others require a protected place. Dahlia, Gladiolus, Lily, Iris and Hemerocallis have all attracted their share of fanciers who have named hundreds of new varieties.

Recommended reading:

PERENNIALS PREFERRED, Helen VanPelt Wilson, Pub. by Barrows.
HARDY CHRYSANTHEMUMS, Alex Cummings, Pub. by Doubleday.
TUBEROUS BEGONIAS, Worth Brown, Pub. by Barrows.
GARDENING WITH HERBS, Helen M. Fox, Pub. by Macmillan.
GARDEN LILIES, Allen and Esther MacNeil, Pub. by Oxford University Press.
ALL ABOUT FLOWERING BULBS, T. A. Weston, Pub. by DeLaMare.
THE HERB GROWERS COMPLETE GUIDE, A. M. Mathew, Pub. by Author.
COLORADO FERNS, Harrington and Durrell, Pub. by Colorado State University.
A LITTLE BOOK OF PERENNIALS, Alfred Hottes, Pub. by DeLaMare.
SPRING FLOWERS FROM BULBS, Claire Norton, Pub. by Doubleday-Doran.
GARDEN BULBS IN COLOR, J. Horace McFarland, Pub. by Macmillan.
WILDFLOWERS AND FERNS, Dr. Edward T. Wherry.

If it is true that there is more pleasure in anticipation than in realization, then February should be the gardener's happiest month.

THE BEST PERENNIALS AND BULBS FOR THE ROCKY MOUNTAIN AREA

Achillea millefolium, COMMON YARROW or MILFOIL. One of the hardiest perennials growing at all altitudes and under wide variety of conditions. Sometimes becomes rather serious weed in lawns. The pink form is attractive in borders if it can be kept in bounds.

Aconitum, MONKSHOOD. A tall perennial similar to delphinium which will grow in sun or shade. It blooms in September and is usually purple in color although there are white and yellow varieties.

Aegopodium, BISHOP'S WEED. Extremely hardy ground cover for difficult places where nothing else will grow. Often becomes a pest because of its persistent growing characteristics. It has white and green leaves.

ANCHUSA. The common italica variety is an extremely vigorous plant, sometimes seeding itself over the garden to become a weed. It grows about four feet tall and blooms with tiny blue flowers from June to September. Usually acts as a biennial plant. A dwarf variety, Anchusa myosotidiflora, is a low plant blooming somewhat earlier with flowers resembling masses of forget-me-nots.

ANEMONE. Many varieties are planted and they make a fine showing when conditions are suitable. Some kinds tolerate shade and all like loose, rich and moist soil. Grows to medium height and has flowers of light shades blooming in September.

ANTHEMIS. Low, daisy-like flowers which will grow in poor soil and hot, dry places. White and yellow in color, it blooms from June until frost.

Aquilegia, COLUMBINE. Many gardeners feel that no border is complete without Columbine. Native plants are blue, yellow and red but they usually hybridize with nearby plants of other colors. The cultivated plants come in a great variety of colors. They prefer loose, moist soil and will tolerate considerable shade. Plants are of medium height and bloom in May. Columbines make excellent cut flowers.

Asclepias, BUTTERFLYWEED or MILKWEED. A hardy, medium height perennial tolerating dry soil. It has interesting orange flowers in the fall.

ASTER, Fall or Michaelmas Daisy. The older varieties are tall, rather ragged looking perennials. They grow in all kinds of soil and tolerate a great amount of heat and drouth. The newer varieties are lower, neater and come in purer colors ranging from pink to red, white and blue. Because they bloom late in the fall they are usually the backbone of the perennial border. Some of the good varieties include Aster frikarti, Beechwood Challenger, Archbishop, Blue Gown, Niobe and Red Rover. Asters should be frequently divided to keep in bounds.

Baptista, FALSE INDIGO. An easily grown, hardy, bushy, medium height plant with small blue flowers in June.

113

TUBEROUS BEGONIA. A most attractive plant which must have a protected shady spot. Soil should be prepared with sand and leaf mold or peat. They should be started indoors in March and set out after the danger of frost. Water sprinkled over their tops frequently will help them to thrive. After frost in the fall bulbs should be brought indoors and stored where there is no danger of freezing. Flowers come in single or double and in all shades of white, pink and red.

Bocconia, PLUME POPPY. A very tall tropical looking background plant which has large plumes of small buff-colored flowers in summer. It likes rich soil and a rather warm place.

BOLTONIA. Similar to fall Aster but of neater appearance. It is extremely hardy and very tall with white or pink flowers in fall.

Campanula, BELLFLOWER. There are many varieties of Bellflowers in various sizes and shades ranging from white to dark blue. The native Harebell which blooms in all seasons and practically all situations is very well known. The Carpathian Bellflower is probably better known in cultivation. Low rock garden forms include Campanula portenschlagiana, isophylla and mayi. The Peach-leaf and Danesblood Bellflowers are among the taller and more useful varieties. The black sheep of the family is the Campanula rapunculoides known as the "cancer of the garden." While it does have pretty blue bells, once it becomes established in the garden, it is almost impossible to eradicate. The Canterbury Bells are classed as biennials.

CANNA. Bulbs must be taken up each fall and set out in the spring when the weather is warm which makes it practically an annual. It has tall green or bronze leaves and red, yellow or pink flowers.

Centaurea, HARDY CORNFLOWER. This perennial is of medium height with blue or pink flowers in the summer which are suitable for cutting.

Ceratostigma, PLUMBAGO. A hardy, low plant with deep blue flowers which appear in late summer.

CHRYSANTHEMUM. Many new varieties of "mums" have been developed in the last few years and the blooming season has been pushed forward until they now make the largest display of color of any perennial, in the late fall garden. They are not too particular as to soil or drouth but prefer a sunny spot. Each grower and gardener has a different list of favorite varieties so we will not attempt to list them here.

Chrysanthemum coccineum, PAINTED DAISY. A very useful addition to any perennial border, it has cheerful shades of red or pink flowers borne on long stems suitable for cutting.

Chrysanthemum maximum, SHASTA DAISY. Another very useful and hardy perennial for the Rocky Mountain area. The medium tall white daisies are suitable for cutting. Plants should be divided frequently. Now some nice double and extra large are available.

Shasta Daisies   **Chrysanthemums**

CLEMATIS. Two of the non-vining Clematis are well known and useful in the garden. They are the C. recta which is white, and C. davidiana which is blue. Both are medium height.

Coreopsis, TICKSEED. A very hardy perennial of medium height, which blooms all summer. It goes very well with Shasta Daisies or Delphinium. The yellow flowers are on long stems suitable for cutting.

Convallaria, LILY-OF-THE-VALLEY. A very low plant which forms solid mats of green leaves. It prefers the shade but will grow in some sun. Has dainty stems of small white fragrant bells in the spring. They are easily started from divisions.

DAHLIA. Tall plants with immense flowers of many colors. Once a great favorite with home gardeners, it is giving way to smaller varieties now started from seeds every spring. The roots must be taken up after frost and carefully stored until spring with temperature and humidity carefully controlled.

DELPHINIUM. A favorite tall perennial with many gardeners. They like good soil and a sunny place and seem to grow even better in high altitude. Fall bloom can be had if the first bloom is cut off as soon as it fades. The new Pacific hybrids are highly regarded.

Dianthus, PINKS or CARNATION. They came in various sizes and variety of colors ranging from the tiny clove pinks to the greenhouse carnations. Several varieties are very hardy and make a good addition to any garden. The Sweet Williams are distinguished by flowers in dense heads and by growing much as a biennial.

Dicentra, BLEEDING HEART. The old-fashioned Bleeding Heart is still a valuable flower. It likes some shade and seems to flourish in mountain towns. Several different varieties have been introduced.

Dictamnus, GAS PLANT. An easy to grow, medium tall perennial with white and pink flowers blooming in June. The plant has a fascinating odor and will stand some shade.

Digitalis, FOXGLOVE. Has beautiful bells in various combinations of red, pink and white borne on tall spikes in June and July. It prefers partly shaded, moist soil and under favorable conditions will naturalize itself.

Echinops, GLOBE THISTLE. Hardy plant which will tolerate heat and drouth. It looks like a thistle with interesting metallic blue heads of flower.

Eremurus, DESERTCANDLE. Another tropical appearing plant with tall stems of white, yellow and pink flowers.

Eryngium, SEAHOLLY. A thistle-like plant with silvery blue, teasel-like flower heads. It will stand drouth and heat and make flowers suitable for cutting.

FOUR O'CLOCK. Usually classified as an annual but they do develop large roots which live over from year to year in favorable spots. It will tolerate more heat than any other flower of its size and has various colored flowers of heavy fragrance opening in the late afternoon.

GAILLARDIA. A medium height, easy to grow plant with daisy-like flowers in tones of yellow, red and brown. It will bloom all summer and flowers are suitable for cutting.

GEUM. Grown in either sun or shade, a medium height plant with red flowers appearing in June and July.

GLADIOLUS. A most popular flower in many gardens. Sometimes scattered among the border flowers but most often grown in rows or beds by themselves, as they have little foliage effects. They come in innumerable colors, sizes and forms. Popular varieties this year may be unknown ten years hence. Gladiolus in many areas are infested with thrips which is the plant's worst enemy. All good gladiolus gardeners arrange to treat their stored bulbs with DDT or a similar insecticide and grow the bulbs in a new spot as often as possible.

ORNAMENTAL GRASS. Grasses of many sizes and characteristics may be used to give character, background or foreground to perennial plantings. Some of the commonly used ornamental grasses include Pennisetum, 3-4 feet tall; Festuca, 10 inches tall; Phalaris or Ribbon Grass, 2 feet; Eulalia, 5-6-feet; and Eranthus, Plume Grass, 5-10 feet tall.

Gypsophila, BABY'S BREATH. A bushy, medium height plant with tiny white flowers which gives a light and airy effect. Used for flower arrangements.

Helenium, SNEEZEWEED. A sunflower-like plant of medium height and yellow flowers which grows in hot places and blooms all late summer and fall.

Helianthus, SUNFLOWER. Some varieties are coarse but all are most useful when planted as a background. They are very hardy and drouth resistant.

Hemerocallis, DAY LILY. Some gardeners have said that if they could only have three perennials in a garden this would be one of them. Day lilies are very easy to grow and have few insect pests. There is a wide variety in season of bloom, colors and sizes. There are now many gardeners who specialize in these flowers as they once did Dahlias and Gladiolus.

Heuchera, CORAL BELLS. Low plants usually used in a rock garden, but may add spots of color to any border with their dainty spikes of red, pink and white flowers.

Hibiscus, ROSEMALLOW. The largest of all perennial flowers. Really a shrub in more southern locations but treated as a perennial in the Rocky Mountain area. It has white, pink and red flowers resembling the hollyhock and blooming all summer.

HOLLYHOCK. Tall, old-fashioned flowers of very easy culture. Sometimes they seed themselves too freely and have the dubious reputation of attracting rats. The secret of growing hollyhocks to avoid all the objections is to cut the stalk down as soon as it is beyond its prime of bloom. Some of the new double varieties are most interesting and attractive.

Hosta or *Funkia*, PLANTAIN LILY. One of the dependable plants for shady places. It has broad leaves and tall stems of white or lavender flowers. Ground snails are their chief pests and these may be controlled by insecticides and sanitation.

Iberis, CANDYTUFT. A low plant with stems of small white flowers which bloom from April to June and are usually used in the rock garden.

IRIS. Sometimes called Flag or Poor Man's Orchid, they are probably the hardiest and most popular perennial. Because they are so easy of culture and survive when other plants die, some people come to think of them as common and unattractive. However, the newer varieties really rival the orchids in beauty. It is possible to move iris at any time of the year except when they are in bloom and they should be thinned and transplanted frequently.

Lathyrus, PERENNIAL SWEET PEA. A very hardy vine which will stand drouth and heat, blooming year after year. The white, pink or purple flowers are present throughout the summer.

Liatris, BLAZING STAR. A very hardy perennial which grows in hot, dry places with a spike of purple or white flowers appearing in the fall. There is one variety which grows to around four feet in height and makes a striking effect in a border.

Plantain Lily, Funkia or Hosta

116

LILY. Most gardeners are familiar with at least a few of the numerous varieties like the Madonna, Regal, Tiger, Umbel and Easter Lilies. Some know the smaller ones like Coral and Henry, but it is practically impossible to make general cultural rules to fit all of them.

Linum, FLAX. Very hardy low plant which is inclined to naturalize itself. New flowers open up each day all summer and fall and blooms are usually blue, although there are white and yellow species.

Lupinus, LUPINE. Because they have definite preferences as to soil and location, these plants are sometimes difficult to establish. This is another plant which comes in a variety of colors and combinations. It is of medium height and has a long blooming season.

Lychnis, MALTESE CROSS. A drouth resistant perennial of medium height and scarlet or white heads of flowers.

Monarda, BEE BALM or HORSEMINT. Has red or lavender flowers on medium height stem and slightly fragrant foliage. It grows in shade or sun and blooms in the summer.

Mertensia, CHIMING BELLS. A medium height perennial which prefers moist, shady places. It has drooping clusters of small bells which make a beautiful combination of blue and pink.

Myosotis, FORGET-ME-NOT. A low plant with tiny blue flowers.

Oenothera, EVENING PRIMROSE. Grown in several colors and sizes and prefers a well-drained, sunny spot. It may become a weed if not checked.

Papaver, ORIENTAL POPPY. It makes one of the most striking effects of any perennial with its large orange, red, white or pink blooms in May and June. Some varieties are very hardy and others do not survive the winter. They may be easily transplanted or propagated by root cutting after the top dies down in August. Oriental Poppies sometimes naturalize themselves.

Papaver, ICELAND POPPY. An ideal plant to grow with tulips. They have dainty flowers in pastel shades on long stems. They bloom in early spring and intermittently all summer.

BEAUTY AND UTILITY

The whole purpose of landscaping is to include as much of beauty in the grounds surrounding your home as is possible without seriously interferring with the necessary utilities. We must live (shelter, food, heating, transportation) but after these essentials, we must make life worth living with as much beauty as we can squeeze in between.

PEONY. One of the standard old-fashioned perennials. Flowers may be double or single and come in shades ranging from red and pink to white. The plant has very few insect pests or diseases. Peonies prefer to remain undisturbed for many years. If necessary to move or divide, this should be done in the fall or very early spring. It is important that they be planted with the buds not more than two inches under the soil.

Penstemon, BEARDSTONGUE. Grown as a biennial and blooms throughout the summer. It has tall or medium spikes of flowers in shades of red, pink, blue and white.

PHLOX. The perennial phlox can be secured in many colors and sizes. They are especially valuable in the perennial border during the fall when few other things are in bloom. They should be dusted with sulphur weekly during the summer to control red spider, mildew and rust.

Physostegia, FALSE DRAGONHEAD. A very hardy and persistent plant with tall spikes of white or lavender flowers which bloom all summer.

Platycodon, BALLOON FLOWER. A medium height plant with white or- blue bell flowers similar to the Campanulas.

POLEMONIUM. Blue or white flowers on medium stems. It prefers shade.

Polygonum, BISTORT. A tall plant with a rather coarse growth that thrives on heat and drouth. Because of its persistence it is valuable in some difficult places.

Primula, ENGLISH PRIMROSE. Low plants preferring moist, shady places. It has a large variety of colors to delight the gardener who is willing to give a little extra care.

Ranunculus, BUTTERCUP. Includes a great variety ‘of plants from low trailing to medium in height and habits from neat to weedy. Gardeners should check the variety to be sure that it fits their conditions.

Rudbeckia, GOLDENGLOW. A tall, fall-blooming, yellow flowered plant suitable for background. It is usually attacked by red aphids which must be killed by spraying with a contact poison. Other species in this group are the Blackeyed Susan and Coneflower which are lower in height but with attractive sunflower-like blooms. All varieties prefer sunny places and bloom in fall.

Salvia, BLUE SAGE. Another good plant for background, growing tall and rank with fall blooming flowers.

Scabiosa, PINCUSHION FLOWER. Attractive and hardy plant of medium height which produces blue and white flowers in the fall.

Solidago, GOLDENROD. A common, tall, yellow, fall blooming flower which is very attractive except to those suffering from hayfever. It may spread and become a weed.

Statice, SEA LAVENDER. Has tiny lavender flowers on spreading stems which give it a misty appearance. When dried it is often used in flower arrangements. One of the difficult perennials to transplant.

Stokesia, STOKE'S ASTER. A medium height, fall blooming Aster of various colors which prefers a dry, sunny spot.

Thalictrum, MEADOW RUE. Has attractive foliage resembling the Columbine which is useful in flower arrangements. Some varieties have dainty purple or yellow bloom. It grows well in shade.

Tigridia, TIGER FLOWER. Little known but a hardy bulb with low flowers resembling Mariposa lilies.

Trollius, GLOBE FLOWER. Has globe shaped yellow flowers in the spring. It prefers moist, shady places,

TUBEROSE. Grown from a tender bulb planted in the spring. It has a tall stem of creamy white, fragrant flowers.

Valeriana, GARDEN HELIOTROPE. Has medium stems of white or rose flowers. It prefers shady, moist places.

Veronica, SPEEDWELL. With a variety of heights and leaf colors, it is useful for borders and perennial beds. Has deep blue small flowers.

VIOLA. Various low plants with violet or pansy-like flowers. Usually they prefer a moist, shady spot and will often be in bloom every month of the year.

Perennials and Bulbs

GENERAL USE

Common yarrow	Tickseed, coreopsis	Marsh mallow	False dragonhead
Monkshood	Lily-of-the-valley	Hollyhock	Balloon flower
Bishop's weed	Dahlia	Plantain lily	Polemonium
Anchusa	Pinks or carnation	Candytuft	Bistort
Anemone	Bleeding heart	Iris	English primrose
Columbine	Gas plant	Perennial sweet pea	Buttercup
Butterflyweed	Foxglove	Blazing star	Goldenglow
Aster, Fall	Globe thistle	Lily	Blue sage
Tuberous begonia	Desertcandle	Phlox	Pincushion flower
Plume poppy	Seaholly	Lupine	Goldenrod
Boltonia	Four o'clock	Maltese cross	Sea lavender
Bellflower	Gaillardia	Beebalm	Stokes' aster
Canna	Geum	Chiming bell	Meadow rue
Cornflower	Gladiolus	Forget-me-not	Tiger flower
Plumbago	Ornamental grass	Evening primrose	Globe flower
Clematis, recta and	Babysbreath	Oriental poppy	Tuberose
davidiana	Sneezeweed	Iceland poppy	Garden heliotrope
Chrysanthemum	Sunflower	Peony	Speedwell
Painted daisy	Daylily	Beardstongue	Viola
Shasta daisy	Coralbell	Flax	

CUT FLOWERS

Common yarrow	Lily-of-the-valley	Coralbell	Balloon flower
Monkshood	Dahlia	Plantain lily	Buttercup
Anchusa	Delphinium	Candytuft	Goldenglow
Anemone	Carnation	Iris	Pincushion flower
Anthemis	Bleeding heart	Perennial sweet pea	Goldenrod
Tuberous begonia	Foxglove	Lily	Sea lavender
Boltonia	Globe thistle	Lupine	Stokes' aster
Baptisia	Seaholly	Maltese cross	Meadow rue
Bellflower	Gaillardia	Chiming bell	Tiger flower
Cornflower	Gladiolus	Oriental poppy	Globe flower
Clematis	Ornamental grass	Iceland poppy	Tuberose
Chrysanthemum	Babysbreath	Peony	Garden heliotrope
Painted daisy	Sneezeweed	Beardstongue	Speedwell
Shasta daisy	Sunflower	Phlox	Viola
Tickseed, coreopsis	Daylily	False dragonhead	

SUNNY, SANDY SOIL

Anemone	Globe thistle	Candytuft	Beardstongue
Yarrow	Desertcandle	Iris	Flax
Anthemis	Seaholly	Perennial sweet pea	Bistort
Butterfly weed	Four o'clock	Blazing star	Buttercup
Aster	Gaillardia	Lily	Blue sage
Boltonia	Geum	Phlox	Goldenrod
Cornflower	Gladiolus	Maltese cross	Stokes' aster
Chrysanthemum	Ornamental grass	Beebalm	Speedwell
Painted daisy	Babysbreath	Evening primrose	Viola
Shasta daisy	Sneezeweed	Oriental poppy	
Pinks	Sunflower	Iceland poppy	

HOLLYHOCKS

It is a queer quirk of human nature that we do not appreciate those nice things that are common or easy to get. If hollyhocks were hard to grow we would probably prize them as highly as orchids. There is no flower that will give a greater display of color for the effort expended, yet they are not planted as often as they should be.

MAY BLOOM

Columbine, BR	Pinks, V	Chiming bell, B	Globe flower, Y
Bellflower, BWP	Daylily, V	Oriental poppy, V	Tuberose, W
Cornflower, B	Flax, B	Peony, V	Viola, V
Lily-of-the-valley, W	Iris, V	English primrose, V	

JUNE BLOOM

Anchusa, B	Pinks, carnation, V	Iris, V	False dragonhead,
Anthemis, YW	Bleeding heart, P	Sweet pea, P	WL
False Indigo, B	Gas plant, WP	Lily, V	Balloon flower, WL
Bellflower, BWP	Foxglove, RPW	Flax, B	Polemonium, BW
Cornflower, B	Four o'clock, V	Lupine	English primrose, V
Clematis, WB	Gaillardia, YR	Chiming bell, B	Buttercup, Y
Painted daisy, RP	Geum, R	Forget-me-not, B	Goldenglow, Y
Shasta daisy, W	Babysbreath, W	Oriental poppy, POR	Globe Flower, Y
Tickseed, Y	Daylily, V	Iceland poppy, V	Garden heliotrope, B
Lily-of-the-valley, W	Coralbell, RP	Peony, V	Speedwell, B
Delphinium, V	Hollyhock, V	Beardstongue, V	Viola, V

JULY BLOOM

Anchusa, B	Delphinium, V	Daylily, V	Beardstongue, BRW
Anthemis, YW	Pinks, carnation, V	Coralbell, RP	Phlox, V
Tuberous begonia,	Bleeding heart, P	Marsh mallow, WRP	False dragonhead, PL
WPR	Foxglove, RPW	Hollyhock, V	Balloon flower, WL
Plume poppy, W	Globe thistle, B	Plantain lily, WL	Polemonium, BW
Bellflower, BWP	Desertcandle, WP	Candytuft, W	Bistort
Cornflower, BP	Seaholly, B	Sweet Pea, P	Buttercup, Y
Clematis, WB	Four o'clock, V	Lily, V	Goldenglow, Y
Cushion mums, V	Gaillardia, YRBr	Flax, B	Tiger flower, Y
Painted daisy, RP	Geum, R	Lupine, V	Viola, V
Shasta daisy, W	Gladiolus, V	Beebalm, RPL	
Tickseed, Y	Ornamental grass	Evening primrose, Y	
Dahlia, V	Babysbreath, WP	Iceland poppy, V	

AUGUST BLOOM

Anchusa, B	Tickseed, V	Sunflower, Y	False dragonhead,
Anthemis, YW	Dahlia, V	Daylily, V	WL
Aster, V	Pinks, carnation, V	Marsh mallow, WPR	Bistort, W
Tuberous begonia, V	Bleeding heart, P	Plantain lily, WL	Goldenglow, Y
Plume poppy, W	Globe thistle, B	Candytuft, W	Pincushion flower,
Boltonia, WP	Desertcandle, WP	Blazing star, PW	BW
Bellflower, BWP	Seaholly, B	Lily, V	Goldenrod, Y
Canna, RYP	Four o'clock, V	Maltese cross, RW	Sea lavender, L
Cornflower, BPW	Gaillardia, YRBr	Beardstongue, BRW	Viola, V
Cushion 'mum, V	Gladiolus, V	Phlox, V	
Painted daisy, RP	Sneezeweed, Y		

SEPTEMBER BLOOM

Monkshood, B	Boltonia, WP	Bleeding heart, P	Maltese cross, RW
Anchusa, B	Canna, RYP	Four o'clock, V	Goldenglow, Y
Anemone, P	Cornflower, BWP	Gaillardia, PRBr	Blue sage
Anthemis, YW	Plumbago, B	Gladiolus, V	Pincushion flower,
Butterflyweed, W	Cushion & English	Sneezeweed, Y	BW
Aster, V	'mums, V	Sunflower, Y	Sea lavender, L
Tuberous begonia,	Dahlia, V	Daylily, V	Viola, V
WPR	Delphinium, V	Marsh mallow, WPR	

KEY TO COLORS: B—Blue, W—White, R—Red, Y—Yellow, L—Lavender, V—Various, P—Pink, O—Orange, Br—Brown.

SHADE AND PART SHADE

Monkshood	Gasplant	Beebalm	Tiger flower
Anemone	Foxglove	Chiming bell	Globe flower
Columbine	Geum	Forget-me-not	Tuberose
Baptisia	Daylily	Peony	Garden heliotrope
Tuberous begonia	Plantain lily	Polemonium	Viola
Bellflower	Iris	English primrose	
Lily-of-the-valley	Lily	Pincushion flower	
Bleeding heart	Lupine	Sea lavender	

HEIGHT OVER 36″

Anchusa	Gasplant	Daylily	Goldenglow
Aster, fall	Foxglove	Hollyhock	Blue sage
Plume poppy	Desertcandle	Perennial sweet pea	Delphinium
Dahlia	Ornamental grass	Blazing star	Goldenrod

HEIGHT 12 TO 36″

Yarrow	Chrysanthemum	Gaillardia	Lupine
Anemone	Painted daisy	Geum	Maltese cross
Anthemis	Shasta daisy	Gladiolus	Beebalm
Columbine	Tickseed, coreopsis	Babysbreath	Chiming bell
Baptisia	Dahlia	Sneezeweed	Evening primrose
Tuberous begonia	Delphinium	Daylily	Oriental poppy
Bellflower	Bleeding heart	Plantain lily	Iceland Poppy
Canna	Globe thistle	Iris	Peony
Cornflower	Seaholly	Lily	Beardstongue
Clematis	Four o'clock	Phlox	Buttercup

HEIGHT UNDER 12″

Anchusa	Pinks, carnation	English primrose	Aster, fall
Bishop's weed	Ornamental grass	Trollius	Phlox subulata
Butterflyweed	Iceland poppy	Tigerflower	
Plumbago	Coralbell	Viola	
Lily-of-the-valley	Iris	Tuberose	

NATURE WAS FIRST

When describing the fruit of our native Mountain Mahogany we often say it is copied after a pipecleaner which has been twisted into a corkscrew. Actually it is the other way around. The mountain mahogany developed this twisted shape and fuzzy character so that the wind would carry its seed far away and it could twist down through the duff into the soil; then we came along and made our pipecleaners and corkscrews like it.

We notice that the seeds of Ash are like little canoe paddles, but actually the canoe paddles made by the Indians were patterned after the seeds of the ash. We think that the Maple and Linden seeds look like little aeroplane propellers. But the seeds of the maple and linden were here long before we ever thought of propellers.

Half an acorn on the ground looks like a Quonset hut, but acorns "invented" this principle of strength in the curve millions of years ago.

We are finding that many of our "modern" discoveries were developed by Nature a long time ago. It is just a matter of our being intelligent and clever enough to adapt them to our modern uses. When we think of these things it makes us mighty humble and gives us greater respect for the Power over all.

Fall Planted or "Dutch" Bulbs

THE REALLY GOOD gardeners could almost be determined by the extent that they planted the Dutch bulbs, for one must have real faith to go to all the work of planting the "dead" looking things in fall when gardening interest is low with the expectation of seeing their bold display of color early next spring. This class of bulbs is most important to maintain a show of color in the garden over a great length of time, for they establish their roots in fall and have their flower stem just ready to break through when they get the signal that spring is near by the ground warming a little. From the earliest snowdrops to the latest Darwin tulips there is a great variety in color, height and form.

As with most other garden practices these bulbs are planted in this area "differently." Because of our drying winds in winter and especially because of the erratic springs we must always plant these bulbs at least 50% deeper than in other areas. This puts tulips down at least a foot and smaller bulbs in proportion. It is also well to avoid planting them in especially hot places such as the south side of a building. When these bulbs are planted too close to the surface or in too hot a place the early spells of warm weather induce them to break through and then they are frozen with the inevitable cold snap that follows. Another real reason for planting them deeper and in a cool place is that they do not break up into small bloomless bulbs as soon. Often they will just form one new bulb after blooming and may remain undisturbed for ten or more years. They do NOT have to be dug each year and left out of the ground before planting back. When they do break up into too many small bulbs it is seldom economy to try to plant them back and grow them into blooming size bulbs. Conditions are so much better in Holland or the Northwest that it is better and cheaper to buy new bulbs.

In most people's minds Tulips top the list of this class of flowers, and to many "tulip" refers to the tall, late Darwins. There are many other types of tulips, however, that can add much to the display of color in a garden.

Tulips have been grown in Holland for so many years that there is an almost limitless list of varieties. Some of the old are still good but every year a few new and different or better varieties are released. If we might select eight as typical Darwins they would be City of Haarlem, scarlet; Clara Butt, pink; Desiree, vermilion; Golden Age, yellow; Insurpassable, lilac; Queen of Night, deep maroon; Zwanenburg, white; Princess Elizabeth, rosy pink.

The single late or Cottage tulips are just a little smaller and earlier than the Darwins. Two good ones would be Marshal Haig, scarlet, and Mrs. John Scheepers, yellow. In the same season and size of the Cottage are the lily flowered. These have long pointed petals instead of the rounded ones of the Darwins and so fit in with perennials or in rock gardens better. Three typical would be Golden Duchess, yellow; Mildred, rose, and Picotee, white, edged pink. The Breeder class of tulips belong with the Darwins in size and season. They are distinguished by their peculiar colors running to bronze, mahogany and purple shades. Four typical might be Dillenburg, salmon-orange; Indian Chief, coppery-red; Louis IV, purple-bronze and Velvet King, purple-violet.

The Parrot class of tulips are liked by some because of their immense size, "broken" colors and irregular "cut" shape. They are generally weak stemmed and do not fit so well for large displays. Blue Parrot, Texas Gold, Parrot Wonder (red) and Fantasy (pink) are typical. The doubles are also used more for specimens than for massing like Darwins. Eros is a good old rose color, Mount Tacoma a pure white, Rocket a cherry red and Schoonoord an early white. The single earlies are not used as much in later years but still have a place because of their earliness, if not size. One variety is still popular, the Keizerskroon, a red and yellow.

Many enjoy the little known species tulips more than any for they come in a variety of delicate sizes and interesting colors. Many are especially appropriate in the rock garden or in small groups among the perennials. The Candystick tulip, T. clusiana, is a favorite. The multiflowered tulip, T. praestans fusilier, gives a lot of bloom for your money. The fosteriana, Red Emperor, really started something with its immense size and earliness. Now there are available several other colors in this size and season. The T. fosteriana, Gold Beater and Zombie; the T. greigi, Bento and Pandour and the T. kaufmanniana, Concerto and Overture are wonderful new kinds. Similar in some respects are the new Peacock tulips, low, early and in a variety of color combinations. The Mendel and Triumph tulips are classes of hybrids between the Darwins and the earlies. The low species tulips like those called "waterlily" are very interesting.

Hyacinths also fill an important place with their immense heads of bright colored flowers. They should have the same care as to deep planting, but generally do not last as many years as the tulips. The number of varieties is not great, generally a red, pink, white, blue and yellow filling all requirements.

Narcissus come in a great variety of sizes, colors and shapes. There seems to be no definite dividing line between those called "Daffodils" and the "Jonquils" so we just call them all Narcissus. The predominating color is yellow and probably the immense King Alfred is the most popular. A good additional assortment might include: Mrs. E. H. Krelage, Mrs. R. O. Backhouse, Dick Wellband, Tunis, Damson and February Gold in the large-cupped kinds, with Twink and Royal Sovereign in the doubles, and Actea, Cheerfulness, Trevithian and Thalia in the small, multi-flowered.

Crocus with their bright colors start the season. They come in blue, white, yellow and striped. They may be planted in borders, among the perennials or even in the edge of the lawn. The very early, small bulbs include the Scillas in white, blue and pink; the Chionodoxas (Glory of the Snow) in blue, white and rose; the Galanthus (Snowdrops) in white; Muscari (Grape Hyacinth) in blue and white and the Leucojum (Snowflake) in white.

The Colchicum or Fall Crocus have the peculiar habit of sending up only foliage in the spring, dying down in summer and sending up large flowers without foliage in the fall.

Annual Flowers for Summer Color

NO PLANTING is complete without including some of the annuals. They are especially valuable during July and August when the best planned perennial borders would look bare without a few appropriate annuals. There is a great variety from which to choose, but for most people it is advisable to stick to the hardiest kinds. Zinnias, Petunias, Marigolds and Cosmos may be grown by almost anyone in almost any kind of a situation. They seem to thrive in the hot, dry air of our summers. Snapdragons and Pansies are usually considered as annuals and fill an important place in the shady spots. Portulacas, Poppies and Four O'Clocks will also tolerate extreme heat. Verbenas, Phlox, Nasturtiums and Sweet Alyssum are old favorites for plant beds while Sweet Peas and Morning Glories are popular annual vines.

Annuals are useful not only to supplement the perennial border, but give temporary bright spots of color in front of the shrubs and to fill in porch boxes. They can also be planted in all kinds of odd places. The old fashioned bed of flowers cut out of the middle of the lawn is no longer considered good taste, but formal beds of annuals in appropriate places may be very attractive. The following list includes most of the annuals which are occasionally grown in the Rocky Mountain area as bedding plants. Some like the Zinnias, Marigolds, Calendulas, Cosmos, Nigella, Nasturtiums, Poppies and Balsam may be seeded in the ground in May when the weather is reasonably settled; but most of the others are more safely started indoors and set out as small plants. It is usually more satisfactory to buy small plants from the nursery at the proper time. Our season of frost-free days is usually short. We can only expect a long season of bloom from the annual flowers when they have been given a head start of about six weeks indoor growth. The first really safe date to put out tender annuals is usually considered about June 1st in the Denver area. Though, if one wants to gamble, annuals will sometimes make it when set out two or three weeks earlier. Gardeners should become familiar with the average frost-free dates in their areas.

Recommended reading:

ANNUAL FLOWERS FROM SEED PACKET TO BOUQUET, Dorothy H. Jenkins, Pub. by Barrows.
THE BOOK OF ANNUALS, Alfred Hottes, Pub. by DeLaMare.
ANNUALS FOR YOUR GARDEN, D. J. Foley, Pub. by Macmillan.

List of Good Annuals

AGERATUM. Low, blue border flower. Now also in white.

ALYSSUM, SWEET. Low, white or lavender border flower.

AMARANTHUS. Tall, highly colored foliage.

ANTIRRHINUM, SNAPDRAGON. Medium, will bloom in shade.

ASTERS, CHINA. Medium, wonderful double flowers in a variety of clolors, but subject to serious diseases.

BALSAM. Medium, various colored flowers.

BEGONIA. Low, green and red foliage. Pink and red bloom.

BLUE-EYED DAISY (Arctotis grandis). Medium, attractive flowers.

CALENDULA. Medium, yellow, very hardy.

CALIFORNIA PINKS (Mesembryanthemum). Low, succulent foliage. Heat resistant.

CALIFORNIA POPPY. Low, yellow, self-seeding.

CALLIOPSIS. Medium, similar to perennial Coreopsis.

CANDYTUFT. Low, white border plant.

CASTOR BEANS. Tall, tropical-like foliage.

CELOSIA, COCKSCOMB. Medium, red and pink.

CENTAUREA, DUSTY MILLER. Low, gray border plant.

CLARKIA. Medium, small flower.

CLEOME. Tall, striking pink heads.

COLEUS. Low, various colored foliage plant.

COSMOS. Tall, hardy, self-seeder.

CYNOGLOSSUM. Chinese Forget-me-not. Medium, tiny blue flowers.

DAHLIA. Tall, easily grown from seed.

DIMORPHOTHECA, AFRICAN DAISY. Medium, good for bedding.

DIDISCUS. Medium, blue-lace flower, good for cut flowers.

EUPHORBIA. Medium, green and white foliage.

FOUR O'CLOCK. Medium, stands extreme heat.

FUCHSIA. Medium, tender bedding plant.

GERANIUM. Low, good bedding plant.

GODETIA. Medium, shades of pink.

GOMPHRENA, GLOBE AMARANTH. Medium, everlasting.

GYPSOPHILA, BABY'S BREATH. Medium, small white flowers.

HELIOTROPE. Medium, fragrant purple.

HELICHRYSUM, STRAWFLOWER. Medium, winter bouquets.

HUNNEMANNIA, SANTA BARBARA POPPY. Medium.

KOCHIA, BURNING BUSH or SUMMER CYPRESS. Medium, formal shape, fall color.

LANTANA. Low, border flower in shades of pink.

LAVATERA, ANNUAL MALLOW. Medium, pink.

LARKSPUR. Medium, blue, white and pink.

LOBELIA. Low, blue border plant.

LUNARIA, MONEY PLANT. Medium, for winter bouquets.

MARIGOLDS. Medium, yellow and orange, hardy.

MIGNONETTE. Medium, very fragrant.

NEOPHILA, BABY BLUE EYES. Low.

NICOTIANA, FLOWERING TOBACCO. Tall, fragrant.

NIEREMBERGIA, DWARF CUP FLOWER, Low, blue.

NIGELLA, LOVE-IN-A-MIST. Medium, blue.

NASTURTIUM. Medium, orange, yellow, dark red.

PANSY. Low, always in bloom. All colors.

PETUNIA. Medium, the most showy annual.

PHLOX. Medium, various colors.

POPPY. Medium, bright colors, showy.

PORTULACA, MOSS ROSE. Low, for hot, dry places.

SALPIGLOSSIS, PAINTED TONGUE. Medium. Many colors.

SALVIA, SCARLET SAGE. Medium, brilliant red.

SCABIOSA, PINCUSHION PLANT. Medium.

SCHIZANTHUS, POOR MAN'S ORCHID. Medium.

STOCK. Medium, various colors.

SWEET ROCKET. Medium, hardy, showy, weedy.

SUNFLOWER. Tall, coarse, yellow.

TITHONIA, MEXICAN SUNFLOWER. Tall, new.

TORENA, WISHBONE FLOWER. Medium, blue.

VERBENA. Low, various bright colors.

VINCA, PERIWINKLE. Medium, pink.

ZINNIA. Medium, very hardy. Many varieties.

ANNUALS
Classified as to Height

Over 3 Feet

Cosmos	Sunflower
Nicotiana	Dahlia
Sweet Pea	

Under 12 Inches

Sweet Alyssum	Pansy
Ageratum	Petunia
Begonia	Verbena
Geranium	Lobelia

One to Three Feet High

China Aster	Zinnia
Cornflower	Calendula
Larkspur	Marigold
Nigella	Nasturtium
Phlox	Four O'clock
Shirley Poppy	Salpiglossis
Snapdragon	

BEAUTY AND BEAST

No perennial makes a greater show than the Oriental Poppies. Even their foliage is attractive when out of bloom, and when their large flowers unfold it is like the unfurling of a flag. Red or flame colors are the most common, but now they may be had in various shades of pink and even white.

We do not like to think of the other side of these beautiful flowers, where their sap is saved to make opium to make beasts of men. How strange it is to find these two widely divergent qualities in the same plant!

Annual Vines

SWEET PEA
MORNING GLORY
GOURD
WILD CUCUMBER
SCARLET RUNNER BEAN

Water Plants

WATERLILY. Plants for pools may be had in the hardy type which may be left out in the pools all winter or the large tropical type which must be brought in to the basement over winter. Other common pool plants are the floating Water Hyacinth, Pickerell Rush, Water Iris and Sweet Flag.

Zinnia

Lawns, the Carpets of the Garden

START THEM RIGHT AND SAVE WORK LATER

WHY does the bluegrass grow better in the perennial border than in the lawn area adjoining. Partly, of course, because it is not mowed, and so is able to produce more food through the action of the sun on its green leaves, and this makes a more vigorous root system and top. This is not always the whole reason, for we will usually find that a gardener will not expect his perennials to thrive unless he works up the soil deeply and adds humus or other fertilizers. Often, little or no advance soil preparation is given the lawn areas and so naturally the grass grows better when it gets over in the areas where it is not supposed to be.

Preparation of the Soil BEFORE Seeding a Lawn

If we would keep up our reputation for having the best lawns in the world, we must learn to put more time and money into preparing the soil for lawns *before* planting. The best fertilizers in the world added to the surface *after* planting can not take the place of the humus that should have been put into the soil *before* planting. At least 50% of the budget for a new lawn should be used in preparing the soil before planting. This will pay big dividends later, for a lawn put in without preparation of the soil will often cost more in the first three years for reseeding, fertilizing and weeding than the extra amount for putting it in right in the first place.

Although a lawn is always considered imperative to a homeowner, there is usually little or no money left after the unexpected expenses of building. Thus, a homeowner feels he has to do the work himself or accept the lowest possible bid to put in a lawn. What usually happens is that the poor soil is leveled off and the surface scratched sufficiently to allow the seed to be covered. Perhaps a surface covering of fertilizer is given and the grass manages to get a start. For the next twenty years or so the homeowner finds a continual fight on his hands to keep the grass watered, fertilized and reasonably free of weeds—a terrible price to pay for a hit-or-miss preparation.

Soils vary in texture and quality, so no general rules can be made, but it is certain that ANY soil will be benefitted by deep loosening and a thorough mixture of humus with it. Humus added to a light, sandy soil will enable it to hold more water and plant food and humus added to a heavy clay soil will break it up and allow better drainage and allow the plant roots to penetrate it better. Adding sand to a clay soil or clay to a sandy soil can sometimes be done if a great enough proportion is used and if it is THOROUGHLY mixed to a sufficient depth. The same amount of time and money for adding humus will usually do more good.

Humus or organic matter may be manure (cow, horse or sheep) it may be peatmoss, leaf mould or it may be composted plant material. Fresh manure has also more chemical value while peatmoss has little or none. Peat may profitably be added to most soils up to 35% while fresh manure must be used cautiously to avoid burning the new roots of plants.

The first procedure in preparing to put in a new lawn should be to thoroughly prospect the area to see what kind of soil (or other materials) is there. Dig a hole at least a foot deep every ten feet and if very poor subsoil or rubbish from the building operations is found it is most profitable to entirely remove this and refill with good top soil. Just a weak soil, if it does not contain too much lime or gypsum, may often be so improved by the addition of organic material that good lawns can be grown.

Rough Grading

After the elimination of poor soil areas the next procedure is to rough grade the ground. This should be carefully worked out to allow drainage away from the buildings and avoid low pockets where water may stand. It is well to have the ground staked out with surveyors' instruments if there is any doubt as to slope. A minimum of one-fourth inch slope per foot is usually desirable. In most cases a very steep slope should be avoided. Sometimes a wall may be necessary to eliminate the necessity of an awkward slope. It also should be recognized that sometimes a slight change of level could be worked out to add interest to an otherwise plain surface.

After the poor soil has been replaced and the ground has been rough graded it would be an ideal arrangement to spread about a two to three inch layer of rough manure and then thoroughly till it in. Then, turn this all under about 8 inches, spread on another inch of well rotted manure or peat and manure and till this in. This would give a seed bed 8 inches deep thoroughly loosened and full of plant food. A lawn should grow in this kind of soil with a minimum of additional fertilizing, a minimum of weed trouble and it should be much easier to keep watered. If lawns were planted in the kind of soil that a market gardener would expect to grow good vegetables in, most of the troubles would be over before they begin. Conditions then would be so favorable for the growth of grass that there would be little room for weeds.

129

The above are IDEAL preparations of soil for a lawn. It may not always be possible to do this, but any work put on loosening up the soil and adding organic matter will be well worth while. Rototilling does thoroughly mix added matter to a soil, but often one is mistaken as to the depth that it cultivates. Small areas may still be worked up with a spade.

Everyone who is considering putting in a lawn should acquaint himself with the qualities of a good organic fertilizer. Needless to say thousands of dollars are spent every year on almost worthless materials. Some fertilizers are known to be loaded with weed seeds, though chemically they are quite rich; other materials may have had the weed seeds "cooked" out of them and have also lost much of their chemical value. Sand, sawdust or just plain dirt may so dilute other fertilizers that they have actually little value.

Topsoil

Another factor the gardener should become familiar with is topsoil.

The term "topsoil" has been much abused and may mean anything from common dirt to very rich manure. Topsoil should apply only to soil taken from the upper few inches of virgin or cultivated land.

It is the sort of material that all lawns, if it were possible, should be built on in the first place. Another thing to remember is that it can do comparatively little good when applied in a thin surface layer.

Fertilization

Some gardeners prefer to apply a complete chemical fertilizer in the place of organic material and avoid the chance of introducing weed seeds. This can be done if care is taken not to over-fertilize. It should be remembered that many chemical fertilizers are highly soluble and though they act quickly, they are soon gone. Chemical fertilizers are usually most effective when applied in small quantities and at frequent intervals. If the soil is highly productive no extra stimulation may be needed. Frequently the weeds that are blamed on fertilizer or grass seed actually come from seeds that were already in the ground.

There is no question but what commercial fertilizer, when applied properly, will benefit a lawn. However, its action is generally temporary and does not in any way take the place of good soil, properly prepared. Lawns built in good soil and properly watered have gone for many years with no additional fertilizer and still remain dense and weed free. Since there are many commercial fertilizers and each manufacturer makes his own claims, it is a good idea to ask the State experiment stations to recommend the proper formulas for a good fertilizer.

The three principal ingredients of the usual commercial fertilizers are Nitrogen, Phosphorous and Potash. The Nitrogen is highly soluble so may be wasted if applied at a time when the grass plants are not ready to use it.

Phosphorus does not readily leach into a soil when applied to the surface, and so, is largely wasted when applied after seeding. It is a good plan to mix in some superphosphate when preparing the seed bed. Potash is seldom needed in new soils and so you are paying for something unnecessary when a fertilizer containing it is used.

Soil Conditioners

There is some little questioning recently as to the actual value of the new soil conditioners. Unfortunately much misleading information was given out when these were first introduced. These soil conditioners are designed to do one thing—keep a heavy soil from becoming hard, WHEN IT IS THOROUGHLY MIXED WITH THIS AT A TIME WHEN THE SOIL IS ALREADY IN RATHER GOOD CONDITION. Application of these materials to the surface of hard soils or to large lumps, or to already sandy soils is not effective. People generally do want simple remedies for their difficulties and this sounds like one, but many good gardeners feel that the application of organic matter to a heavy soil will do all that the soil conditioners will do, at possibly a lower cost and with the addition of many intangible benefits that tend to encourage the important soil micro-organisms.

Finish Grading

With preliminary grading and fertilization out of the way it is time to start the finished grading process. This is the place that a cheap lawnmaker begins and cuts the cost in half at the expense of a good lawn. Preparing the final grade and raking can be fun if you enjoy taking a rough piece of ground and molding it as a sculptor might. While some of the preliminary work may be done with power tools, it is hard to get away from the final hand raking. If this raking is carefully done the soft spots will be rather well compacted so that there will be little sinking after the seed is sown. It is well, however, to run over the area with a lawn roller even after it looks to be in perfect condition, checking to be sure that no sunken spots develop. In most cases this is the only use for a roller in lawn making. If the seedbed is too loose the grade may still sink out of shape. On the other hand, a too-firmly compacted seedbed will often resist the entrance of water and cause some surface erosion. Many a home owner makes a practice of rolling the lawn after the seed is in, and while this has a tendency to make the job look well, it often makes watering difficult.

Where it is possible a better way to assure that the seedbed for a new lawn is properly settled is to thoroughly soak the area. This will require that a few days be lost while the ground is drying sufficiently to again loosen up the surface, but it is time and water well spent for it assures that there will be no further settling after the grass is planted and it will save much water later which would be sprinkled on the surface over a dry subsoil.

Seeding

After the area has been properly prepared, and checked, the surface should again be loosened with a light raking prior to sowing the seed. The seed may be broadcast by hand in small areas or various types of seeders may be used. The important thing is to have the seed evenly distributed, and this is rather difficult to do by hand. Rate of seeding varies from 3 to 4 pounds of Bluegrass seed for each 1,000 square feet of lawn. Another very light raking with just the weight of the rake will allow the seed to be slightly covered. Then a top dressing of some well-rotted manure, peat or compost will make the watering job easier and perhaps give a bit of stimulation to the grass. Heavy applications of commercial fertilizer should be avoided at this time.

Watering Up

Immediately after the seed is in the ground and the manure, peat or the surface mulch is applied, the area must be carefully watered. Many gardeners prefer to do this first watering by hand so that it is done thoroughly with no soil erosion. Once the planted soil is wet, great care should be taken to keep, especially, the surface soil from drying out, at least until the lawn is well started. No actual watering rule can be given for this process because soils and temperature vary considerably. Conditions may require watering once, twice or three times a day. As the grass begins to green up, the watering should be gradually done less often but more thoroughly. The important consideration in watering now is to see that moisture gets into the lower soil.

Thorough preparation before planting and proper watering are the most important considerations in building a good lawn. When the roots of a suitable grass are forced to go deeply for food and moisture there is usually a dense top growth which will discourage most of the weeds and pests of lawns.

The proper time to seed a new lawn is a subject of much discussion. In general the best times of the year are after the soil warms up in the spring and before the weather gets severely hot, or the fall period after the weather cools and before severe winter. This means in much of the Rocky Mountain area the period from April through June and from the middle of August to the middle of October.

The old idea of seeding a lawn on the snow may save some work but seldom gives a good lawn in this area. There are some advantages of fall seeding, in that many weed seeds have already sprouted and been eliminated and those that do start are soon killed by frost.

Kind of Seed

The kind of lawn seed used is very important. Many people with lawn experience in this area have come to the conclusion that straight Kentucky Bluegrass is most satisfactory. However, some prefer the addition of a small amount of White Dutch clover. This merely depends on individual preference. It is true that the clover will start quickly, but it may make a spotty lawn. A small amount of Redtop may not harm a lawn, but it seldom is beneficial to it. Ryegrass has been used in mixtures, but it is a coarse grass which adds little to the value of a lawn. In some very sandy locations Fescue has been known to do better than Bluegrass, but on normal soils, it also, adds but little. The rough-stalked Meadowgrass, *Poa trivialis*, usually does a little better in shady places than regular Kentucky Bluegrass.

Merion Bluegrass has been widely advertised as a much superior lawn grass to Kentucky Bluegrass. It is supposed to stand dry weather better, to tolerate closer mowing and to choke out competing weeds. Actually, side by side tests in many areas, simply show this new strain of bluegrass to be about as good as ordinary Kentucky Bluegrass. Many of the superior results claimed for it are probably the result of more care being given it because the seed cost much more.

The Bent grasses make fine, dense carpets for certain requirements, but are generally difficult to establish and maintain. It should be noted that experiment stations are working on improved grasses which may be available in a few years. For very dry conditions, where little water other than rainfall is available and where it is not necessary to mow the lawn often, some of the native grasses such as Wheatgrass or Buffalo grass may be used. There are some grasses which spread from underground runners like the Bermuda or "Salt grass" which may be adapted to lawn use under certain conditions. A little investigation of grasses which have succeeded in each locality will demonstrate those most suitable for varying altitudes and exposures. It should be kept in mind that there is some kind of grass which will grow in almost any part of the Rocky Mountain area where there are human dwellings.

After a lawn is well established, watering becomes the most important maintenance chore. Probably the greatest mistake made in lawn care is that of watering too frequently and not enough applied at one time. This generally uses more water, and at the same time produces a lawn which is shallow-rooted and not able to stand difficult weather or weed competition. Watering by hand seldom does the job properly, simply because few people have the patience to do it thoroughly. While overhead sprinkling does freshen a lawn, it is a bad practice to train it to expect moisture and nourishment in the two top inches of soil. Shallow watering allows the soil to dry out quickly and it actually wastes water. Many improved sprinklers have been put on the market which throw a large circle of water and can be left for a long time without overwatering the lawn. Some gardeners enjoy the convenience of underground sprinkling systems which do a good job when properly engineered and installed. In rural areas where irrigation is available, lawns may be built on such a level that they may be flooded.

It is usually a good practice to delay regular watering of the lawn in the spring. However, when it gets really dry as indicated by its brown color, a thorough watering should be given whether it be December or March. Regular waterings begun too early in the season will simply encourage shallow rooting and cause more work later on.

MODERATION

One of the most common mistakes made by new gardeners is the thought that if a little water or fertilizer will do a garden good, larger quantities will make it grow still better. Some careful cultivation will keep the weeds down but too much deep cultivation may harm the root systems. A little trimming of a tree may improve its appearance and prevent it being broken in a storm, but excessive trimming may cause soft, rank growth which will later be broken off or killed by frost. Too much 2,4-D may kill your dandelions all right—and perhaps the trees and shrubs around the lawn. Neatness may be a characteristic of a good garden, but over neatness can keep a gardener so busy that he will have no time to enjoy the fruits of his labor.

Learning that there is a proper balance between too much and too little is one of the valuable lessons the gardener gets in addition to the more obvious benefits. Nature teaches us, through gardening, things that we might apply to all our activities.

Often there is a "six week's slump" noticed after a new lawn comes up. This is caused by a nitrogen starvation brought about by the beginning of decomposition of the humus used, and this condition may be corrected by the application of a small amount of commercial fertilizer containing nitrogen. One-half pound to the 100 square feet of 20% ammonium sulphate is a most economical treatment though the "complete" fertilizers will do the job at a greater cost.

Mowing

Mowing is another perennial chore in the maintenance of a good lawn. Reliable power mowers have considerably lightened this task. There is always some discussion among gardeners as to the proper height to mow a lawn and whether the clippings should be removed. Experience has shown that it is usually better to cut the grass fairly high—about 1½ to 2 inches. There are many reasons for leaving all the clippings possible on the lawn. Clippings do create a mulch to hold moisture and keep the surface of the soil in good condition. Of course, if the grass is left to grow too long, clippings may appear unsightly. However, when mowed at frequent intervals they will drop down among the standing grasses and not be a menace to appearance. It should be noted here that there may be some benefit in leaving the lawn a little longer at the last mowings in the fall.

Raking

Perhaps it is only natural that many home owners seem to have the urge to rake the lawn in the spring. While raking does make the lawn look neat and allows a new growth of grass to make a quicker showing, it does remove all the good mulch that has accumulated the previous season. This practice is also rather hard on lawns as it exposes bare patches of soil where weeds are anxious to get started, and allows water to run off as well as increasing evaporation. There are many advantages to a mulch on the lawn surface which vigorous raking removes.

Weeds

As mentioned before, proper preparation of the soil and proper watering should eliminate many of the weed problems. However, many times these conditions cannot be controlled and weeds will do a great deal of damage to the lawn. Maintaining a dense, vigorous stand of grass is the best way to prevent weedy lawns. Should weeds get a start, effective measures should be taken at once before they have a chance to choke out good grass.

Two of the worst weed pests in lawns, Dandelions and Plantain, may now be removed with 2, 4-D weedkillers. Extreme caution should be used in applying these weed killers since they may do damage to the other growing plants. Under some circumstances Crabgrass is even more damaging than Dandelions. Many chemical weedkillers have been used in an attempt to eradicate Crabgrass, and unfortunately some have done almost as much damage to the Bluegrass as to the Crabgrass. However, some of the latter preparations have been reported to kill the Crabgrass and its seed without seriously damaging Bluegrass. It should be remembered that Crabgrass is an annual and killed by frost so it is seldom worthwhile spending much time or money combating it in the late fall when it is the most conspicuous. The best time to eradicate it is soon after it comes up in June or July.

See the chapter on weeds for a more complete discussion of the control of lawn weeds especially crabgrass. The control of crabgrass is more a matter of prevention than elimination after infestation.

Other weeds which may become established in lawns are Chickweed, Creeping Euphorbia, Yarrow, Japanese clover and annual Bluegrass. Again the best control of these is a vigorous stand of grass and careful inspection to remove these pests as soon as they get started. Moss also may become a pest in damp, shady places. It does not always indicate a "sour soil" but is usually associated with poor soil, shade and improper watering.

PLANT GROWTH

One of the most common misconceptions of plant growth is that a certain point on a tree's trunk will move up as the tree grows. This is actually impossible.

The only expansion made by a tree as it increases in size is by the development from buds and the addition of annual rings of growth throughout the trunk, branches and roots.

The top of the tree, which might have been exactly three feet high when it was five years old, will be at that exact height for the remainder of the tree's life, but will be surrounded by annual layers of wood until this point is deep in the heart of the tree.

A nail driven in the trunk of a tree will remain at that exact height until it is surrounded and covered up by succeeding years' growth.

Roots will force up sidewalks because new growth will expand in a vertical direction.

An understanding of this principle of plant growth will make it understandable why it is better to put a bolt in a broken tree than to encircle it with a wire.

Insects and Diseases

Eastern areas are sometimes troubled by insect pests such as chinch bugs, grubs and Japanese beetles. Fortunately, there are few lawn insect pests as yet in the Rocky Mountain area. Earthworms or nightcrawlers are blessed by some and cursed by others. Their presence is an indication of humus in the soil and sometimes a sign of over-watering. Earthworms or night-crawlers may do comparatively little good to the soil and may be a decided nuisance by their unsightly piles of castings. Perhaps, the safest remedy for them is a half to one pound of arsenate of lead applied to the surface of each one hundred square feet of lawn. This may be easier to apply evenly if mixed with sand or fine soil, and should be watered in at once. The poison may be more effective if applied just before dark.

Chlordane is also an effective treatment when applied according to directions.

Common lawn diseases of the East are less known here. Fairy ring may cause some damage to Rocky Mountain lawns and there is no known chemical which will easily destroy its growth. However, aerating the soil and watering may help, or the soil may be completely removed in areas affected and replaced with new.

Dithane Z78, Captan or other of the new fungicides can be used to thoroughly saturate the remaining soil after removing the sterile, gray material under the Fairy rings. This will often stop the growth of the fungus if bad watering practices are also corrected.

Dollarspot and other fungus diseases may occasionally be seen here but are seldom serious. The presence of toadstools in a lawn is usually an indication of some buried woody material such as roots of trees which have been cut down. These toadstools, however, will disappear when the humus in the ground has completely decayed and is not being supplied with moisture. In general, any chemical strong enough to kill this fungus growth might sterilize the soil for any other plant growth. Often the problem arises as to what to do for old lawns which will not grow vigorously and have bare spots or excessive amounts of weeds. In many cases the most satisfactory procedure is to spade up the whole area, properly prepare the soil, and reseed. If this is impractical it is possible to go over an old lawn and reseed the worst spots or add seed to thin stands. Much the same procedure should be used as in seeding a new lawn except that small spots cannot be dug as deeply. Sodding can sometimes be done effectively, but it is often difficult to find good sod. When good sod is available, it may be peeled off and relaid to make a very quick and effective job.

Repairing an Old Lawn

When an old lawn needs some patching up, it is seldom advisable to prepare the soil or seed so that the new places will be much different from the old parts. Dig up the bare spots enough to give the necessary loose soil to cover the seeds. Use the same mixture of seed as is already growing in the lawn. After seeding, rake lightly and, if possible, spread on a thin layer of some good mulch; then water carefully for several weeks, just as though you had a new lawn.

House Plants

BRING THE GARDEN INDOORS

MOST people who love to work with plants in a garden also like to bring a few plants into the house, when freezing weather comes along. This allows them to keep their thumbs green over winter and enjoy blooms and foliage while the outdoors is covered with snow.

While it is becoming increasingly easy to have a small greenhouse with plenty of room and controlled conditions for growing a variety of plants over winter, the majority of people must grow only those plants which will tolerate the conditions usually found in their living room. House plants may require a variety of conditions. Some prefer full sun, others no sun, while many like a little of both. Some plants like a lot of water, others, a little and most of them are in between in their moisture requirements. Temperature requirements of plants vary a great deal, too. Extreme heat can be tolerated by some plants while others require it. Soil and fertilizer are also variable factors with house plants.

In the Rocky Mountain area, conditions for house plants are different for many of the same reasons that out-of-doors conditions are different. The air has less humidity, the average soil is more alkaline and there are more sunny days. Since most house plants are in small pots it is rather easy to prepare the soil for each plant's requirements. The amount of water given plants may be carefully controlled and the light available will depend largely on what window space can be used for growing plants. The temperature, however, may be more difficult to control, because we humans usually demand a rather uniform temperature of around 70° Fahrenheit.

The condition that most restricts the variety of house plants that can be grown is likely to be the lack of humidity in the air of the living quarters. This may be partially corrected by leaving a pan or kettle of water on the

137

stove, register or radiator; or allowing a teakettle to steam on an electric plate for a few hours a day.

Large windows may have small plant boxes built on the sill and glass shelves attached above. Pots may also be suspended from brackets or set on tables or stands.

Insect pests on house plants must be carefully controlled before they become numerous enough to cause severe damage. The common pests and diseases with which house plant growers are faced can be found with the general list of insects and disease on other plants.

What might be termed a basic soil for the average house plant contains about the proportions of one-half good garden soil, one-fourth sand and one-fourth peat or leaf mould. Variations in proportions of these soil ingredients will depend upon the plants to be grown. For example: ferns, African violets and similar things prefer a greater proportion of leafmold, and cactus or succulents will thrive better in a soil containing more sand or gravel.

Regardless of the average amount of water needed by plants, none of them like to be continually overwatered, so that the soil remains soggy. On the other hand, no house plants like to be completely dried up, except such as the cactus and amaryllis which require a complete rest at certain times. Temperature preferences can often be humored by growing certain plants in different rooms of various average temperatures.

Most house plants appreciate some additional fertilizer occasionally, especially when they are in the blooming stage. It is a good idea to study the requirements of each plant you plan to grow and give it as nearly as possible conditions with which it can thrive and be happy.

We will not attempt in this little book to explain all the tricks of growing house plants, nor list all of those that may be easily grown. Many other writers have covered this subject thoroughly and since house plants are grown under controlled conditions, their directions will be sufficient for the average grower.

PLANTS GROWING IN A LITTLE SUN AND
A LITTLE SHADE

AFRICAN VIOLET, *Saintpaulia.* Everyone seems to grow African Violets, though they are rather tempermental. However, good results can be obtained when their requirements are fulfilled. African Violets prefer a light, well-drained soil with plenty of moisture, but, they should not be watered to the extent that they remain soggy. Uniform temperature and diffuse sunlight, as from an east window, are other preferred conditions. Some people think that they bloom better when crowded, though others prefer to keep them separated. The leaves may be easily damaged by rough handling, from letting them stand in the sun with water on them or by watering with cold water. Providing they are carefully dried, the leaves may be washed with room temperature water. Some African Violet fanciers prefer to water with almost hot water, when applied at base of plant.

BEGONIA. These may include many varieties from the hardy "Angel wing" types to the more particular Christmas varieties. Here again, experiment to see which grows best for you.

GRAPE IVY. It may be used in almost any room of the house for trailing from fancy pots. Grown in either water or soil, it needs little sun.

WAX PLANT *(Hoya).* A popular vine which sometimes has fragrant waxy heads of bloom. It needs some sun and appreciates being sprayed with water.

DRACAENA. There are many forms, some resembling corn or yucca. They are tolerant of most abuses to which house plants are subjected.

ASPARAGUS FERN. These plants give a light airy effect. Since they have water reservoirs on their roots, they tolerate irregular watering. Asparagus Ferns are often used in pots or hanging baskets.

IMPATIENS (or Sultana). Old-fashioned succulent-stemmed plants that bloom very early and persistently. They are easily started from cuttings in soil or water.

PANDANUS (or Screw Pine). They have white and green, tough, sword-like leaves with thorns on edges.

CROTON. Another plant with odd shaped varicolored leaves. It likes moisture.

CALADIUM (Elephant Ears). This common plant has large, variegated, colored leaves and likes a great deal of moisture. The tubers may be saved to grow again after a rest period.

STRAWBERRY BEGONIA. It is neither a strawberry nor a begonia, but a saxifrage. Described as a frail little vine with small round leaves, it has interesting habit of small plants coming out on long streamers over edge of pot.

MARANTA. An interesting tropical looking plant with variegated leaves. It is called prayer plant from its habit of raising its leaves at night.

CALLA LILY. No plant is more interesting to watch grow; it almost seems that you can see it develop. Started from a bulb, it requires a great deal of water and a reasonable amount of heat.

OXALIS. This plant is easily grown from small bulbs and has clover-like leaves and small cheerful blossoms.

139

COMMON PLANTS FOR A WARM SOUTH WINDOW

Listed in About the Order of Popularity and Easy Growing Characteristics

WANDERING JEW *(Tradescantia)*. Green or variegated vines which are easily rooted in water. Cuttings may be taken from old plants when they become too ragged.

GERANIUMS *(Pelargoniums)*. Includes the common bedding type with variously colored bloom or the cut leaf and scented kinds. All may be easily started by taking cuttings from growing tips when old plants become too coarse and leggy. Geraniums bloom best after they have become somewhat potbound. They like some good fertilizer at blooming time.

CACTUS. A vast variety of shapes and sizes can be grown as house plants, including the popular Christmas cactus. Cacti, like most succulent plants, prefer to be given a rest period at which time they can be rather well dried up for a few weeks. Then they require more water as growth and blooming begins. Christmas cactus failures may often be charged to erratic watering, lack of rest period, irregular temperatures, drafts or too little sun.

AMARYLLIS. Rather temperamental plants, sometimes giving wonderful results and sometimes very disappointing. Some of the same cultural conditions as mentioned under CACTUS may influence their blooming.

OTHER SUCCULENTS: This includes a great variety of plants all of which tolerate heat and drouth because of their fleshy nature. Included in this group are the Crassula, Aloe, Sempervivum, Sedum, Kalanchoe, Mesembryanthemum, Euphorbia, Echeveria, Agave, Haworthia, Stapelia and many others. Most of these have small but interesting bloom and are grown chiefly because of their tolerance of dry indoor conditions and their interesting foliage and bloom.

BEGONIAS. Some varieties are easily grown under the difficult conditions found in a south window. We suggest that you experiment and see which will be happy in your window.

PETUNIAS. Sometimes a few young plants of Petunias brought into the house during the fall will give even more cheerful bloom than the common house plants. Other tender annuals like Marigolds and Larkspur will serve the same purpose.

COLEUS. Because of their bright foliage colors, they are the favorite house plants of many. Chief disadvantage is that they are usually attacked by mealy bugs. These insects, however, can be controlled by washing the leaves or touching visible bugs with a little alcohol on a toothpick, or spraying with Malathion.

FUCHSIAS. These are old favorites, coming mainly in combinations of the reds and purples. They prefer considerable shade and must be kept growing vigorously, for once retarded they seldom amount to much.

OLEANDERS. Another old favorite which often becomes so large that even when potted in a tub they are difficult to care for over winter. Must be watched carefully for infestations of mealy bug and scale.

HOUSE PLANTS GROWING WITHOUT DIRECT SUNSHINE

ENGLISH IVY *(Hedera helix)*. Often used to trail from small wall pots or is trained around the ceiling. Chief enemy is scale which may be effectively controlled by washing or spraying with a safe miscible oil.

PHILODENDRON. A popular plant for many uses. It must have well drained soil. Is easily started from tip cuttings. There are many forms of Philodendron which are equally useful.

MONSTERA. This plant has large leaves with holes in them. It likes sprays of water on its leaves, light soil, support. Do not cut off aerial roots.

SANSEVIERIA. This plant, which has many common names such as Snake Plant or Bowstring Hemp, tolerates much abuse and neglect. It seldom blooms and has practically no pests.

FERNS. Many of the attractive ferns may be grown with little but reflected light. They require very light soil and frequent watering.

ASPIDISTRA. As easily grown as the Sansevieria, it likes frequent watering and to have its leaves washed.

CHINESE EVERGREEN *(Aglaonema)*. It has large leaves and occasionally small Jack-in-the-pulpit-like flowers. Will grow in soil or water with no direct sun.

NEPHTHYTIS. An interest climbing vine which has arrow shaped leaves. Similar in cultural requirements to Chinese Evergreen.

FIGS *(Ficus)*. They have large leathery leaves in a variety of patterns depending upon variety. Sometimes grow out of bounds so should be kept a little potbound. Moderate watering satisfies them.

PEPEROMIA. Another plant with large variegated leaves. It is easily grown. This plant does prefer moist air.

DIEFFENBACHIA. A tropical looking plant; it likes average growing conditions and a light soil.

SCHEFFLERA. An Australian plant with compound leaves. Will grow quite large in time.

POTHOS. A small vining plant that will grow in shade or some sun. Similar to the philodendrons. Do not overwater. Will thrive on neglect.

AUCUBA. An upright plant with large leaves. Interesting variegated foliage. Must be checked frequently for insects.

TRICHOSPORUM. A small, slow-growing vine with leathery leaves. Trails rather than climbing.

PLANTS FROM THE FLORIST AT CHRISTMAS OR EASTER

How to take care of plants from the florist, often given during the holidays, is always a question in the minds of folks who would like to keep them as long as possible. Usually the best advice is to throw them away when they are no longer beautiful. Many such plants have been "forced" or grown out of their natural season. Thus it is difficult to give them the controlled care that they have become accustomed to in the greenhouse. Everyone wants to try to grow them on or at least hold them as long as it is practical. The following are some general directions for culture.

AZALEA. It must have frequent watering, uniform rather low temperatures, rather humid air, acid soil and a rest period after blooming.

CYCLAMEN. Requirements of this plant much the same as with the Azalea. No water should be allowed in the crown.

EASTER LILY. Plants may be set outside and will sometimes bloom again in the open. Don't expect, however, to bring them in again in the fall and have another bloom. It is dangerous to put these lilies in a garden with other lily species as they may be carriers of the deadly mosaic disease.

HYDRANGEA. This plant should be cut back to six inches in the spring, repotted and set outside to rest for a few months. Then it may be brought inside during the fall, watered and given more heat and fertilizer. It needs heavy watering and light while blooming.

POINSETTIA. Should be treated about the same as the Hydrangea, but more sensitive to sudden drops in temperature.

GARDENIA. Uniform temperature, careful watering and high humidity are imperative for these temperamental plants.

BABY RAMBLER ROSES. They may be kept growing after bloom is gone, then cut back and set outside in a sunny place, in spring. Check frequently for aphids and red spider.

GLOXINIA. Needs treatment similar to African Violets, but is more sensitive to lack of humidity and varying temperatures. It will set buds but drop them before blooming unless conditions are just right. Spidermites and thrips often attack them.

CHRYSANTHEMUMS. They may be gradually dried up after all bloom is gone and put outside when warm weather comes. Some varieties may be hardy enough to bloom again in the open.

TULIPS, HYACINTHS and NARCISSUS. If the foliage is left on these plants and they are allowed to grow and ripen more or less naturally, a new bulb sufficiently large enough to bloom again next season may be formed. They may be set out after they are dormant or, if still growing, moved without disturbing the soil around them.

Recommended reading:

ALL ABOUT HOUSE PLANTS, Montague Free, Pub. by American Garden Guild and Doubleday.

PICTURE PRIMER OF INDOOR GARDENING, M. O. Goldsmith, Pub. by Houghton Mifflin Co.

GARDEN IN YOUR WINDOW, Jean Hersey, Pub. by Prentice-Hall.

THE TRICK OF GROWING HOUSE PLANTS IN EVERY WINDOW, Sophia Naumberg, Pub. by Floral Art, West Englewood, N. J.

THE AFRICAN VIOLET, Helen VanPelt Wilson, Pub. by Barrows.

BEGONIAS, HOW TO GROW THEM, Bessie R. Buxton, Oxford Univ. Press.

GERANIUMS-PELARGONIUMS, Helen VanPelt Wilson, Pub. by Barrows.

CACTI FOR THE AMATEUR, Scott E. Hazelton, Pub. by Abbey Garden Press.

SUCCULENTS FOR THE AMATEUR, J. R. Brown, Pub. by Abbey Garden Press.

THE COMPLETE BOOK OF FLOWER ARRANGEMENT, Rockwell and Grayson, Pub. by Doubleday.

FLOWER ARRANGEMENT FOR EVERYONE, Dorothy Biddle and Dorothea Blom, Pub. by Barrows.

Plants for Shady Places

MUCH of the existing horticultural literature refers to shady spots as very difficult places. This may be true in England or Pittsburgh, but in our area many plants listed as preferring full sun will do better in half sun and those listed as growing in half sun will like it in a spot where the sun only hits them in the early morning or late afternoon. Because here the sun shines more days in the year and there are generally less clouds and smog to filter it, we need to plan for shady nooks where the weather is tempered both for us humans and the plants.

Actually, some of the nicest things grow here in those shady places, and by using care in selecting plants and caring for them some very attractive nooks can be made from otherwise neglected spots.

Here are some suggestions for suitable plants for a shady spot. Others may be added to this list if the soil is especially favorable.

EVERGREENS

Native Low Juniper
Arborvitae
White Fir (Dwarfed)
Dwarf Alberta Spruce
Douglas Fir
Yew (sometimes)

SHRUBS

Forsythia
Elderberry
Privet
Viburnum, carlesi, burk-woodi, carcephalum, dentatum and lentago
Ribes aureum (Flowering currant) and other currants
Common Snowberry
Coralberry
Chenault Snowberry
Honeysuckles, native and cultivated
Euonymous atropurpureus, alatus, radicans and others
Bush Cinquefoil
Hydrangeas
Mockoranges
Dogwoods
Winter Jasmine
Jetbead
Weigelia
Pearlbush

PERENNIALS

English Primroses	Anchusa myosotidiflora	Trillium
Bleeding Hearts	Lily-of-the-Valley	Hemerocallis
Monkshood (Aconitum)	Mertensia virginica	Monarda
Foxglove (Digitalis)	Anemones	Valeriana
Saxifraga cordifolia	Plantain Lilies	Campanulas
Columbines	Violas	Polemonium
Meadow Rue (Thalictrum)	Lobelia cardinalis	Platycodon (balloon)
Globe Flower (Trollius)	Gas Plant (Dictamnus)	Heuchera
Christmas Rose	Cimicifuga	

FERNS

Colorado Male	Rock Fern	Ostrich Fern
Lady Fern	Maidenhair	

BULBS

Tuberous Begonias	Tulips	Lilies
Tigridia	Snowdrops	Lycoris

VINES

Vinca minor	English Ivy	Boston Ivy
Euonymus	Clematis	Honeysuckles

BROADLEAF EVERGREENS

Mahonia or Oregon Grape	Pryacantha or Firethorn	Euonymus, Vining or Upright

WILDFLOWERS IN SHADY NOOKS

We all enjoy the brilliant masses of color from the wildflowers that grow on the plains or open hillsides, but for those things of rare and delicate beauty we go to the moist, shady nooks under the trees. There we may find the Columbine in blue, red or yellow, or if we are very lucky we may see a flashy Wood Lily, Yellow Ladys Slipper or Coralroot. Sometimes we might find the ground carpeted with Twinflowers, Dwarf Cornel or Pyrolas. Several other rare orchids may be found in such a place.

Tough Plants for Spots Where "Nothing" Grows

SUITABLE plants for especially hot, dry or alkaline places will always be one of the number one problems for gardeners in the Rocky Mountain area. Just because we have tried the ordinary plants in these places, and failed, does not necessarily mean that we must give up and leave unattractive bare ground around our homes and businesses. If we will hunt, we will find many plants that will enjoy these difficult places. (And I don't mean just cactus and soapweed, though these may even be appropriate in certain places.)

First of all, there is that strip of parking which resists all attempts to be covered with lawn. Try one of the low sedums or the lovely portulaca. I have seen some very attractive plantings of both of these.

Suppose the problem is a narrow strip along the foundation on the south, and everything has failed. Try Four O'clocks. They love this kind of place and provide cheerful bloom every afternoon, all summer. In a little less severe situation you might try Zinnias, Calendulas, Cosmos, Marigolds, Hollyhocks, Iris or Castor Beans.

If you want a more permanent planting, there is a variety of shrubs which will delight in these difficult places. The Sumacs, Tamarix, Caraganas, Lilacs, Peking Cotoneasters, Shrub Roses and Leadplants are all tough, and, when everything else fails, the Matrimony Vine will grow and give a little touch of green.

There are several trees which will thrive under difficult conditions. Honeylocust and Hackberry have demonstrated their ability to grow in difficult places. Green Ash and Russianolive will do with very little water. Out on the dry, windy plains and up in the steep mountains, we will find that the Pines and Junipers will thrive and be happy. The groves of Pinion Pine and Oneseed Juniper found growing naturally at the edge of the desert, prove their ability to grow with little care. Ponderosa Pine and Rocky Mountain Juniper make beautiful trees but ask little in the way of soil or water.

We could increase the chances of these things growing where little water is available, by improving the soil so that it will most effectively use the water that is available. We can also make a special effort to give newly transplanted things an extra amount of water, until they get their deep roots established.

If we can't grow many of the things that we like, let us learn some other things that we CAN grow under adverse conditions. Even the desert places will support some Cactus, Sagebrush or Yucca.

GAMBLING

It may be that one of the unrecognized attractions in gardening is that it gives us a legitimate outlet for our inherent instinct for gambling. The difference between this kind of gambling and playing the horses or the "one-armed bandits" is that in those man-made forms of gambling we are sure to lose and in gambling with Nature we have a good chance of winning.

More Plants for the Plains

A LARGE proportion of the Rocky Mountain area is known as the High Plains, where there is little rainfall and much wind. The soil is more or less alkaline, the sun is hot in the summer and the wind is cold in the winter, making planting conditions difficult at best. While this area probably will not support a large population any more than our rugged mountain country, with improved methods of culture, there can be grown much better crops, as well as ornamental plants. Of course, the first consideration here must be to make a "living" from the soil, but too little attention has been given in the past to making homes which were worth "living for."

General conditions are much the same over this plains area, but there are variations such as the valleys where irrigation is possible and southern areas where some things which are not so winter hardy can be grown. The following are four steps which the home gardener in this area may take to develop more and better home grounds:

1—A carefully devised plan for each place, indicating where various trees and plants are desirable to provide shade, fruit, windbreak, screening, timber, or just beauty. 2—Selection of plants which are adaptable to conditions found in the area. 3—Learning the practices which will give these plants the best chance of survival, such as proper watering, shade, soil improvement, and protection from the wind. 4—Learning and practicing all possible methods of conserving natural rainfall through reservoirs and mulches or cultivation and, where practical, development of additional water from wells.

There are in most communities some gardeners who have gone beyond their neighbors in experimenting with possible plants and developing methods of successfully growing them. Seek out these people and learn from them.

Hardy Things to Plant First
EVERGREENS

Ponderosa Pine	Limber Pine	Rocky Mtn. Juniper
Austrian Pine	Bristlecone Pine	(Cedar)
Pinyon Pine		Utah and Oneseed Juniper

DECIDUOUS TREES

Native Cottonwood
Siberian (Chinese) Elm
Honeylocust
Russianolive

Boxelder
American Elm
Silver Poplar
Hackberry

Green Ash
Treeofheaven
(Poplar and Willows must
have plenty of water)

TALL SHRUBS

Siberian Peashrub
Tamarisk
Bush Honeysuckle
Russianolive
Sumac

Peking Cotoneaster
Privet
Persian and Common Lilac
Rose Acacia
Forestiera

Skunkbush Sumac
Chokecherry
Wild Plum
Buckthorn

LOW SHRUBS

Leadplant
Indigobush
Spirea
Cotoneaster

Currant
Matrimony Vine
Dwarf Peashrub
Wild Rose

Yucca
Alpine Currant
Flowering Quince

HEDGES

Russianolive
Siberian Elm

Lilac
Bush Honeysuckle

Cotoneaster

PERENNIALS

Achillea
Fall Aster
Boltonia
Painted Daisy
Chrysanthemum
Baptisia
Helenium

Hemerocallis
Iris
Liatris
Blue Flax
Nepeta
Echinops
Plume Poppy

Goldenrod
Salvia
Saponaria
Hollyhock
Veronica
Sedum
Thermopsis

ANNUALS

Zinnia
Marigold
Calendula
Petunia
Cosmos

Cleome
Sweet Alyssum
Bachelor Button
Four o'Clock
Nasturtium

Poppy
Portulaca
Sunflower

VINES

Engelmann Ivy
Halls Japanese Honeysuckle

Silverlace Vine
Morning Glory

Native White Clematis

FRUIT

Sour Cherries

Sand Cherries

Hybrid Plums

Desirable Plants to Add Later

EVERGREENS

Douglasfir (In Favored
  locations)
Pfitzer Juniper
Savin Juniper

Mugho Pine (Winter burns
  in exposed places)
Blue Spruce (Needs extra
  care)

Chinese Arborvitae (For
  southern part)

TREES

Flowering Crab
Black Walnut
Willow
Soft Maple
Kentuckycoffeetree

Bur Oak
Poplar
(In Southern Areas)
Sycamore
Mulberry

Osageorange
Catalpa
Linden

147

SHRUBS

Elderberry	Flowering Plum	Hawthorn
Snowball	Redleaf Plum	Rock Spirea
Snowberry	(Last four need care like	Althea
Coralberry	orchard trees)	Pin Cherry
Forsythia	Redosier Dogwood	Hibiscus
Shrub Roses	Buddleia	Buffaloberry
Flowering Almond	Japanese Barberry	Redbud
Flowering Quince	Mockorange	

PERENNIALS AND BULBS

Tritoma	Delphinium	Goldenglow
Peony	Bleeding Heart	Monarda
Phlox	Columbine	Penstemon
Gladiolus	Coreopsis	Viola
Dahlia	Dianthus	Hibiscus
Lily	Campanula	
Oriental Poppy	Gaillardia	

ANNUALS

Verbena	Nasturtium	Snapdragon
Stock	Nicotiana	Calliopsis
Salpiglossis	Morning Glory (Very good)	Cockscomb
Sweet Pea	Phlox	Bachelor Button
Larkspur	Aster	

FRUIT

Peach (Hardy only in fa-vored locations)	Plum	Everbearing Strawberry (Berries must have lots of
Apricot (Rarely sets fruit)	Manchu Cherry	water)
Apple	Gooseberry	Buffaloberry
	Everbearing Raspberry	

VINES

Purple Clematis	Boston Ivy	(All above need pro-tection)
Goldflame Honeysuckle	Climbing Roses	

SWEET CORN

An early-maturing sweet corn planted in mid-June will usually pro-duce roasting ears in early September. Maturing at that time, when the weather is cooler, the corn is sweeter and the corn worms have usually given up in disgust and quit so that most ears are clean and worm-free.

Sweet corn deteriorates rapidly after being picked, so, if you would complete the recipe for really good sweet corn, it must be picked, cooked and eaten quickly. Wise gardeners discovered this fact many years ago, but many people still do not know of it.

I plan each year to plant a sizable patch of sweet corn in June so that I can invite my friends to enjoy really good corn in September. I wait until the guests arrive, and not until then do I gather the corn. It is quickly husked by the assembled people and plunged into kettles of boiling water for from three to five minutes, only. Then, with a little salt and melted butter, it is really something to make one drool. People who claim that they do not like sweet corn have been found later trying to hide six or seven empty cobs. The grocery stores do not like me for no one who has ever eaten this kind of corn can ever again enjoy the tough, tasteless sort that has been several days from patch to plate.

Plants for Mountain Homes

LANDSCAPING of home grounds at altitudes of over six thousand feet has been neglected generally because it does offer some difficulties. When suitable plants are selected, however, the advantages of carefully planned plantings often outweigh the disadvantages.

In the higher altitudes, the rainfall is usually more adequate, there are more cloudy days, and more snow in the winter. Then, too, the soil has better drainage and there is less alkali present. The limiting factors, as far as plant growth is concerned, are the rather severe cold weather, the high winds, together with the fact that the growing season is often very short.

While some plants used successfully in the irrigated areas at four to six thousand feet will kill back in the higher altitudes, still others will grow with greater vigor and produce larger blooms at high altitudes than when the season is longer.

Protection from wind and sun and the direction which the planting is facing make considerable difference in how it will thrive. Gardeners should note the types of plants which naturally grow under their conditions and use similar things in native and imported plants.

Residences in the higher towns may be landscaped much the same as those at lower elevations, making effective use of hardy material. Mountain cabins, however, which are located in the wilds, should be carefully planted to preserve all of the charm of the native landscape. As many as possible of the native plants which grow in the neighborhood or similar altitudes should be used, though many imported things which are equally hardy and fit the situation are available. It is well to avoid conspicuously cultivated plants such as lilacs, iris, and cannas.

149

Since buildings must be definitely man-made, it is possible in keeping with good taste to make the immediate design of the grounds conform to the lines of the house and be somewhat formal. The planting farther out, however, should blend well with the native landscape. Views of distant mountains and closer valleys should be carefully preserved.

At Elevations of 7,000 to 9,000 Feet

Exposure to wind and sun as well as elevation will determine which will be hardy. Figures given are average height under cultivation. Arranged more or less in order of their usefulness.

EVERGREENS, Native

Colorado Spruce 80'	Engelmann Spruce 80'	Douglasfir 70'
White Fir 60'	Alpine Fir 80'	Limber Pine 40'
Bristlecone Pine 40'	Lodgepole Pine 60'	Colorado Pinyon Pine 15'
Colorado Juniper 40'	Oneseed Juniper 15'	Mtn. Common Juniper 3'

Introduced

Scotch Pine 80'	Pfitzer Juniper 5'	Tamarixleaf Juniper 2'

DECIDUOUS TREES, Native

Narrowleaf Poplar 60'	Smoothbark Poplar 70'	Balsam Poplar 40'
Quaking Aspen 30'	Plains Poplar 70'	Boxelder 40'

Introduced

Siberian Elm 60'	Common Hackberry 60'	Honeylocust 60'
American Elm 80'	Soft Maple 80'	Green Ash 60'
White Willow 40'	Russian Willow 40'	Bigtooth Aspen 40'

SHRUBS, Native

Bush Rockspirea 4'	Bunchberry Elder 4'	Colo. Redosier Dogwood 6'
Boulder Raspberry 5'	Mountain Snowberry 3'	Wax Currant 4'
Serviceberry 8'	Western Chokecherry 10'	Water Birch 12'
Thinleaf Alder 15'	Greenes Mountainash 12'	Bush Cinquefoil 2'
Bearberry Honeysuckle 3'	Beaked Filbert 8'	Wild Rose 2'
Wild Gooseberries 3'	Wild Currants 3'	Cliff Jamesia 4'
Bluestem Willow 8'	Coyote Willow 6'	Shrub Willows 8'
American Red Raspberry 2'	Rocky Mtn. Maple 10'	Pachystima 1'
Russet Buffaloberry 3'	American Plum 8'	Colorado Hawthorn 15'
True Mountainmahogany 4'	Antelope Bitterbrush 3'	Bog Birch 3'
Mountain Ninebark 3'	Pin Cherry 8'	Golden Currant 5'
Mooseberry Viburnum 3'	Western Thimbleberry 3'	Creeping Mahonia ½'
R. M. Smooth Sumac 4'	Skunkbush Sumac 5'	Scrub Oak 6'
Snowbrush Ceanothus 2'	Fendlers Ceanothus 1'	Intermediate Ceanothus 3'
Bearberry Kinnikinnick 3"		

Introduced

Common Lilac 10'	Persian Lilac 8'	Late Lilac 8'
Hungarian Lilac 8'	Chinese Lilac 10'	Alpine Currant 3'
Siberian Peashrub 10'	Dwarf Peashrub 3'	Shrub Roses, various 6'
Vanhoutte Spirea 6'	Frobel Spirea 3'	Anthony Waterer Spirea 2'
Tartarian Honeysuckle 10'	Common Snowberry 3'	Coralberry 3'
Peking Cotoneaster 6'	Kashgar Tamarix 8'	Snowball 8'
Korean Barberry 4'	Manchu Cherry 8'	Matrimonyvine 4'

VINES, Native

Western Virginsbower	Rocky Mountain Clematis	Oriental Clematis
Hop	Thicket Creeper	

Introduced

Halls Honeysuckle	Silvervine Fleeceflower

PERENNIALS, Native

Penstemon 2'	Sedum ½'	Sieversia 1'
Gaillardia 1'	Gentian 1'	Aster 1'
Solomonplume 1'	Goldenglow 3'	Violet ½'
Harebell 1'	Twistedstalk 1½'	Fairybell 1½'
Allium 1'	Anemone 1'	Alumroot ½'
Wallflower 1'	Corydalis 1'	Purple Fringe 1'
Thermopsis 1'	Mertensia 1'	Valerian 1½'
Lupine 2'	Thalictrum 2'	Horsemint 1½'
Geranium 1'	Gilia 1½'	

Introduced

Coral Lily 1½'	Phlox 1½'	Pinks 1'
Bleedingheart 1½'	Hesperis 1½'	Columbine 2'
Iris 1½'	Peony 1½'	Daylily 2'
Shirley Poppy 1'	Iceland Poppy 1'	Oriental Poppy 2'
Saponaria 1½'	Shasta 2'	Tansy 2'
Gypsophila 1½'	Delphinium 4'	Statice 2'

FRUIT, Native

Wild Gooseberries 3'	Serviceberries 6'	Sand Cherries 3'
Wild Currants 3'	Wild Raspberries 2'	

Introduced

Hybrid Plums 6'	Hardy Crabapples 10'

Plants for the Southwest

THE WESTERN area of limited rainfall, which extends from the north to the south boundaries of our country, might be divided in two general divisions determined by the average temperature and length of growing season and the resultant difference in ornamental plants that will thrive. This line would roughly be the state lines east and west from the Four Corners or the line between Utah and Colorado on the north and Arizona and New Mexico on the south. The southwest area would include Arizona, New Mexico, western Texas and southeastern California. Conditions of drouth, and alkaline soil are similar in the whole western area, but, because of longer season, the plants used in the southwest are quite different. Of course, no definite line can be made because the change in climate is gradual. In some of the higher elevations well south into New Mexico much the same plants can be grown as would be at Denver, a thousand or more feet lower. The line shown on our plant zone map is average and many exceptions occur. The near tropical area in these southern states is rather well indicated by the native plants. Where the Saguaro cactus, Sotol, Beargrass and "Skirt" Yucca grow, there a much different and almost tropical list of ornamental plants is called for.

Perhaps the southern third of Colorado and the northern third of New Mexico could be called the transition zone where most all the ornamental plants in our general lists would be suitable, but many on the borderline list would begin to appear and thrive.

These would include things like the Arborvitaes and Yews among the evergreens; Flowering Cherries, Flowering Peaches, Flowering Dogwood, Redbud, Smoke tree, Golden chain, Prunus pissardi, Tree Wistaria and some of the Mulberries in the small trees; some of the borderline Coton-

151

easters and Barberries, Deutzias, Euonymus patens, Firethorn, Hydrangeas and Weigelias, among the shrubs.

In this transition area, some of the plants only half hardy farther north begin to dominate, especially, the Firethorns and Euonymus and some of the broadleaf evergreens.

In the southern and lower parts of the area where almost tropical climate prevails, the things like various palms, Italian Cypress, Arizona Cypress, Magnolias, Pecans, Texas Walnuts, Arizona Ash, and occasional Pepper-trees, Pomegranates and Figs begin to be seen.

Along with these dominant things will be found occasional specimens of Desert Willow, Mexican Elder, Orange, Abelia, Albizza, Crepe Myrtle, Jasmine, Nandina, Shrub Myrtle, Oleander, Photinia, Poinciana, California Privet, Baccharis, Desert Broom and the Tree Tamarix.

Plantings over the area might still include the old standbys among the evergreens such as Blue Spruce, Douglasfir, Austrian Pine, Pfitzer Juniper, Colorado Juniper, Eastern Red Cedar and White Fir. Deciduous trees might include the easily grown and weedy things like Chinese Elm, Lombardy Poplar, Tree-of-Heaven Ailanthus, Black Locust, Silver Poplar, Cottonwood, Box Elder, and Weeping Willow; the better trees like Hackberry, Honeylocust, Western Catalpa, American Elm, American Linden, Arizona Ash, Soft Maple, Sycamore and the small or flowering trees like the Hawthorns, Russianolive, Crab, Apricot, Apples and Flowering Plums. In favorable places, there will be grown some of the better, and longer-lived trees like the Sugar Maple, Norway Maple, Schwedler Maple, some of the Oaks, Mountainash, Birch and Buckeye.

Many of the old standbys in shrubs are still effectively used here. These might include the various Lilacs, many Spireas, Barberries, Honeysuckles, Forsythias, the aristocratic Viburnums, Shrub Roses, several Mockoranges, Vitex, Pussy Willows, Beautybushes, Buddleia or Butterfly bush, Cotoneasters, Redtwig and other shrub Dogwoods, Flowering Quinces, Hibiscus, and Caryopteris or Blue Spireas.

As with most comparatively new areas, the nice things among the natives are generally considered as weeds and have not been used as they should have been. Some of the things which grow naturally in this area and give an appropriate character to the landscape include: Palo Verde trees, Agave, Sotol, Beargrass, Ocotillo, Barrel Cactus and many smaller cacti, Manzanita, Alligator Juniper, several of the really wonderful evergreen Oak, Ceanothus, many of the Yucca, Madrone, Mexican Pinion Pine, Three leaf and five leaf Sumac, Thimbleberry, Mountain Spirea, Mock-orange, Arizona Sycamore, Mountain Mahogany, Wild Cherry, Desert Willow, Bigtooth Maple, Aspen and various pine.

We strongly recommend that residents in this area get a copy of that delightful little book, "Southwest Gardening" by Rosalie Doolittle and Harriet Tidebohl, Published by the University of New Mexico Press.

Even garden vegetables may be beautiful as well as useful. Carrots make a nice border for a flower bed. Rhubarb and Asparagus are quite ornamental when not cut back too severely. Chives and Mint are also useful for this double role.

Plants for the Arkansas Valley

IN SOME areas of our Rocky Mountain-Plains region there are specialized conditions which require an additional plant list. Typical of one
important situation is the Arkansas Valley, where there is little rainfall
and conditions similar in general to the surrounding plains but a slightly
longer season because of the lower altitude and being farther south; more
alkalinity in the soil and supplementary irrigation water.

The lists of plants suitable for the plains areas will be useful here, but
because of the mentioned differences the following additional plants will
often thrive. These lists will also apply, with modifications, to others
similar areas such as the Grand Valley and parts of Utah.

EVERGREENS

Tamarix Savin Juniper	Vonehron Savin Juniper	Eastern Red Cedar
Mountain Common Juniper	Black Hills Spruce	Scotch Pine

DECIDUOUS TREES

Sugar Maple	White Ash	Pin Oak
Schwedler Maple	European Mountainash	Red Oak
Norway Maple	Black Cherry	English Elm
Cutleaf Weeping Maple	Downy Hawthorn	Cork Elm
Cutleaf Weeping Birch	Native Aspen	Moline Elm
European White Birch	Horsechestnut	

FRUIT

Late Apples	Grapes

VINES

Wistaria	Trumpet Vine	Wintercreeper Euonymus

SHRUBS

Cranberry Bush	Devils Walkingstick	Manchu Cherry
Floribunda Rose	Mountain Alder	Bladder Senna
Austrian Copper Rose	Arrowwood	Vitex
Euonymus	Gray Dogwood	Frobel Spirea
Late Lilac	Common Ninebark	Firethorn
Prairie Rose	Smoketree	Wayfaringtree Viburnum
Bush Cinquefoil	Jetbead	Japanese Tree Lilac
Redleaf Barberry	Garland Spirea	Amur Maple
Winged Euonymus	Chenault Snowberry	Nannyberry
Desmodium	Pussy Willow	Lemoine Mockorange
Lodense Privet	Beauty Bush	Lilac Honeysuckle
Bluestem Willow	Hydrangea	Sandcherry
Glossy Buckthorn	Mountain Birch	
Mentor Barberry	Buffaloberry	

PERENNIALS AND BULBS

Lycoris	Alyssum saxatile	Euphorbia
Sweet Pea	Violet	Lythrum
Trailing Phlox	Babysbreath	Valeriana
Maltese Cross	English Primrose	Statice
Flowering Tobacco	Redhot Poker	

ANNUALS AND TUBERS

Dahlia	Canna	Castor Bean
Sweet Rocket	Buttercup	Mexican Burning Bush
Salvia	Pansy	Mexican Torch Flower
Lobelia	African Daisy	Candytuft

153

Sedum   *Myrtle*

Ground Covers—Other Than Grass

THERE are often ground surfaces, such as steep banks, shady places under trees or especially hot spots where grass would grow only with difficulty, where some ground cover is needed. There are a number of low trailing plants, which will grow under these difficult conditions, and require little care and no mowing. The most desirable things are those which retain their foliage over the greatest part of the year. Such things as trailing Myrtle and English Ivy are good, but require a shady spot to avoid sunburn. When we learn to propagate and transplant them, there are several good natives like Kinnikinnick and Oregon grape that are very effective. Sometimes slightly taller plants like some of the wild roses and snowberries will fill the requirements. Several of the plants generally considered as rock garden plants will make a hardy and dense mass when used as a ground cover. The Cerastiums, Trailing Phlox and Sedums are in this class.

We need to learn, also, that some spots may have ground covers other than living plants. The ancient Roman gardens and the more modern gardens of California used flagstone paving, brick terraces, gravel court-yards and shallow water areas to serve the same purpose of framing and foreground as would be done with a lawn or other living ground covers.

Below are listed some of the most useful plants for use as ground covers in this area:

Aegopodium podograria variegatum, BISHOP WEED or GOUTWEED. This is a rather coarse plant with green and white leaves. It is very effective where it can be confined to limited areas.

Aethionema, PERSIAN CANDYTUFT. A delicate little rock plant with pink flowers.

Ajuga, BUGLE PLANT. This is a popular ground cover for shade or part sun. There are varieties with green leaves and those with bronze. The flowers are usually blue, but there are some variations.

Alyssum saxatile, MADWORT. Taller, gray foliage, yellow flowers.

Arabis alpina, ROCK CRESS. Mats of gray foliage and white flowers.

Arctostaphylos uva-ursi, BEARBERRY. A beautiful evergreen native. Hard to transplant and requires well drained soil.

154

Arenaria, SANDWORT. Small rock garden plant with white flowers.

Armeria, THRIFT. Small rock garden plant.

Asperula odorata, SWEET WOODRUFF. Forms mats in the shade with small white flowers.

Aster alpinus, ALPINE ASTER. Low purple daisy.

Aubretia deltoides, ROCK CRESS. Thrives in part shade.

Campanula, BLUEBELLS. There are several varieties that do well around rocks and walls in part shade.

Cerastium tomentosum, SNOW-IN-SUMMER. Here is a really aggressive perennial that will cover banks, rocks or slopes in the sun. Gray foliage and white flowers.

Convallaria majalis, LILY-OF-THE-VALLEY. This is the old standby for the north side of the house where no sun shines, but it will grow well with some sun. Nice white flowers, fragrant.

Dianthus, GARDEN PINKS. The smaller types are the hardiest. Some will make nice mats on the ground. Spicy, fragrant flowers.

EUONYMUS. There are several species very suitable for ground covers in partial shade. The tiny minimus or kewensis is beautiful and hold its foliage all year.

Hedera helix, ENGLISH IVY. This and the Baltic Ivy is one of the best ground covers in the shade. Evergreen.

Iberis sempervirens, HARDY CANDYTUFT. Taller perennial, almost evergreen. White flowers.

Lysimachia nummularia, MONEYWORT. A beautiful trailing vine with small yellow flowers.

Mahonia repens, CREEPING HOLLYGRAPE. Another fine native evergreen. The difficulty again is in transplanting. Holly-like leaves with yellow flowers and purple fruit.

Phlox subulata, TRAILING PHLOX. Cheerful flowers covering the plants in spring. Comes in shades of pink, blue, red and white.

Sedums in great variety, STONECROPS. Some good ones are stoloniferum, acre, coccineum, album, seiboldia, dasyphyllum and many others. Sedums will grow in hot places.

Sempervivum, HOUSELEEK. Similar to the sedum in hardiness and ability to stand hot places.

Thymus serpyllum, THYME. A nice low ground cover. Will stand some traffic.

Veronica, SPEEDWELL. Usually low and with small blue flowers, but some variations.

Vinca minor, MYRTLE or PERIWINKLE. One of the best ground covers as it holds its foliage throughout the year, has cheerful blue flowers and is easy to grow, especially in shady places.

VIOLETS and VIOLAS. Sometimes run wild and look very nice.

Ajuga

Trailing Phlox

We Love the Sunshine States

WE LIVE HERE because we like it here. We love the mountains for their beauty and wildness. We love the trees and flowers and rocks and streams that are in the mountains.

We love the vast plains with their grass and ranches.

We even believe that the cities and towns in this area are more pleasant to live in.

We love the cool breezes and we love the sunshine.

We recognize that many of the qualities that make up this country that we love are perishable and we would do everything possible to keep this wonderful area just as nice for our descendants as we found it when we came here.

We know that water is the one thing that makes much of this area livable and so we will learn how to conserve this water, and we will avoid pollution of our streams.

We know that our forests are important for they help us to collect and distribute our valuable water and they provide us with necessary recreation and beauty.

We know that we must learn to keep our soil in place to provide food for an increasing population.

We know that when we have earned a living from the bounties provided here that we need the inspiration from our wilderness areas in the mountains and deserts, so we will see to it that a few of these beautiful places are left "as is" for all time.

We know that the charm of these wild places is in their primitive naturalness and so we will always avoid unnecessarily destroying any of the trees, flowers, wildlife or rocks. We will not leave foreign matter at our camp sites or along the highways and will not be litterbugs.

This is practical conservation as it applies to us in these states where the sun shines bright and the breezes are cool.

WALLS AND WINDBREAKS

Some feel that the walled English gardens are too exclusive and unfriendly, but the English are garden-loving people and do like to get the utmost possible enjoyment from their outdoor areas. The degree of pleasure obtained from a garden is often in direct relation to its privacy.

The farmers on the plains are beginning to learn that a properly designed and planted windbreak may actually increase yields of crops as well as making a sheltered place around the residence where a few attractive trees and flowers may be grown. Residences in towns or cities on these same plains may often profit from the same principle and plant windbreaks on the windward side of the property.

Fruits and Vegetables for Every Garden

INCLUDED in the Rocky Mountain Area are some irrigated valleys where fruit growing is one of the chief horticultural enterprises. However, over most of the territory, growing of the standard fruits is very difficult due to the short season, lack of rainfall, and soil conditions. Suggestions which are given here concern climate and soil conditions similar to that of the Denver area, and it should be recognized that only the hardiest of these things can be expected to be worthwhile in the higher altitudes or on the dry, high plains.

Fruit Trees

Late-season apples are restricted to the lower valleys, though there are some mid-season varieties which some times bear well in the Denver area. The Yellow Transparent has been a very popular apple, but is losing favor because it is attacked by fire blight in most seasons. Hybrids of this apple and the McIntosh, such as Early McIntosh, and Cortland, have been gaining in favor. Two newer varieties, Haralson and Anoka, have received some attention. The Jonathan, Delicious and its variations, such as Golden Delicious, Northwest Greening, Roman Beauty, and Sheriff are occasionally planted. The Dolga Crabapple is classified as an ornamental, but produces small apples which, like its beauty, are greatly appreciated. All apple trees must be carefully sprayed, at proper times, if fruit of good quality is expected.

Sour cherries are probably the most dependable fruit over a great part of the Rocky Mountain area. Leading the list of varieties by far is Montmorency. A small, but earlier, variety is the Early Richmond; while the English Morello is later and produces darker fruit. Only a few favored valleys can successfully grow sweet cherries.

Plums do not always bear well in this region, but the trees take up little space and their occasional good crops are much appreciated. Of the prune type, the Stanley variety seems to be the hardiest. Another variety is the Green Gage, which is known by some as the "White Prune." Superior, Omaha, Underwood, and Lombard are varieties of good quality but erratic in bearing under Rocky Mountain conditions. The hardier hybrids include the Waneta, Kahinta, and Kaga, and are usually considerably smaller but more reliable kinds. In really difficult places, the small sand cherry hybrids with such Indian names as Sapa, Opata, and Oka may bear.

Raising peaches is a gamble except in favored valleys. Peach trees have the characteristics of wanting to bloom at the first sign of warm weather and then the buds are often killed off by late freezes. Where some protection can be given, the Polly variety will bear better than most and some times the Elberta will surprise its owner with a good crop.

Apricots are generally more unreliable than peaches because they usually bloom at an even earlier date. Pears are seldom worth the space they occupy in the garden.

The home owner or gardener who is interested in fruit trees may write his State Agricultural College for free bulletins on care of fruit trees in his particular area.

Small Fruits for the Rocky Mountain Area

GRAPES. Perhaps the best known all-around grape for Colorado is the Beta (or Alpha). It is a hybrid of wild grape and the Concord variety. Its size and quality are intermediate and, while it is not much for raw eating, the juices and jam are considered very good. The hybrid varieties will bear almost everywhere, while Concord, Niagara, or Diamond will do well to produce a crop once, in possibly, three years.

RASPBERRIES. Spring bearing red raspberries are raised commercially, but the work of covering and uncovering them is a rather severe handicap. The Latham and Chief varieties seem to give good results. Black raspberries will sometimes grow, but many home gardeners feel they are not worth the effort. Blackberries and dewberries are also not practical in most of the Rocky Mountain area. The everbearing red raspberries are generally considered the best kind for home gardeners. The St. Regis variety is a small well-flavored berry, but a rather short cropper. Indian Summer or September varieties are preferred by many gardeners because they produce good summer and fall crops, even when the plants are not covered and are allowed to freeze back each winter. The fruit is of good size and fair flavor.

STRAWBERRIES. Here is one small fruit which should be in every garden. Most standard one-crop varieties will do well here in the Rocky Mountain area, but the favorites for the home gardener seem to be the everbearers. Gem and Mastodon are well-liked, while Streamliner, Twentieth Century and Red Rich are among the newer varieties which show promise. For high altitudes, the Experiment Station at Cheyenne has developed several new hybrids of wild and cultivated stock, one called Radiance. They have the hardiness of the wild strawberry and the fruit is about half the size of the cultivated varieties.

GOOSEBERRIES. Wild gooseberries grow at all altitudes. While they are small and tart, they do have certain value for mixing with other fruit. Cultivated kinds, occasionally produce good crops but are not reliable. The Pixwell variety is an especially good one for difficult places.

CURRANTS. Another small fruit, not reliable every year, but which will occasionally produce crops is the currant. Favorite varieties include Red Lake and Perfection. While, wild species will grow well, their fruit is inferior.

MANCHU CHERRIES, sometimes called Nanking Cherry, or Chinese Bird Cherry, is a beautiful, tall ornamental shrub. The fruit has flavor and character superior to large cultivated cherries, but the plants do not always bear because they bloom very early and fruits are frequently killed by frost.

SANDCHERRIES. The Hansen Bush Cherry is an improvement over the species in quality of fruit. They are of low growth, beautiful in flower, and every few years will bear immense quantities of fruit. Furthermore, they are hardy almost everywhere.

ELDERBERRIES. When they bear fruit, elderberries are especially appreciated by the birds and are also good for pies and sauce.

AMELANCHIER, called the serviceberry or Juneberry, produces delicious fruit but grows very slowly and is difficult to transplant. It will, however, tolerate drouth and poor soils.

BUFFALOBERRIES are hardy native shrubs used chiefly as ornamentals They do, however, bear quantities of small red berries which are rich in pectin and valuable for jelly making.

CHOKECHERRIES. A very hardy slow-growing native, which bears fruit almost every year. It is useful for jams and jellies, especially when mixed with apples.

Most of these plants that we have mentioned for their fruit bearing qualities are also good ornamentals, when they are planted in a place where they will grow to the right size. They are also valuable plants to attract birds to the garden, even if the fruit is not wanted for human use.

Vegetables

Most of the agricultural colleges issue excellent bulletins on the growing of vegetables in their area; so we will not attempt to duplicate their services. The home gardener may write directly to his agricultural experiment station for free bulletins.

The permanent plants, such as rhubarb, asparagus, and horse radish, can be planted in connection with the orchard or ornamental garden and may attain beauty, as well as usefulness. Since they are long-lived plants, they should have the soil well prepared before planting.

Parts of the Rocky Mountain area have become famous for certain vegetables such as lettuce, celery, and peas. The cool nights of the higher altitude seem to give them a superior quality. Cantaloupes, onions, cabbage, dry and string beans, tomatoes, and potatoes are raised commercially in many areas.

Radishes, beets, carrots, parsnips, turnips, chard, spinach, broccoli, cauliflower, and kohlrabi all do well over much of the area. Often a late seeding of these things may be made so they can be harvested during the cool fall weather. In the lower valleys, sweet corn, squash, cucumbers, watermelons, and pumpkins will mature. Under irrigation, most of these vegetables may be grown on the plains and the shorter-season plants will do well in the mountains.

Your local seedsman can usually recommend the varieties of vegetables that are likely to do well in your area and can suggest those kinds that are good for the home garden rather than the commercial grower. New names appear each year in the list of vegetables. Some of these may be simply an old variety with a new name but each year there are some really good new things, especially in the hybrids.

Recommended reading:

GROWING BETTER FRUIT IN COLORADO, Bulletin 396A Extension Service, Colorado State University, Fort Collins, Colo.

GROW YOUR OWN VEGETABLES, Paul W. Demsey, Pub. by Houghton-Mifflin.

Herbs for Taste and Fragrance

HERBS have been used for generations to flavor food and drinks, and their culture dates back to ancient gardens. Since many part time gardeners are also full time cooks, there is a close relationship between these two home making practices.

They may be grown in formal gardens as our grandmothers grew them, or they may be tucked in the garden in many odd places, preferably within easy access to the kitchen.

Most herbs are easy to grow and their main requirements are full sun and rather poor soil. Some are easily started from seed, but others must be propagated by division. Good gardeners usually develop a hobby of growing some particular kind of plant, and the growing of herbs is a very suitable outlet for this urge.

The list of plants used as herbs includes most of the known plant families and have been assembled from around the world. Some of them are quite familiar and commonplace; others may not be recognized by many gardeners. Most of us remember the rich fragrance of mint as we have crushed it underfoot along streams. We are familiar with the odor of catnip as it grows around old gardens, and we can hardly go far in this Rocky Mountain area without smelling some species of sage. We also may remember the faint minty odor of horsemint or monarda or the anise odor of Washingtonia as we walk through Aspen groves in the mountains.

Listed below are a few of the more common and easily grown herbs of the Rocky Mountain area.

Allium schoenoprasum, CHIVES. For a mild onion flavor. Easy to grow in the garden or as a pot plant indoors. Attractive lilac flowers. This is one herb that prefers rich soil. Propagation by divisions.

Anethum graveolens, DILL. Rank growing herb, much used for flavoring pickles.

Anthriscus cerefolium, CHERVIL. Similar to parsley. Prefers shade. Plant early.

Artemisia dracunculus, TARRAGON. Hardy perennial grown in full sun. Much prized by good cooks for use in sauces, vinegar and with fish and chicken.

BETONY or Applemint. Spreads rapidly from underground runners.

Borago officinalis, BORAGE. Coarse self-seeding annual. Cucumber flavor.

Carum carvi, CARAWAY. Seeds have been used in cookies and cake.

PEONIES

Peonies are one of those slow-growing, long-lived plants. While Iris and Shasta Daisies must be thinned and divided every few years, the peony likes to be left alone, and it grows bigger and better with the years. Available in many colors and forms, they produce some of the largest and most beautiful flowers that it is possible to raise in the Rocky Mountain region. Few insects or diseases bother them.

Let us hope that more and more people over the area, in large cities and small towns, will learn to appreciate this fine flower and plant more of them.

Chrysanthemum balsamita tanacetoides, COSTMARY. Old fashioned herb sometimes called Sweet Mary. Used for salads and beverages.

Coriandum savitum, CORIANDER. Seeds are used for flavoring similar to dill or caraway.

Foeniculum dulce, FENNEL. An easily grown annual used for flavoring fish.

Hyssopus officinalis, HYSSOP. Easily started from seed.

Lavandula vera, LAVENDER. Easily grown low plant with tiny flowers. Gives pleasant fragrance to linens.

Levisticum officinale, LOVAGE. Large perennial with celery flavor.

Origanum majorana, SWEET MARJORAM. Very popular tender perennial used to flavor many dishes.

Melissa officinalis, LEMON BALM. Spreads rapidly from underground runners.

Mentha spictata and others, MINT. Various flavors for various uses. The most easily grown and common herb; sometimes becoming a pest.

Myrrhis odorata, SWEET CICELY. Licorice flavored perennial. Use for salads and drinks.

Ocimum basilicum, SWEET BASIL. Tender but easily grown annual. Used for flavoring many dishes.

Petroselium hortense, PARSLEY. Leaves used as a garnish for meats. Usually treated as an annual.

Pimpinella anisum, ANISE. Easy to grow. Seeds used for flavoring.

Rosemarinus officinalis, ROSEMARY. Half-hardy perennial, started from seed. Used to flavor meat.

Rumex scutatus, SORRELL. Coarse perennial used for flavoring soups and salads.

Salvia officinalis, SAGE. Leaves used in dressings. Grown in sun.

Sanguisorba minor, BURNET. A biennial grown from seed. Cucumber flavor.

Satureia hortensis, SUMMER SAVORY. Started from seed in early spring. Used for flavoring beans and meat.

Satureia montana, WINTER SAVORY. Perennial of similar use as above.

Teucrium chamaedrys, GERMANDER. Used for flavoring or as a neat border plant. Easily started by divisions.

Thymus vulgaris and others, THYME. Low mat plant used for rock gardens or for seasoning. Likes a dry, sunny spot.

FALL COLORS

It is commonly thought that the action of frost on the leaves in the fall of the year causes their brilliant red and yellow colors. When we stop to observe that some leaves begin to turn before frost, we realize that this cannot be entirely true. The coloring is really caused by a natural ripening of the plant and a chemical change in the leaves which destroys the chlorophyll or green coloring matter. Chlorophyll has been present in the leaves all summer and it is thru the action of the sun (photosynthesis) on this green matter that the water and carbon dioxide are transformed into starches and sugars which the plant can use for growth.

Shortening of the days, completion of the natural life cycle of the plant, or other factors may have as much to do with the ripening which results in the coloring of the leaves as cool weather or frost. Some plant scientists believe part of this change is caused by the preparation of the leaves to separate from the plant thru a change of cell structure at the point where the leaves are attached. When the green matter is no longer needed for the manufacture of food it disappears and allows other pigments to color the leaves.

Scientific explanations of fall leaf color need not detract from the pleasure you get from the grand autumn display of color. If you get more pleasure from thinking that it is an act of Nature just for your benefit, why think otherwise?

Birds Form Important Part of Garden Beauty

B IRDS and gardens go together and we should plan our gardens with birds in mind. Many of the better birds do not take kindly to civilization, so we must make special arrangements for their comfort if we hope to attract them.

We must provide suitable food at proper times and places, we must provide water for bathing and drinking, we must provide shelter and protection.

I know of some bird lovers who will bake many pans of cornbread to feed their feathered friends on bad winter days.

Various kinds of birds eat different things, so no sprinkling of crumbs will attract all birds. Some birds prefer things like suet tied to a limb, others prefer fruit, while many are seed eaters. Some prefer to eat only high up in a tree, while others may be ground feeders.

Insect Supply Difficult

It would be difficult for most gardeners to supply the insects necessary to attract certain kinds of birds, but anyone can supply fruit by planting those trees and shrubs which produce fruit attractive to birds.

Mulberries are probably number one fruit for birds, with elderberries running a close second. The native pin cherries and chokecherries may be planted to attract birds away from the cultivated cherries.

Wild grapes, woodbine, buffalo berries and currants are attractive to birds, as well as being good ornamentals. Flowering crabs, gooseberries, honeysuckles, thimbleberries and mountain ash all furnish edible fruit.

Hawthorns Good

Some plants furnishing fruit which hangs on for winter use include the cotoneasters, hawthorns, roses, viburnums, sumacs, snowberries, privets and russianolives. Apples may be tied to trees in winter.

Birds must have water to drink and to bathe in. This must be provided in such a place that they can use it with the minimum of risk—they must be able to look around and not be liable to ambush by some cat.

A conventional bird bath may be the central feature of one section of the garden. Many birds enjoy a little shallow bowl of water right on the ground. Especially in winter do they appreciate a constant source of water.

Shelter Needed

They must have shelter for bad weather and roosting at night. Junipers and spruce provide excellent hiding and nesting places for many kinds. (Whisper this to the landscaper)—many birds prefer dead trees in which to build their nests and homes, but what good landscaper would leave a dead or hollow tree standing?

In most cases we must provide substitutes by fastening up sections of logs or carefully constructed houses.

Most birds prefer those made of naturalistic and neutral colored material.

Many birds may set up housekeeping in the gaudily colored and elaborately constructed houses but these are not always the most desirable kinds. Each bird has its own preference for a nesting place and will use no other.

Protection Important

Protection from enemies is a most important consideration, but one most often neglected. Cats and birds do not go together, or rather, from the cats' viewpoint, they go together too well. Choose between them, and if the neighborhoods' cats bother too much you may be compelled to put tin collars on your trees.

Unappreciative children, magpies, sparrows and squirrels are other pests that birds must be protected against if you would have them feel at ease on your premises.

I know of one bird lover who controlled all these with a .22 rifle, but this method is too drastic for use in the city.

Corn shocks, feeding platform, water and various types of food, consistently supplied in the winter, will do much to attract birds to your grounds.

ORNAMENTAL FRUITS ATTRACTIVE TO BIRDS

PREFERRED

Soft fruits eaten when ripe by such birds as Robins, Finches, Bluebirds, Solitaires and Grosbeaks.

Mulberries	Elderberries
Pie Cherries	Manchu Cherries
Pin Cherries	Raspberries
Black Cherries	Wild Grapes
Chokecherries	

EATEN LATER AS SECOND CHOICE

Buffaloberries	Mountainash
Currants	Sand Cherries
Crabapples	Wild Plums
Gooseberries	

PREFERRED

Dry or persistent fruits eaten in winter or spring by such as Waxwings, Robins, Flickers, Starlings.

Russianolives	Nannyberries
Engelmann Ivies	

ALSO EATEN AS SECOND CHOICE

Dogwoods	Euonymus
Privets	Hawthorns
Rose Hips	Highbush Cran-
Barberries	berries
Buckthorns	Sumacs
Coralberries	Junipers
Snowberries	Hackberries

Dry fruit important for such as sparrows, finches and grosbeaks.

Ash   Boxelders

Important for Woodpeckers, Waxwings and Finches.

Inferior apples left on the tree to dry and decay.

Toxic, but not always lethal. Eaten by immature robins.

Bush honeysuckle berries.

Highbush Cranberry

Hedges for Every Garden

THERE are few landscape plans that cannot profitably use a hedge of some form. These may be formally clipped or unsheared; they may be of deciduous material or evergreen. Hedges may be used to mark boundaries, to carry out the architectural lines of the house into the garden, to confine children or dogs or to screen out objectionable views. The secret of growing good formal hedges is to shear them frequently so that they become full and dense. However, if good results are to be obtained, the plant material which adapts itself to shearing is necessary. This means plants which will send out new branches from just below the cut point so that each shearing will make them more dense. Shrubs which only send out new growth from the ground or which are naturally sparse-stemmed and open can seldom be used effectively for clipped hedge purposes. A great deal of the effectiveness of hedges depends upon the form to which they are trimmed. Formerly most hedges were trimmd with only vertical and horizontal lines. Experiment has shown that a design which slopes out at the bottom will allow the sun to hit all parts of the hedge and avoid much of the bare-around-the-bottom effect so often seen in hedges. Material which grows rapidly should not be used for a hedge that is expected to be kept very low. Each community and situation calls for a particular plant which will most nearly fill the individual requirements.

Small size plants are most often used to start hedges. This reduces the cost, makes the hedge easy to plant and gives the gardener a chance to cut the plant back severely so it will have many stems coming from the bottom. Medium height hedges are most often planted by digging a continuous trench about a foot deep and a foot wide the whole length of the proposed site. Plants are then spaced about a foot apart in a single, straight line or may be staggered in a double line. Plants for low or very tall hedges may be planted closer or farther apart depending on the kind of plant and denseness desired.

The material for informal, unsheared hedges must be carefully selected so that it will grow as quickly as possible to the desired height, but will never get too tall or of too great a spread. For unusual or different places, special care should be taken to select plants which will thrive best. The

plants listed below will generally grow in reasonably good soil and with a moderate amount of sunshine and moisture at the altitude of Denver. Those which are especially tolerant of drouth, alkaline soil, shady places, wet spots or high altitude are also indicated in the list.

Evergreen hedges are of much greater value than those of deciduous material. However, they take much more time to develop into an effective size and if large plants are used in starting the hedge, much greater expense is incurred.

LIST OF PLANT MATERIAL FOR EVERY KIND OF HEDGE

CODE

D—Especially useful for dry, hot or alkaline conditions on the plains or elsewhere.
W—Will grow in wet places.
H—Suitable for use at 7,000-9,000 feet elevation.
S—Will grow in shady places.
Most of the shrubs listed below are also suitable for informal, unclipped hedges which would be of greater height and spread than where clipped.

TALL, 4-8 FEET, Arranged Approximately in Order of Preference

RUSSIANOLIVE (DH). Gray Foliage, hardy, drouth resistant.

SIBERIAN ELM (DH). Fast growing, drouth resistant.

PERSIAN (Chinese) LILAC (H). Dense, not as coarse or liable to sucker as common lilac.

SIBERIAN PEA SHRUB (DH). Drouth and alkali resistant, coarse.

BUSH HONEYSUCKLE (HSDW). Fast growing, tolerant of poor soils.

HAWTHORN, THICKET and ENGLISH (H). Dense, thorny, slow growing.

AMUR (Ginnala) MAPLE. Beautiful, coarse, sometimes chlorotic.

COMMON BUCKTHORN (SD). Hardy and dense.

MULBERRY. Coarse, not hardy north, tolerant of difficult situations.

HONEY LOCUST (D). Coarse, slow growing, very hardy.

BOXELDER (DH). Coarse, grows where nothing else will.

EUONYMUS, EUROPEAN, NATIVE (S). Needs good soil, good fall color.

PURPLE PLUM (D). Contrasting foliage.

JAPANESE TREE LILAC. Slow growing, does not sucker.

LATE LILAC (H). Slow growing, does not sucker.

COMMON LILAC (SH). Coarse, very hardy, suckers.

COLORADO SILVER CEDAR (D). Winter effects, slow growing.

SPRUCE *(Black Hills and Colorado)* (W). Coarse, slow, winter effects.

MEDIUM, 2-6 FEET

PRIVET *(English, Polish, Thompson)* (S). Dense, and holds leaves late.

COTONEASTER *(Peking, European)* (SDH). Slow, dense and hardy.

SAKHALIN, HONEYSUCKLE. Nice foliage, flowers and fruit.

SPIREA, ARGUTA. Neat, small leaves, tolerates clipping.

SPIREA, *Vanhoutte*. Hardy and easy to grow, not as tolerant to clipping.

SPIREA PRUNIFOLIA and THUNBERGI. Not as effective as the above.

PFITZER JUNIPER. Year 'round effect, slow, remains dense to ground.

VONEHRON JUNIPER. Quick growing, may be readily clipped.

FORESTIERA. Native of S.W. Colorado, hardy, slow.

MOUNTAINMAHOGANY (DH). Native in dry situations, slow.

FLOWERING QUINCE. Slow, subject to chlorosis.

SILVERBERRY. Drouth resistant, suckers, grey leaves.

THREELEAVED SUMAC (D). Native of dry places.

ONE SEED JUNIPER (D). Tolerant of poor, dry soil, shears well.

MUGHO PINE (D). Slow growing, tolerates some shearing.

JAPANESE TABLE PINE. Slow growing, may be pinched back.

FONTANESIA. Somewhat similar to Privet.

REDTWIG DOGWOOD (SH). A little coarse, red twigs, hardy.

WINGED EUONYMUS. Slow, dense, good fall color.

LEMOINE MOCKORANGE (S). Naturally rather formal in growth, and dense.

DWARF NINEBARK (S). Good foliage, fruit and flower.

WESTERN MOUNTAINASH (H). Slow and coarse, but beautiful.

LOW, 1-3 FEET

TRUEHEDGE COLUMNBERRY. Naturally dense and upright, takes little shearing.

LODENSE PRIVET (S). Slow growing, shears well, holds foliage late.

ALPINE CURRANT (SDH). Naturally dense and low, shears well.

JAPANESE BARBERRY (SD). Thorny, sometimes chlorotic, does not shear well.

REDLEAF BARBERRY. Much like the Japanese but less vigorous.

MENTOR BARBERRY (S). Stiff and dense, not as hardy as Japanese.

CARAGANA, PYGMAEA, AURANTIACA, MICROPHYLLA (DH). Low growing, beautiful in summer but unattractive in winter.

BUSH CINQUEFOIL (SDH). Native yellow flower, damaged by red spiders.

WHITE FLOWER BUSH CINQUEFOIL. Better shape and hardier than the native.

GOLDDROP BUSH CINQUEFOIL. Better shape and flower than native.

SNOWBERRY AND CORALBERRY (SH). Suckers and does not shear well.

CHENAULT SNOWBERRY (S). Neater than the common and shears better.

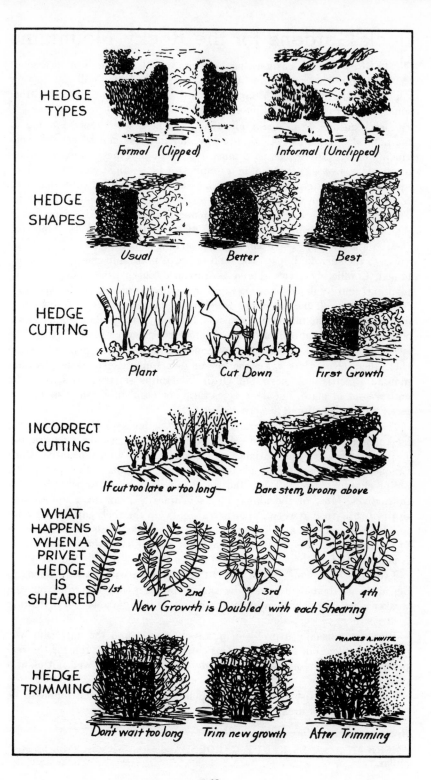

HEDGE TYPES

Formal (Clipped) *Informal (Unclipped)*

HEDGE SHAPES

Usual *Better* *Best*

HEDGE CUTTING

Plant *Cut Down* *First Growth*

INCORRECT CUTTING

If cut too late or too long— *Bare stem, broom above*

WHAT HAPPENS WHEN A PRIVET HEDGE IS SHEARED

1st *2nd* *3rd* *4th*

New Growth is Doubled with each Shearing

FRANCES A. WHITE.

HEDGE TRIMMING

Don't wait too long *Trim new growth* *After Trimming*

Rock Gardens for the Rocky Mountains

INTEREST in rock gardens has been more or less periodical in the last few years. Those which are well designed and planted still can be very appropriate in this Rocky Mountain area, but many have been so bad that some gardeners have lost all interest in them.

A rock garden, to be really effective, must be a small representation of the natural mountains with their rocks and flowers; and to get this convincing effect, those rocks used must look as though they belong together, or in other words, arranged in groupings which might have been done by nature. A rock garden should not be simply a geological collection. The rocks should act in relation to the plants as a frame for a picture. Usually a few large rocks are necessary with smaller ones surrounding them rather than the most generally used collection of a few dozen all of the same size.

After the rock garden itself has been arranged consideration should be given to the surroundings if the total effect of natural-likeness is to be obtained. Conflicting views should be screened out by the background of plantings and by flank plantings; and the actual garden with its surroundings should be planned as a unit which will give the desired effect of being a little piece of the mountains transplanted into your garden. Sometimes a small pool can be effectively worked into a rock garden plan.

Plants used in the rock garden should be as carefully planned as the rocks themselves. Here again the low or dwarf characteristics to give that mountain feel is most desirable. Ordinarily tulips or large lilies would be entirely out of place, but the species tulips or coral lilies could fit in perfectly with other alpine flowers.

A rock garden of considerable size needs a few woody plants to give backbone to the planting. Some of the creeping Junipers like Andorra and J. procumbens are appropriate; also dwarf shrubs like the native Bush Cinquefoil or Oregon Grape are to be considered. Plants of the appropriate alpine character from all over the world may be used along with many of the natives. Most of the alpine plants ordinarily grow in a loose, well-drained soil. So it is very important to build up the rock garden site with this kind of gravelly and leaf-mold soil. Many books stress the importance of locating them where they will have the most sun, however, in this region it is better to face them north or east where they will not get the full sun.

Even the best planned and planted rock garden will not stay good indefinitely as there will always be rank growing plants to crowd out the weaker ones. Frequent dividing of these rank growing plants and replanting of the weaker is suggested.

Weeds are usually a problem in a rock garden and the only safe way of keeping them out is by hand. This can be an interesting job for the real plant lover, but if you do not like to do this—you may as well not plant a rock garden.

Following is a list of some of the plants which have been found to be most useful in this area.

Recommended reading:

AMERICAN ALPINES IN THE GARDEN, Anderson McCully, Pub. by Macmillan.

ROCK GARDEN PLANTS FOR SUN OR SHADE
THE LIST THAT FOLLOWS IS FOR SUN

These lists do not aim at being complete. They are to assist the average rock gardener in planting a garden in "The Rocky Mountain Empire."

Name	Color of Flowers	Height	Time of Flowering
Achillea argentea	White	4"	Summer
Achillea umbellata	White	4"	June
Achillea tomentosa	Yellow	9"	June-September
Aethionema, var., sp.	Pink	1'	Summer
Ajuga, vars., sp.	Blue	4-5"	Spring
Alyssum, var., sp.	Yellow	6"	Spring
Androsace, var., sp.	White and Rose	3-6"	Spring and Summer
Arabis, var.	White	4"	Spring
Arenaria montana	White	6"	Spring and Summer
Armeria, vars., sp.	Rose and White	6-12"	Spring and Summer
Aster alpinus	Blue	9"	Summer and Fall
Ceratostigma plum.	Blue	8"	Autumn
Campanula, dwarf	White and Blue	3-12"	Spring and Summer
Cerastium tomentosum	White	6"	Spring
Corydalis vars.	White	6"	Spring
Dianthus, Alpine pinks	White to Rose	5-12"	Spring and Summer
Epimedium mac.	Yellow	Low	Spring
Erigeron villarsi	Violet	12"	Summer
Erinus alpinus	Purple	Low	April to June
Gypsophila, dwarf	White to Pink	6-12"	Summer
Hedera, var.	For evergreen foliage	6-8"	
Helianthemum, vars.	Various	6-8"	Spring and Summer
Hemerocallis, dwarf	Yellow	Med.	Spring
Iberis, vars.	White	6"	Summer
Iris, dwarf bearded	Various	6-15"	Spring and Summer
Linum flavum	Yellow	12"	Summer
Leontopodium alpinum	White	6"	Summer and Fall
Nepeta mussini	Blue	12"	Summer and Fall
Papaver alpinum	Various	6"	Spring
Papaver nudicaule	Various	8"	All Summer
Phlox subulata	Various	Low	Spring
Saponaria ocymoides	Red	Creeping	Summer
Silene, var., sp.	White and Red	5-15"	Summer and Fall
Thymus, vars., sp.	Various	Dwarf	Summer
Tiarella cordifolia	White	6-8"	Early Summer
Tunica saxifraga	Pinkish White	3-5"	Summer
Veronica, car., sp.	Blue	6-14"	Summer

ROCK PLANTS FOR SHADY SITUATIONS

Name	Color of Flowers	Height	Time of Flowering
Aconitum anthora	Yellowish White	12-14″	Summer
Anchusa myosotidiflora	Blue	12″	Summer
Anemone alpina	White	14-16″	Summer
Anemone sylvestris	White	12″	Spring
Aquilegia glandulosa	Blue and White	12″	Early Summer
Aquilegia coerulea	Blue and White	15″	Summer
Ajuga	Blue	4-5″	Spring
Arenaria balearica	White	2-4″	Summer
Dodocatheon sp.	White to Purple	12″	Spring and Summer
Epimedium, vars., cp.	Ornamental foliage	6-12″	
Erinus, car., sup.	White and Rose	3″	Spring and Summer
Funkia, vars.	Lavender and White	8-14″	Late Summer
Helleborus niger	White	12″	Winter
Iris cristata	Blue	4″	Spring
Linaria cymbalaria	Lilac	3″	Summer
Polemonium reptans	Blue	7″	Spring
Primula, various forms		6-9″	Spring
Saxifraga, vars.	Various	12-18″	Spring and Summer
Sedum spurium	Rose-Pink	3″	Summer
Stachys lanata	Pink	12″	Summer
Thalictrum minus	Ornamental foliage	6-12″	
Thalictrum adiantifolium	Ornamental foliage	6-12″	

BULBS FOR THE ROCK GARDEN

Grape Hyacinths, Daffodils, Hyacinths, Crocuses, Snowdrops, Snowflakes, Tulip species, Trilliums and Tenuifolium Lilies.

Ferns for Shady Places

FERNS fill a place in the garden in which no other plant can be substituted. Shady places on the north side of buildings can be beautiful when planted with appropriate Ferns, Columbines, Meadow Rue, Hosta, Lily-of-the-Valley, and such things.

Those familiar with eastern native woods and flowers miss the presence of many ferns here in the Rocky Mountains. Our dry soil and low humidity over much of the area is definitely not favorable for fern growth. By supplying additional moisture, humus in the soil, and shady spots, we can grow a few of the good kinds.

The Colorado Male Fern, *Aspidium filix-mas*, is rated as one of the most useful by many gardeners. The Ostrich Fern, *Pteretis nodulosa*, gives favorable response, while the Lady Fern, *Athyrium filix-femina*, is especially hardy in this area. The Cinnamon, *Osmunda cinnamonea*, and the Christmas Fern, *Polystichum acrostichoides*, have been grown successfully by some gardeners also. Where conditions permit, the distinctive and beautiful Maidenhair Fern, *Adiantum pedatum*, is hardy. Bracken Fern, *Pteridium*, is easily grown and may even become a pest under some conditions. Among the rocks where a small, dainty fern is needed, the Native Rock or Brittlebladder Fern, *Cystopteris filix*, or the Woodsia Fern, may grow.

Ferns are easy to plant and require little care if requirements of shade, soil and moisture are met. Most gardeners could make good use of them.

We might learn to plan our "back yards" more for beauty as well as simply utility. More people see the back yard than is often thought, and when a highway or railroad abuts the rear of a lot, it is especially important to keep it attractive. A visitor's impression of a community is often influenced considerably by the ugly or neat back yards that they see as they drive by.

Wildflowers to Domesticate

DURING the summer months, in this area, we all spend more time in the mountains than we do in our gardens. When we look at our gardens after we return from a trip among the beautiful wildflowers, we wonder if we might grow some of those nice natives in our garden where we might see them more often.

In considering native wildflowers for use in city gardens, we must remember that they naturally grow under a great variety of conditions, mostly quite different than the environment that we intend to put them in. Unless we can approximate the natural conditions in which a wild plant has developed, we can not hope to grow them successfully.

Many wild flowers have such deep and complicated root systems that it is extremely difficult to successfully transplant a mature specimen. Other wildflowers are accustomed to well-drained, leafmold soil and cannot tolerate the heavy, alkaline soil common around many communities. Many of the wildflowers of the mountains are happy only when they receive frequent rains and much cloudy weather. Other nice things, especially those from the lower foothills, will accustom themselves to cultivated conditions as well as those plants that have been used for ornamental plantings for many years.

Everyone is attracted to some of our fine native Orchids, Gentians, Lupines, Lilies, and Paintbrushes but few can provide proper conditions for their growth. These difficult and delicate things had better be enjoyed where they grow naturally.

If you can provide marshy conditions or cold running water, you might be able to grow some Shooting Stars, Marsh Marigolds, Little Red Elephants, White Anemones, Globeflowers or Wild Iris.

If you have a dry place, well drained, you could try some of the Daisies, Golden Smoke, Sedum, Malvastrum, Wild Onions, Pussytoes, Blazing Stars or even the weedy, but beautiful Prickly Poppy.

Moist, shady nooks might welcome some Meadowrue, Spring Beauties, Violets of blue, white or yellow, Alum root, Harebells or Rock Ferns.

There is a long list of our native wildflowers that will grow quite happily under ordinary garden conditions. There is a wide variety in the native Penstemons, the native Gaillardia is a beautiful thing, Spiderwort will grow almost anywhere, Gilias, Coneflowers and Wallflowers will grow easily. The native blue Columbines, several species of Mertensias, Monardas, Larkspurs, Goldenglow and Solomon's Seal will grow easily in a moist, shady place.

For a rockery there are many nice, dwarf plants that will nestle in among the rocks very well, if it is remembered to provide them with well-drained soil, full of humus. The true alpines are a challenge to grow.

Unfortunately, very few of these nice natives are available from commercial sources. When the demand becomes sufficient, someone will make it a business to learn how to propagate them and have them for sale. Very few can be safely collected when they are seen in bloom. At this time, they are in the poorest possible condition to be moved, and it is not possible to collect flowers without the consent of the owner of the land where they are growing. Sometimes, it is possible to make notes and mark the spot where certain desirable plants grow, and come back at the right time to collect a few seeds. Certain very attractive wildflowers including the Wood Lily, Yellow Ladies' Slipper, and Alpine Forget-me-not are almost extinct because of the many attempts (mostly unsuccessful) to transplant them to gardens when they are in bloom. These are all on the "taboo" list and are not to be collected.

Following are lists of several different classes of wildflowers that might be successfully used in certain types of gardens.

The wildness of the mountains and the peace of working with growing things in our gardens are two places where we might get the greatest benefit in relaxation from our daily grind, yet we often lose much of these benefits by taking them too seriously.

LOW PLANTS SUITABLE FOR ROCK GARDENS IN DRY, SUNNY PLACES

Allium in variety, WILD ONION. White, pink or purple heads of flowers on erect stems. Propagated by bulbs. Easy to grow.

Anaphalis subalpina, PEARLY EVERLASTING. Creamy white flowers which dry for winter bouquets.

Anemone globosa, RED ANEMONE. Erect stems. Woolly seed heads.

Antennaria in variety, PUSSYTOES. Low plants with low heads of white or pink flowers.

Arenaria fendleri, FENDLER'S SANDWORT. Small white flowers on slender stems.

Calochortus gunnisoni, MARIPOSA LILY. Beautiful tulip-like flowers on slender stems. From small bulbs. Also grow in shade.

Campanula rotundifolia, HAREBELL. Delicate blue bells on slender stems. Also grows in shade.

Cerastium arvense, CHICKWEED. Small white flowers in dense, matted growth. Good, easy to grow, rock garden plant.

Corydalis aurea, GOLDEN SMOKE. Canary-like yellow flowers in smoke colored foliage. Like loose well drained spots.

Erigeron in variety, DAISY. Cheerful little daisies in various heights.

Eriogonum effusium, PRAIRIE BABY'S BREATH. From the dry plains. Tiny flowers which may be dried and used like Gypsophila.

Eriogonum umbellatum, SULPHUR FLOWER. Heads of small yellow flowers, gray matted foliage. On dry slopes.

Erodium cicutarium, STORKSBILL. Small pink flowers and long-pointed seed pods. Easy to move.

Fragaria americana, WILD STRAWBERRY. White flowers and (sometimes) edible fruit. Good rock plant.

Geranium caespitosum, WILD PINK GERANIUM or CRANESBILL. Cheerful pink flowers. Easily grown in sunny places.

Liatris punctata, BLAZING STAR or GAYFEATHER. Heads of purple flowers on erect stems, in fall. Deep rooted.

Leucocrinum montanum, SAND LILY. White star-shaped flowers in early spring. Fleshy roots, easy to move.

Linum lewisi, BLUE FLAX. Easy to grow, often naturalizing itself. Bright blue flowers opening each day.

Malvastrum coccineum, FALSE MALLOW or COWBOY'S DELIGHT. Tomato colored flowers on low, gray mats of leaves. Tolerates extreme drouth and heat.

Pachylophus macroglottis, FRAGRANT MORNING PRIMROSE. Immense white flowers opening each day. Fragrant. Must have well drained sunny spot.

Penstemon in variety, BEARDSTONGUE. Blue, pink, lavender and white. One half to two feet high. As easy to move as Shasta Daisies.

Phacelia sericea, PURPLE FRINGE or PINCUSHION. Large spike of purple flowers.

Potentilla in variety. CINQUEFOIL. Very common yellow flowers.

Scutellaria brittoni, SKULLCAP. Small purple, snapdragon-like flowers. Spreads by underground runners.

Sedum stenopetalum, YELLOW STONECROP. Tiny star-like yellow flowers and low fleshy foliage. Easily transplanted and grown.

Tradescantia occidentalis, SPIDERWORT. Purple lily-like flowers. Easily transplanted and grown anywhere.

Zigadenus elegans, WAND LILY. Stems of greenish flowers and grass-like foliage. On dry slopes.

When plants or animals become highly specialized or refined, a change of usual living conditions may find them unprepared to survive.

TALLER MEADOW FLOWERS THRIVING IN
DRY, SUNNY PLACES

Abronia fragrans, PRAIRIE SNOWBALL. Clusters of fragrant white flowers on bushy plant. Hard to transplant.

Achillea millefolium, YARROW. Flat heads of small white flowers. Grows at all altitudes and sometimes becomes a weed in lawns.

Anogra in variety, WHITE EVENING PRIMROSE. Large white flowers, growing often as a weed in vacant lots.

Argemone intercedia, PRICKLY POPPY. Very large white flowers. Gray, prickly leaves. Likes heat and sun.

Astragalus and *Aragallus* in variety, LOCO. Pea-like flowers in a variety of sizes and colors.

Artemisia in variety, SAGE. Rank scented, gray leaved desert plants.

Clematis douglasi, BUSH CLEMATIS. Large purple bells on bushy plant.

Cryptantha virgata, MINER'S CANDLE. Tall stems of tiny white flowers. Stems remain overwinter covered with hoary white hairs.

Delphinium in variety, LARKSPUR. Spikes of blue or white flowers in varying heights and various exposures.

Epilobium angustifolium, FIREWEED. Tall spikes of red flowers.

Erysimum asperum, WALLFLOWER. Yellow to bronze flowers in spring.

Euphorbia albomarginata, SNOW-ON-THE-MOUNTAIN. Weedy plant but beautiful green and white striped leaves. In dry places.

Frasera speciosa, GREEN GENTIAN. Tall stems of beautiful greenish flowers.

Gaillardia aristata, GAILLARDIA. Large, attractive brown and yellow sunflower-like flowers.

Gilia attenuata and *aggregata*, FAIRY TRUMPET. Red, white or pink trumpet flowers on tall stems. Seeds and naturalizes easily.

Helianthus pumilis, PERENNIAL SUNFLOWER. Many stems of yellow flowers.

Ipomea leptophylla, BUSH MORNING GLORY. Large bush with pink morning glory flowers. Enormous root that holds water for years.

Linaria vulgaris, BUTTER & EGGS. Yellow and white, snapdragon-like flowers. Easy to naturalize.

Lithospermum angustifolium, PUCCOON. Crinkly yellow flowers.

Lupinus in variety, LUPINE. Blue or white flowers on large plant. Deep rooted and hard to move.

Petalostemon purpureus, PRAIRIE CLOVER. Thimble-like heads of purple flowers on tall stem.

Phacelia heterophylla, SCORPIONWEED. Interesting fiddleneck heads of greenish flowers.

Ratibida columnaris, CONEFLOWER. Yellow flower with high center.

Senecio, in variety, GROUNDSEL. Weedy appearing, drouth resisting yellow flowers in various heights.

Solidago in variety, GOLDENROD. Spikes of yellow flowers in fall.

Verbascum thapsus, MULLEIN. Woolly leaves. Tall Saguaro-like stems with small yellow flowers.

Verbesina encelaoides, GOLDWEED. Large weedy plant with nice coreopsis-like flowers in fall.

Vernonia fasciculata, IRONWEED. Tall stems of purplish flowers.

The common cattails of swampy places are picturesque plants, a favorite subject for artists. The blackbirds find them indispensable for nesting places. Small boys who have never known the adventure of torchlight parades lit by the kerosene-soaked seed heads have missed something.

But the cattail has more valuable uses than these. Its roots furnish valuable food, one of the major vegetable foods of the primitive Indians that modern peoples have not commercialized. The Indians also used the down to cradle their babies.

FOR MOIST SHADY PLACES—LOW ROCK GARDEN PLANTS

Anemone canadensis, NORTHERN ANEMONE. Woolly seed heads following flowers, on erect stems.

Arnica cordifolia, HEART-LEAVED ARNICA. Yellow sunflower-like bloom.

Claytonia rosea, SPRING BEAUTY. Small delicate white and pink flowers, blooming the first thing in spring.

Clematis pseudoalpina, ALPINE CLEMATIS. Beautiful lavender-purple flowers on frail vine.

Cornus canadensis, DWARF CORNEL. Single white flower on trailing plant in shady, moist places.

Cystoperis fragilis, BRITTLE FERN. Delicate little ferns growing in the shade under rocks.

Disporum trachycarpum, FAIRY BELLS. Large, branched, lily-like plant with twin white bells and red fruit.

Erythronium parviflorum, DOGTOOTH VIOLET or SNOW LILY. Bright yellow "lilies" growing from small bulbs. Blooming very early.

Galium boreale, BEDSTRAW. Fine white flowers and foliage. Easy to grow.

Geranium richardsoni, WILD WHITE GERANIUM. Hardy plant growing in moist places.

Heuchera in variety, ALUMROOT. Matted in shady cracks of rock. Small white flowers.

Linnaea americana, TWINFLOWER. Dainty twin, pink bells on slender stalk. Trailing plant in dense shade and woodsy soil.

Saxifraga rhomboidea, SNOWBALL SAXIFRAGE. Early blooms of small white flowers on top of bare stem. On moist north slopes.

Smilacina amplexicaulis, FALSE SOLOMON'S SEAL. Small white flowers on leafy stem. Lily-like foliage.

Stellaria longifolia, STARWORT. Very small white flowers similar to chickweed.

Streptopus amplexifolius, TWISTED STALK. Similar to Solomon's Seal.

Viola canadensis, CANADA VIOLET. Growing in shady, moist places.

Viola in variety, BLUE VIOLET. Beautiful in shade.

TALLER MEADOW FLOWERS PREFERRING A SHADY, MOIST PLACE

Actaea arguta, BANEBERRY. Heads of white flowers followed by clusters of red or white berries.

Apacynum androsaemifolium, INDIAN HEMP. Small pink flowers on low plant.

Aquilegia coerulea, ROCKY MOUNTAIN COLUMBINE. Colorado State Flower. One of the showiest.

Aquilegia elegantula, RED COLUMBINE. Small brilliant red flowers.

Asclepias incarnata, PINK SWAMP MILKWEED. Heads of orange flowers.

Eupatorium masculatum, THOROUGHWORT. Flowers small, foliage purple spotted.

Gentiana barbellata, FRAGRANT GENTIAN. Beautiful blue flowers.

Heracleum lanatum, COW PARSNIP. Enormous rhubarb-like leaves and tall stems of white flowers.

Lilium montanum, WOOD LILY. Large orange lily growing in rich shady places.

Mertensia in variety, CHIMING BELLS. Drooping clusters of bells in blue with pink base.

Monarda menthaefolia, HORSEMINT. Shaggy heads of purple flowers.

Polemonium in variety, JACOB'S LADDER. Fine foliage and heads of blue bells.

Thalictrum fendleri, MEADOW RUE. Not much flower but nice foliage, like columbine.

Thermopsis montana, GOLDEN BANNER. Stems of large yellow, pea-like flowers.

Valeriana sylvatica, VALERIAN. Heads of small white flowers.

179

PLANTS GROWING BY WATER

Caltha rotundifolia, WHITE MARSH MARIGOLD. Low, white, marsh flowers.

Cardamine cordifolia, MOUNTAIN CRESS. Small white flowers on medium stems growing lush along streams.

Dodecatheon radicatum, SHOOTING STAR. Like a purple dart. Will grow along streams of water.

Eustoma andrewsi, TULIP GENTIAN. Blue tulip-like flowers in swamps.

Gentiana elegans, FRINGED GENTIAN. Beautiful blue flowers.

Mimulus guttatus, YELLOW MONKEY FLOWER. Small yellow flowers growing by water.

Nuphar polysepalum, YELLOW PONDLILY. Floating leaves in shallow ponds.

Pedicularis groenlandica, LITTLE RED ELEPHANT. Stems of purple flowers like little elephant heads.

Primula parryi, PARRY PRIMROSE. Beautiful purple flowers at timberline.

Ranunculus in variety, BUTTERCUP. Small yellow flowers with various leaves.

Sisyrincium angustifolium, BLUE-EYED GRASS. Tiny dwarf iris.

Swertia palustris, STAR GENTIAN. Small star-flowers in moist places.

Trollius albiflorus, GLOBEFLOWER. Low marsh plant with white flowers.

Veronica americana, SPEEDWELL. Grows in and by water, blooms all winter.

Recommended reading:

MEET THE NATIVES, M. Walter Pesman, Pub. by Author (Denver, Colo.)
MANUAL OF THE PLANTS OF COLORADO, H. D. Harrington, Pub. by Sage Books, Denver.

A series of three small books:

    FLOWERS OF SOUTHWESTERN MESAS, Pauline Patraw
    FLOWERS OF SOUTHWESTERN MOUNTAINS, Leslie P. Arnberger
    FLOWERS OF SOUTHWESTERN DESERTS, Natt M. Dodge
    all published by the Southwestern Monuments Assn., Santa Fe, N. Mex.

PLANTS OF ROCKY MOUNTAIN, Yellowstone, Glacier, Grand Canyon, Mesa Verde or other National Parks and Monuments.

DANDELIONS VS. TARAXACUM

Weeds are still "plants out of place," and it is very possible for the same plant to be a weed in one location and a valuable flower or vegetable in another. One of the best known examples is the common dandelion. No weed is more hated when found in lawns, but dandelion seed is actually sold in many of our mining towns. The European miners plant little beds of dandelions for greens.

Over much of our mountain park area the dandelion has naturalized itself. It seems to be able to grow anywhere and everywhere. Some of the most beautiful scenes of Colorado which have been much published have foregrounds of "beautiful mountain flowers" which consist chiefly of dandelion. If we can forget our hatred for the plants, they really produce some beautiful displays in the mountains. I have taught people to forget its connection with the hated weed and call it by its botanical name when found in the mountains.

Taraxacum officinale might be the name of a very rare flower, so let's not remember that it is a dandelion when it is found in the hills and call it taraxacum.

Inanimate Landscape Materials

WHEN planning desired effects in landscape designing, we naturally think of the living materials first—trees, shrubs, flowers and lawns but no garden is complete without appropriate inanimate materials. Often, these materials give character and interest to a garden as many months of the year as do the living plants, and gardens should be planned for year-'round interest. Stone, wood, concrete, brick, tile, gravel, iron, plastics and water all may be used in appropriate places to give livability and beauty to a garden.

These materials may be used to construct patios, platforms, porches, walks, fences, gates, fireplaces or barbecues, screens, walls, pergolas or shades, pools, rockeries, fountains, statuary and many other garden conveniences or ornaments. Often the garden work can be put on a yearly basis by planning construction of the inanimate things in fall, winter, or mid-summer when the living plants need little attention.

The following pages will give a few suggestions both as to basic materials and desirable features that may be constructed of these materials. Unlimited ingenuity may be used here, always keeping in mind that there should be a certain unity in the design of all features of a garden, and avoiding the "museum" effect of unrelated things.

THE NATIVE FLAGSTONE FITS IN ROCKY MOUNTAIN GARDENS

Inanimate garden accessories may be of many materials, both natural and synthetic, but of all the possibilities flagstone seems to "fit" in the greatest number of places. It has good color and texture and under the hands of a skilled stone mason beautiful things may be created. If one has a strong back and a slight artistic temperament he may learn to cut stone himself. One of the interesting things about laying flagstone is that it is a combination of art and science. There is a thrill to piecing together irregular pieces of flagstone to make a pattern, equal to that of working a jig-saw puzzle.

The first use that we generally think of for flagstone is for laying platforms—large areas where tea can be served, or small nooks where one may sit and read. These may be flush with the lawn and fit in informally or be on the house floor level with a supporting wall. In this latter type of construction rather thin surface stone may be used for a solid base of concrete is needed anyhow.

If stones are laid on dirt they must be large and heavy enough to resist being tipped out of place when they are walked on.

This is an ideal material for garden walks and steps. These may be laid informally with cracks filled with grass or laid with narrow and carefully cut joints. Even steps and house entrances may be built of flagstone if the work is planned to fit the existing architecture and the construction is carefully done. More and more builders are learning to use carefully cut flagstone for trim on brick houses. A feature seldom considered is that of tying the house to the garden by using this same material in the house trim and in the construction of various garden features.

Flagstone has been used for stepping stones for many years. The common mistake often made in this use is in the practice of using too small pieces and not lining up these pieces to look as though they might have naturally fit together. They should be set high enough that they are not soon covered with grass and hold puddles of water rather than being a dry place to step, as intended.

Curbings, finishes for walls of brick or concrete and often garden gate posts may appropriately be made of flagstone if good design is used. Formal pool curbs may be made of carefully cut and fit pieces of flagstone.

Fireplaces and incinerators may be designed and built which are useful as well as beautiful. If they are likely to be used much it would be well to give them a lining of fire brick. The tendency has been to make garden fireplaces too tall and top-heavy looking. A good, simple design is the first consideration.

Another very delightful use for our native flagstone is for the construction of rockeries with supporting ledges, walls and steps made of weathered and lichened stone found on the surface of the ground over flagstone quarries. Here unlimited artistry and ingenuity can be used. This is a separate subject which will be treated further in another chapter.

Perhaps the most valuable use of flagstone is in the construction of garden walls. It is often good design to put a wall where now a steep, useless bank exists. Walls may be tall and backed with concrete or they may be only a foot high to give the "feeling" of a change in level. The most interesting kind of wall is the English "dry" type.

This is laid up with dirt rather than cement between the stones. It is necessary in this type of wall to let it lean back against the bank at the rate of about one foot in five. Pockets of good soil may be left all through a dry wall in which to plant all manner of interesting rock plants. Contrary to the common directions found in all the English rock garden books a north or east facing wall will grow more plants, and better, than a south wall, for our winter sun is so much hotter here.

WOOD

Wood still has many uses in a modern garden. It is one of the easiest materials for the inexperienced handy man to work with. It may be used to tie in the material and design of the residence with the garden features. Its chief difficulty is in the fact that it requires frequent painting to keep it from rapidly deteriorating, and this is sometimes a problem when vines and shrubs are on or close to it. Pergolas, shelters, garden houses, shade houses, fences, gates and screens may be effectively made of wood. Some screen or fence material may be made of the weather resistant woods such as cedar, redwood or cypress, which might last a long time without painting.

CONCRETE

Concrete is one of the most versatile and easily handled of the construction materials, but it is difficult to get away from the artifiicial and "concrety" color and effect, so it is seldom appropriate in garden construction unless it is used chiefly as a base where it can be covered or hidden with more appropriate materials.

For the main framework of pools, platforms and walls it gives a sturdy base and is easy and inexpensive to handle. Some attempts are occasionally made to disguise concrete by adding color or texture lines. It is seldom very convincing—it is still concrete.

BRICK

Brick has been used in gardens for the construction of platforms, walls and various ornaments for as long as there have been gardens and brick. If the house is of brick, often the adjoining platforms and walls might appropriately be made of brick to give a unity with the house, rather than to introduce a new feature, such as stone, where it was not used in quantity enough to create a feature of itself. Brick now comes in a great variety of colors and textures and may be laid in a number of interesting patterns. Brick platforms laid "dry" on tamped sand are very successful and inexpensive.

TILE

Tile really includes a great variety of materials, which may be used to lay up walls, surface platforms or ornament various features of a garden. Tile of some kind has been used for many years in gardens, notably the Spanish and Italian.

Since there is such a variation in tile character it is especially important to use it with judgment and restraint. Examples of the use of tile will be found in garden pictures throughout this book as well as the few typical examples seen here.

GRAVEL

The typical picture of the old time gardener was a man with a rake "neatening up" a drive or walks. This was at one time a great proportion of garden work. Gravel surfaces for drives, walks and service areas are not being used as much as formerly largely because of the great amount of labor continually needed to keep them neat looking. In our area, however, where water is at a premium we might well think of gravel instead of bluegrass in many places. Lawn may be prettier and softer and give off some humidity, but gravel surfaces will serve for foreground effects equally as well as grass.

In arranging gravel surfaces it is best to first apply a small layer of gravel and when that is worked into the surface of the soil by traffic, occasionally, add more. Putting a 3-inch layer of gravel on the surface is uncomfortable to travel in and is unnecessary.

WATER

In the old Spanish and Italian gardens where natural rainfall was about like ours water was used in a great many ways. It was the chief thing that made gardens comfortable and livable, and because it was naturally scarce it gave one the feeling that he was mastering Nature to some extent to create favorable living places. Broad and shallow water surfaces may serve as would a lawn or gravel surface for foreground effects, water may be used in pools of many sizes and characters, and a little trickle of flowing water will add life to any garden. Water may be used in pools or streams in a naturalistic effect copied after the scenes from the mountains or it may be used in very "civilized," man-made formal pools and rills.

Because water can not be wasted in this area, the small effects of running water will usually be obtained through the use of a circulating pump hidden somewhere out of sight. Sometimes an existing flow of water, such as an irrigation ditch, can be so arranged and planted that it gives the appearance of a natural streamway.

We might well bring back the ancient garden custom of ornamental fountains springing from an otherwise uninteresting garage wall or in connection with a pool.

Under the heading of "Pools and Streams" will be found other examples of the appropriate use of water.

METALS

Wrought iron may be used in the garden in the form of a gate, as a garden lamp to mark your entrance, as a plant bracket or design against a blank wall. A personal touch may be given the garden by working out a design in iron that represents some distinctive character or hobby of the owner, such as a conventionalized iris for an iris fancier or dogs for a dog lover. Designs of flowers, leaves or vines can be worked out that will give interest to spots in the garden all year through. Wrought iron legs for tables and stands or bases for pots and planters can be made to fit in with other ironwork in the garden or house.

Aluminum is now available in a variety of forms and may be used in the construction of many garden objects. Its great advantages include its light weight, and bright, unrusting surface.

SYNTHETIC MATERIALS

Recently, there have been developed several new plastics or fibreglass materials that adapt themselves to use in gardens as screens, windbreaks and backgrounds. They come in a great variety of characters and colors which adapt themselves to many interesting uses.

189

PATIOS, PLATFORMS AND PORCHES

The modern garden design revolves around the patio. As now used, the term "patio" includes any partly screened or roofed garden area which is essentially open to the outdoor air and used as an outdoor living or dining room. Their usefulness depends much on their design which should give a maximum of outdoor feeling with many of the indoor conveniences. A good floor underneath, screening from neighbors' eyes, partial protection from the wind and sun are essentials. Suitable embellishments with vines, flowers and interesting inanimate features add to their pleasure.

The term platform might apply to simply the floor part of a patio or to a solid floor used for other purposes. Porches might refer to the old fashioned open air areas which were under the house roof and essentially a part of the house. Here are additional illustrations of what others have done which might supplement the article earlier in this book and give ideas for developing new or remodeled gardens.

WALLS

Walls may be essentially to hold up steep banks or might even be quite low to give an illusion of change in level where little actually exists. They may be made in a great variety of designs and materials from the informal dry walls of weathered stone to the formal walls of brick or tile. Suggestions are given here which might be modified to meet other conditions.

WALKS

There really are other materials from which to make walks, than concrete. A concrete walk along the front of the property or even to the front door or ash pit may be appropriate, but in the garden-proper less formal and more attractive materials are desirable. Flagstone in all styles from the simple stepping stone to the carefully fitted designs laid on concrete are most appropriate. Good brick walks may be suitable in some places and even gravel may fit in others. Walks properly designed and carefully executed may add much to the general appearance of a garden through the added beauty of ground pattern. Careful grading should precede the laying of a walk so that it will shed water and be dry in stormy weather.

FENCES AND GATES

The design and materials for fences and gates should be the same and so they are treated together here. Fences originally were largely to keep stray stock out and kids or dogs in. Now many fences are chiefly to mark boundaries, furnish some screening or wind protection or just for the beauty and interest which their design adds.

Woven, chainlink or other wire fences are very practical, as they last indefinitely with little or no maintenance, and are easy to erect. Fences of split cedar or similar decay-resisting woods are the most pleasing, generally adjoining a garden. They usually weather in time and fit right into the garden picture. The rather coarse "basket weave" fences are mainly constructed because they are cheap or because the neighbors all have them. Fences of wrought iron, as in the past, are largely antiques now. Some attractive fences are made with masonry posts and various materials fastened between these. Tile or cinderblocks have been used in different designs, but these usually we would class with the walls. Ranch type fences of poles might be appropriate for a ranch type house.

Gates are made of the same material as the fences, but may be elaborated, enlarged and beautified in many interesting ways until they are a definite point of interest in the garden picture.

195

FIREPLACES AND BARBECUES

A few years ago, we occasionally saw fireplaces of stone or brick set in a corner of the "yard" to furnish heat for cool evenings outdoors or on which to cook a picnic meal. Now these have been largely replaced by the "barbecue" which often is a portable metal affair which lends little to the general design of the place. Fireplaces, to be most useful, should be easily accessible from the outdoor areas or patio, should not be so close to the house as to make a nuisance of their inevitable smoke. The massive top-heavy, monstrosity often built in the past is passing fortunately. Stone and brick are still suitable materials to build these fireplaces, and the design may be so simplified and fitted into the general plan that they add much and are not eyesores. Actual designs and uses still vary to fit the desires of the family.

Those shown may not all suit any one gardener but will furnish ideas which may be adapted to any given requirement.

There have been wall gardens, natural or accidental, for hundreds of years. It is only recently, however, gardeners have been definitely planning them. With the mountains a main feature of Nature's landscape in this area, it is very appropriate that we carry out the same theme in our gardens.

A wall suitable for growing plants should be laid up dry. That is, soil should be between the stones instead of cement. Flat stones, like our native flagstone are most stable and effective and they should be laid tipping back so they will remain in place. Although English wall gardens do best when facing south, Rocky Mountain wall gardens seem to do best when facing the north or east. There is a wide choice of rock garden plants which will grow and be happy in a wall garden.

SCREENS

"Screens" may include any material that is used to block out undesirable views or give a feeling of intimacy to a patio or outdoor area. Living screens of shrubs, vines on fences, solid or almost solid fences and walls may each be suitably used under varying circumstances. Recently the new plastics and fibreglass materials with their great variety in texture and color, have been used in appropriate framings of wood or masonry to give that up-to-the-minute effect in a garden.

Here is where your imagination and taste may run riot if you always keep in mind the general design and unity of your plan.

SHADES, PERGOLAS AND SHELTERS

These features of a garden usually refer to structures apart from the house as contrasted to the modern patio effects, which are usually a modified extension to the house. They were used largely in older and larger gardens before the time of the attached patio. There may still be occasions when and where they may be appropriate.

POOLS

The landscape effects obtained from pools have been stressed previously. Here we will give some additional suggestions as to designs and materials used. None of these may exactly fit any particular situation, but each may give an idea, which, when modified and adapted, may make a very suitable effect.

Pools can not be constructed cheaply. They must have walls solid enough to resist cracking from settling of surrounding soil and they must hold water without excessive leakage. Informal pools that attempt to represent natural pools in the mountains should be given a natural setting and have the rim so built that any incongruous cement or other construction material may be hidden with sod or overhanging plants. For reflection only, they may be only a few inches deep, but the minimum depth for fish or lilies would be two feet. If fish or lilies are to be left out all winter, at least twice this depth is necessary.

FOUNTAINS

Fountains were a common feature in the ancient Roman and Spanish gardens. Their use in appropriate places is again becoming popular. Where a garden area is small and must be screened to be usable often a wall fountain may be the most attractive feature included.

Materials may vary greatly, using brick, tile, stone or other materials. Sometimes these ornate backgrounds may not even have a stream of water available but are still very effective.

GARDEN OR YARD

The word garden as we use it is meant to include the grounds surrounding your home. To some the word "garden" means only the vegetable garden, and to others the word "yard" refers to a railroad yard or coal yard, so no one word can convey the whole meaning of beautifying the grounds surrounding your home.

ROCKERIES

Rockeries or rock gardens have been mentioned before under general design and other places. A well designed, constructed and maintained rock garden will always be beautiful, but rock gardens have come and gone because of the many horrible examples that have failed to include one or more of these three essentials. If rock gardens are supposed to be a representation of Nature they should not have disturbing features near or visible from them. Rock gardens of formal material might be beautiful in their way but might properly be called dry walls, or geological collections partly covered with plants.

We burn a stick of wood and it disappears, but it is not gone, it has just changed form. It has been transformed by the action of combustion into its simpler forms of gas and minerals. The particles of carbon-di-oxide given off in this burning process may be used again by our maple tree to help form more wood. Nature wastes nothing, just changes it to fit the greatest need.

STATUARY AND ORNAMENTS

The large gardens of the wealthy in Europe, many years ago, very often featured statuary of many forms. Good statuary appropriately placed will be effective, but in small gardens it must be selected and placed with extreme care.

PICKING WILDFLOWERS

We all love Mountain Wildflowers. Most of them are only really beautiful in their natural surroundings. To pick some of the rarer kinds is not only thoughtless but selfish.

Too often we have seen people pick armloads of Columbine and then a few hours later seen these wilted flowers thrown from the car. There are, however, plenty of varieties and many places where wild flowers can be picked with no danger of seriously limiting future bloom. Our common sunflowers and Spiderworts are usually plentiful in season. And, they make fine table decorations. There are many kinds of Asters, Senecios, Penstemons and Locos which can be found growing in such profusion that anyone may pick all he pleases and run no risk of reducing their numbers for next year.

Preserving the beauties that we have in the Rocky Mountains may be more necessary than bringing in exotic plants from faraway places.

GARDEN FURNITURE

Under this head would be included many of the features of an out-door living room or patio which correspond to indoor furniture or are portable, as contrasted to permanent features like posts and walls. Much garden furniture of recent years is highly colored, made of new materials such as aluminum and plastic and is designed in a modern manner. Garden furniture properly selected may add much to the general design of the garden or if unsuitable it may be awful. Being portable, however, any unpleasing effects may be corrected by rearranging or substituting more appropriate pieces.

Culture and Maintenance

Let's Begin with the Soil

Composition, Preparation, Fertilizers, Humus

GOOD soil is the basis of all good gardening. Every gardener should learn what constitutes good soil and how poor soils can be improved. He should recognize that various plants prefer various kinds of soil—sandy, clayey, alkaline, or acid. If a plant is grown in soil which is suited to its requirements, it will be more inclined to grow so vigorously that it will resist many common disease and insect pests.

Physical properties and chemical composition are the two main qualities of soil which must be considered. Physical properties might be described as light sandy, heavy clayey, compacted, or friable, depending upon the amount of available humus. An ideal soil with a good proportion of sand, clay, and humus can be easily cultivated. Some plants prefer a well-drained, sandy soil which must be watered frequently while other require a heavier, clayey soil which retains moisture longer, once it has been absorbed. A very heavy, clayey, type soil may be made looser and easier to work by addition of sand and humus, making it able to absorb water quickly and retain it over a longer period of time. Barnyard manure, leaf mold, peatmoss, and compost, may be profitably added as humus to heavy soil. If nitrogen is added, sawdust can also be used. These materials should be mixed with the soil thoroughly and deeply if they are to do the most good. Humus with very little chemical properties, like peat, may be mixed with the soil up to one-third volume with beneficial effect. But usually it is more desirable to mix smaller quantities over a period of years.

Of recent years there has been much written about the use of soil conditioners such as krillium to loosen up a heavy soil. When they are properly and thoroughly mixed with a soil already friable they tend to keep it that way, but are of little value when applied to the surface of a hard soil, applied to sandy soils or used in any way where they are not thoroughly mixed with the soil. Generally the application of suitable humus will do all that these chemicals will do, and at less expense and may supply other values such as hormones and plant food.

Hydroponics or water and gravel culture has captured the imagination of many recently, some feeling that this soilless plant culture will someday supplant the ordinary cultivation of plants in soil. Much has been learned of the actual chemical requirements of plants through this experimentation with hydroponics, but it does not now seem that the time is at all close when this method will take the place of growing crops in Nature's soil. Under specialized conditions it is a valuable new science.

Sandy soil may be made more retentive of moisture by the addition of humus, particularly peat. Proper addition of humus on rather light, sandy soils can make them surprisingly productive and easy to work. It is not generally understood that soil must contain some air as well as moisture to enable plants to grow properly. Plants vary in this requirement, but roughly we might say that one-half of garden soil should be sand or clay, one-fourth water, and one-fourth air.

Subsoil

While many plants have shallow roots and are concerned chiefly with the top eight inches of soil, the character of subsoil determines to a great extent the growth. Petunias and barberries, for example, may prosper if there is a two-foot depth of good soil. Maple trees, on the other hand, may become chlorotic, should there be shale, gypsum, clay, or hardpan below this depth. A subsoil which contains some gravel is usually advantageous because it provides better drainage and prevents the topsoil from becoming waterlogged. One of the several important reasons many trees grow better in Boulder, Colorado, than in Pueblo, about a hundred miles away, can be explained by the usually better-drained subsoil in the Boulder, Colorado, area.

It should be recognized that subsoil is much more difficult to improve than topsoil. While sometimes a hardpan subsoil may be broken up by a deep "rooter" or dynamite, greater care should be used to avoid attempting to grow things in soggy soil if it is known that there is a heavy subsoil underneath.

Some times just cultivating a "gumbo" soil, allowing the weather elements to break it up, is beneficial. Great care should be taken to avoid working or trampling a heavy soil when it is wet. Much of the trouble in new lawns is caused by brick-like areas of heavy soil which have been run over by heavy trucks, following rains, during building operations. Some of the rotary cultivators are very effective in thoroughly mixing and pulverizing humus with soil. A method of preparing soil somewhere midway between the old, fixed system of turning a layer completely upside down and the new plowless method of scratching the natural litter into the surface seems to be most desirable.

A LIVING FOSSIL

The Ginkgo or Maidenhair-tree is the oldest existing type of tree, a veritable living fossil.

It is the sole survivor of a family which was distributed over the temperate regions of the earth as long ago as the Reptile Age. No living wild specimens have ever been found, the ancestors of the present trees having come from old Chinese gardens. Apparently they had some religious significance and were preserved beyond their time by the ancient Chinese priests. Over other parts of the world they are only remembered by the fossil remains.

They are difficult to establish in Colorado's climate, but several specimens have grown to a fair size in Denver. The leaves are different from that of any other tree, being parallel-veined and fan-shaped much like the leaf of a Maidenhair fern.

Organic Gardening

Perhaps it should be noted here that there is a certain amount of fanaticism here in the Rocky Mountain area, as everywhere else, concerning organic gardening and earth worms. Certainly our soils need humus badly, but this should not prevent us supplying chemical deficiencies when such exist. The idea that earth worms make great quantities of good soil may be good business to the "pedigreed" earth worm dealers, but it is stretching a point. Earth worms live on decaying vegetable matter in the soil and thus a certain amount of humus must be supplied. Chemical fertilizer in the soil, when applied with judgment, does not kill earth worms. It is hard to say that earth worms do more than move and transform a certain amount of soil and the presence of earth worms in the soil is principally an indication of the presence of humus. Earth worm holes may have some aerating value, but a soil with sufficient humus generally will already contain enough air.

Alkaline Soils

In most areas of restricted rainfall, the soil is inclined to be more or less alkaline. This alkalinity is caused by an excess of mineral salts coming from breakdown of original rocks from which the soil came. These salts may be in excess because there hasn't been enough moisture to grow plants which would have used this material; because there have not been heavy rains to wash out excess salts; or because there has been little vegetable growth which might counteract alkalinity by falling back to the earth and decaying.

Air in Soil Is As Vital As Water to Plant Roots

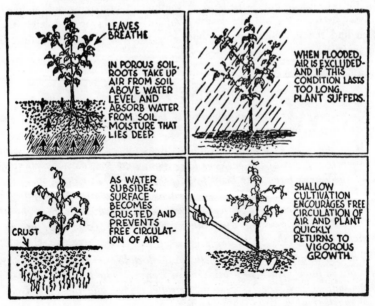

One of the best remedies for this adverse chemical condition is the identical treatment given to correct poor physical condition; namely, the addition of humus. Humus decaying in the soil will tend to create an acid condition. Many soils which are naturally in bad chemical condition or those which have been mistreated by repeated croppings of the same kinds of plants may be greatly benefited by the application of the deficient elements. Under ordinary conditions, soil testing of the average Rocky Mountain garden does not reveal anything not already known—that it is more or less alkaline. However, a careful test of over-cropped soil in such concentrated areas as florists' benches or certain peculiar soils, may indicate elements which are in excessive or deficient amounts. Many times an excess of some chemical such as some of the alkalis may prevent a plant obtaining necessary elements which are actually in the soil.

Soil acidity or alkalinity is commonly expressed in a pH number, 7 being neutral and acidity being indicated by smaller numbers and alkalinity by larger. A pH of 5 being quite acid and 9 very alkaline.

The acid soils of the East are generally benefited by application of lime while here in the Rocky Mountain area there may be a number of chemicals needed which will counteract the opposite condition—alkalinity. Certain chemicals may be important to make other elements available to plants. Chlorosis, or an interference with the natural cholorphyll (green matter) in leaves, often indicates a deficiency of some elements in the soil. Often this deficiency is iron and addition of iron sulphate may prove to be beneficial. It should be noted here that plain iron, as from buried tin cans and nails, is not readily available for plant growth; so the application of the sulphate form is necessary. Sometimes aluminum sulphate is beneficial, especially in the case of oak trees. Addition of small amounts of other chemicals may give remarkable results, when a deficiency or improper balance of the essential elements is present.

Recently there has been some successes in treating difficult cases of chlorosis with the iron chelates or sequestrene. Very small amounts of this product will often cause yellowing leaves to green up in a few days.

It has been generally proven that the deficiency of certain trace minerals seriously interferes with the proper development of plants. Treating deficient soils is a job for a soil chemist of long experience.

Many "miracle" trace minerals products have come on the market recently from which the introducers have hoped to profit from the scant publicity about the importance of trace minerals. Sometimes, especially in the older soils of the east, these products may contain minute amounts of some element which is deficient in some particular soil and spectacular results may be seen. Generally in our "newer" soils, there are few real deficiencies (at least that these miracle products can correct.) It is wise to consult an impartial authority who has nothing to sell before going overboard with these unproven products.

Chemicals Needed for Plant Growth

The three chemicals most often deficient in soils are nitrogen, phosphorus, and potash. Nitrogen is most generally needed in our Rocky Mountain soils since it seems to vary much in relation to the humus content. Nitrogen can be readily supplied in highly soluble form with such

207

materials as ammonium sulphate and urea. Every gardener should be familiar with the method of learning the exact content of any given fertilizer. Each bag of fertilizer must list on the tag the content of the principal elements. For example, a 4-12-4 fertilizer would indicate four percent nitrogen, 12 percent phosphorous, and four percent potassium. Phosphorous is often needed in small quantities and may be readily supplied by the addition of super-phosphate. Phosphate does not seem to travel very far when applied to the soil; so it must be placed down in the soil where it will do the plant the most good. Potash is one of the alkaline materials; so it is not generally as greatly needed in our soils as other elements. Some of the other chemicals which may occasionally be deficient include sulphur, iron, aluminum, boron, magnesium, copper, zinc.

Three elements, generally in gaseous or liquid form are also essential to plant life and growth. They are Oxygen, found in air and water; Hydrogen, found in water; and Carbon, from the carbon-di-oxide, a by-product of combustion found in air.

At the present time, there is much interest in the processes of supplying necessary elements by liquid fertilizers and by injection into the plant or spraying on the leaves. These methods are still in the experimental stage and we should know more about their value to the home gardener in a few years. At present the application of fertilizers in the dry form is still the most popular method. Much information on this subject can be found in the regular soils books so that it is not necessary to repeat it here.

Avoiding too frequent light watering of the surface, cultivation to break up hard crust following a watering and addition of a mulch to the surface are all methods which allow a sufficient amount of air to enter the soil.

"Miracle" fertilizers in many forms have been advertised recently even in reputable garden magazines. These promise wonderful results and give the impression that an "easy" application of these secret and marvelous preparations will grow plants under all conditions and without the usual work, or consideration of the other usual growth factors. Some of these do have the necessary chemicals that plants need for growth, but their cost is all out of proportion to the good that they do. Some might contain only a small amount of some form of soluble nitrogen and an inert filler, like sand, but sell for several times the price of the one valuable ingredient if bought under its well known chemical name. Again, the only safe course is to learn a little about values and deal with those who will give you the facts regardless of sales made.

Two facts should be emphasized—one, soils should be thoroughly prepared by the application of humus; and two, surface mulching is a valuable practice. It should be kept in mind that surface applications of fertilizers can never take the place of mixing these materials deep in the soil before planting. Mulches are usually more beneficial for the moisture they conserve or their modification of soil temperature than for the actual fertilizing value, though this may be eventually very beneficial.

Any gardener can make mulch of manure, leaf mold, peat moss, leaves, straw, sawdust, or similar materials. Mother Nature herself attempts to form a mulch over the surface around plants—a system which we could profitably follow.

Dirt or Soil

SOME people are proud to be called good "dirt" gardeners. I am not so sure that this title is any complement. Dirt is some useless, grimy material such as the layer that accumulates on the windowsill in a large city or the various rubbish that is often left around a new home when the contractors leave.

Soil is something different. It is the material that plants grow from and is a live substance composed of minerals, chemicals, humus and millions of living organisms.

Many are confronted with the problem of transforming the "dirt" that they have been left around their homes into "soil." This is not an impossible job, but sometimes very difficult. If this inherited dirt contains impossible things like plaster, bricks, lumber scraps and gypsum subsoil it is most economical to completely remove it, even though this is an expensive operation. Just a weak, sandy soil or subsoil can be made into productive material by the addition of peat, compost, manure or green crops turned under. A heavy clay soil can be improved by the addition of these same materials and large quantities of sand thoroughly mixed. (Small amounts of sand are worse than nothing.)

In our area the addition of some superphosphate will be of benefit, as it cannot be profitably added to the surface of the ground after planting. Nitrogen, on the other hand is best added to the surface after plants are in, as it leaches in readily, and if applied when there are no plant roots to absorb it much will be wasted.

Good Soil Is Full of Life

MOST gardeners know that the basis of all soil is disintegrated rock, which contains various necessary minerals and chemicals. They may realize that added to this base is much partly decayed vegetable matter called humus, and they may even realize that about one quarter of this mass must be water and one quarter air if plants are to grow well in it.

Few people, however, realize that this apparently lifeless material is really full of millions of living organisms. We can see the angleworms, wireworms, ants, centipedes and some of the nematodes, but a handful of soil may contain millions of microscopic bacteria, algae, moulds or other minute organisms—all important to a good soil. Many microbes are found grouped in various parts of the soil mass, and they are vigorously making lifeless soil into something that will support plant life. By-products of bacterial decomposition and other soluble materials flow into the growing plant roots and into all parts of the plant.

Moulds bring about a partial decomposition of the organic matter in the soil and make it available for plant growth.

Algae are capable of manufacturing their own starch, and this starch is used by the bacteria who also do valuable services for plant life.

When these soil organisms decompose the organic material in the soil a number of growth promoting hormones may be made which are also important for proper plant growth.

The mystery of a seed developing into a fruiting plant when placed in soil, under other suitable conditions, is partly explained when we know of the action of some of these billions of tiny soil organisms. Size is just relative in Nature after all.

Hormones

MUCH has been done in recent years with the effect of hormones on plant growth. These mysterious things which are produced naturally in many plants for specific purposes have been produced synthetically as chemicals and may be used to produce desirable effects in plants. One hormone may encourage plant growth, another induces the rooting of cuttings, another helps a newly transplanted plant to quickly survive the shock of losing many of its roots, another may induce fruit to drop prematurely, hold it on longer or prevent its formation.

Carried one step further these hormones may so encourage plant growth that it may literally grow itself to death. These are called the 2,4-D, 2,4-5T and such, weed killers. They can be very dangerous when used carelessly, for they do not have the power of distinguishing between an undesirable weed and a desirable plant. Much can be expected from these hormones in the future when more is known about them and they are developed for more selective use.

Learn to Water Properly

PROPER watering is probably the most important cultural practice for Rocky Mountain gardeners to learn. The rules are simple, yet many do not go to the trouble to learn them. We must keep in mind that one of the principal factors which makes gardening different in the Rocky Mountain area is lack of natural rainfall. Therefore it is necessary to supply the subsoil with moisture which is supplied naturally in many other areas. Gardeners should recognize that there are various factors which govern the frequency and amount of water which is necessary. Soils vary in textures, thus requiring varied amounts of water and holding the moisture for various lengths of time. The slope of the ground influences the ease of watering and retention of moisture. Humus content of the soil makes a great deal of difference in its water-retaining ability. Mulch or cover crops may make much difference in the amount of water absorbed after a hard rain, and also the rapidity with which it is evaporated from the soil. Certain plants seem to be more greedy for moisture than others. Still other factors are temperature and humidity of the air. It would be difficult to determine just how often a certain area should be watered and how much water should be applied at one time without making a careful study of existing conditions.

As an illustration, let us assume that an area of level, open lawn in soil of medium texture, containing an average amount of humus, having a suitable mulch on the surface, requires thirty minutes of watering a week to keep it in good condition. These same conditions, but in the shade, might require ten minutes less watering time. A heavy soil might also need ten minutes less and cool, cloudy weather, as compared with bright sunshine, might mean five minutes less. A combination of these conditions might only require five minutes a week watering. A location on the south side of a building or on a steep south slope might require thirty minutes more watering. And very sandy soil or the presence of greedy shallow-rooted trees might each require an additional thirty minutes to give equal results. The lack of sufficient humus in the soil or lack of mulch on the surface might require ten minutes extra watering, and extremely hot, dry weather fifteen minutes. A combination of all of these unfavorable conditions might require a total of an hour or two more watering a week to keep the soil sufficiently moist and in ideal condition.

Test the Soil

The only sure way to determine the correct amount of water needed is to test the condition of the soil in various locations. Running a pencil into the ground almost to its entire length is usually a good test for lawns. If it goes in easily, the chances are the ground is moist enough. To determine if enough water is being given larger trees and shrubs, it may be necessary to dig test holes occasionally. Unless this is done, you may find that some spots of ground thought to be properly watered will be wet only half as deep as necessary and other spots will be wet and soggy.

Many cities have ordinances prohibiting the use of an open hose in the irrigation of a garden or lawn. Yet this method properly controlled will require much less water than sprinkling. In the sprinkling process, often much water is lost by evaporation. There is also a tendency among some gardeners to sprinkle until the water runs off the surface and assume the soil is sufficiently wet. Yet the water may actually have soaked in only a few inches and the ground may be as dry as before by the middle of the next day.

When the soil is soaked deep by proper irrigation, there is a subsoil moisture which will return to the top by capillary action as the surface water is used up or evaporated. Here again we should work toward the objective of WATERING LESS OFTEN AND MORE THOROLY.

Under this method of watering, much less time is involved and most plants will thrive a great deal better. Though the practice of holding the hose to water the ground every day a few minutes after supper gives one a fine feeling of having done his duty by the lawn, it does the lawn very little good and is actually just a method of killing time. Furthermore, this kind of watering in poor soils tends to encourage shallow rooting of plants, making them susceptible to poor growth during the difficult summer days.

Recent introduction of several new sprinklers which throw a wide circle of water and which may be left running a long time without overwatering is an improvement on the old sprinklers which could only be left in one place a few minutes. Automatic underground sprinklers are now available and they do a fine job if properly engineered and installed.

Shade Trees Suffer

Probably our shade trees suffer more than any other class of plants from the lack of water, since their roots reach far in search of nourishment and moisture. The old rule that the roots of a tree extend only as far as the spread of its limbs is correct only in generalities. Shallow-rooted trees like the willows, poplars, and Chinese Elm may send their masses of surface roots a much greater distance than the spread of their limbs. On the other hand, very deep-rooted trees like the walnut and buckeye may not spread so far on the surface, but go to extreme depths. Most gardeners find that street trees planted in narrow parkings have difficulty in surviving. Often these parkings build up until it is difficult to supply enough water for even the lawn. Roots from these trees range out under the street, under the sidewalk, and up into the front yard, but still may not be able to gather enough moisture.

A thorough soaking three or four times a year which reaches out and down to the farthest root is of much greater value than the traditional sprinkling three times a week, for most trees. The small "bowl" around the trunk of the tree may barely keep the tree alive, but that alone cannot make it thrive. Each plant has its own distinctive root system and its own requirements for water. Most of the plum family, for example, have only a few far-reaching shallow roots. Chinese Elm, willow, and poplar trees have a wide system of small shallow roots, while the slower-growing trees have especially deep roots. Roughly, we might figure the bulk of the lawn grass roots along with annuals and small bulbs to be in the first eight inches of soil. Many perennials, large bulbs, and vegetables may reach down to eighteen inches, small shrubs and roses to thirty inches, large shrubs and small trees to four feet, and large trees to eight feet or more. Most of these plants will send a few roots to much greater depths than this but the bulk of their system will be in this range, depending upon soil conditions and variety of plants.

Over-watering may be as detrimental to plants as lack of watering. This is especially true where we have considerable alkali in our soil and water. As water absorbs these alkaline salts and then evaporates, it may leave concentrations of alkali on the surface.

Some care is necessary to avoid damage from watering at wrong times. Roses may suffer from mildew if watered overhead late in the day, so that the foliage does not dry before sundown. There may be damage to some leaves from watering during the heat of the day. Sprinkling simply to wet the tops or add to the humidity of the air is some times desirable; especially in cases of newly transplanted plants, or moisture-loving things like tuberous begonias and ferns.

When to water and when not to water may be an instinct with some gardeners, but any one can learn it, at least with some degree of success, if he actually wishes to.

HOW PLANTS GROW WITHOUT RAIN

Plants native to the Rocky Mountains have to be able to survive with very little rainfall. It helps us to appreciate the difficulties native plants experience here when we learn how those which grow naturally "get by" with this little moisture.

Take the cactus, for example. It has large fleshy "leaves" which hold moisture for a long time after a rain. Some natives, like the Yucca, have tough, waxy type leaves through which little water can evaporate. Still others have practically no leaves at all, for the same reason. The Bush Morning Glory has an immense underground root system, which could store up enough water to last a year or two. Some plants send down very deep roots in times of plentiful rainfall so they can obtain sufficient moisture from the deep subsoil in times of drouth. Many annuals, like the Russian Thistle, are able to sprout their seeds, grow leaves and blossoms, and mature seeds with the moisture from one good rain. The Downy Brome Grass gets a good start in the fall, lives through the winter, and matures its seed in late spring, to take advantage of more plentiful moisture in the winter.

When plants from the more moist section of the country are brought to this Rocky Mountain country, we must remember that they usually have no such provisions for surviving without much rain. We must give them some of the same treatment they got in their native places, if they are to thrive and remain happy.

How much or how little to water a plant is something which cannot be told in a rule book. One indication of a person with a green thumb is his ability to instinctively know when a plant needs a drink.

The Importance of Water to Plant Growth

All life is dependent on water and cannot survive without it, but it is especially important to the growth of plants. Plants growing in swamps where there is always a plentiful supply of water have very different structures from those which grow on the desert. Compare waterlilies with cacti for instance. About 50 gallons of water are required to produce one pound of dry matter in some plants. Much of this water is used as a solvent or carrier for minerals and is required to complete the miraculous process of photosynthesis which is necessary to all life, plant or animal. After being used to transport the necessary elements much water is evaporated into the air helping to increase humidity.

Although plant growth depends on several things, such as sunshine, proper temperature, air, minerals and such, water is near the top of the list in importance.

In our area of limited rainfall at least 25% of the proper growth of ornamental plants depends on how well we learn to use the water that we have available. Without the additional water collected in the mountains as snow in winter and diverted to our use in summer. on the lower, more level lands where most of us live, we would still be living in practically a desert.

"When Shall I Stop Watering?"

Good gardeners should learn that there is *no time* to completely stop watering, or no time to "begin" watering. Living plants should have the soil moist around their roots at all times.

This idea of a time to stop and start watering came from the East with us, and had a good reason there, for in the fall when the weather was cooler, the plants slowed up in their growth and there was generally much precipitation and cloudy weather, so that seldom was additional moisture needed until the next spring when the weather became warmer and the plants sprang into renewed growth.

In our area of limited rainfall, and open, dry winters we should learn that while we may reduce our watering considerably we should never stop it. In an average winter (if there is such a thing) our lawns, trees and other plants would benefit greatly by at least three thorough soakings between November first and April first. If the soil is thoroughly soaked after plants lose their leaves and stop active growth in the fall and the ground remains frozen, no more watering is necessary or desirable; but

---

LEARN ABOUT PLANTS FROM PLANTS

If one person could accumulate in his head all the horticultural knowledge from books, he might still be missing the best part of horticulture. Real joy in gardening comes from learning about plants from plants themselves. Nothing can take the place of the personal experience of sowing seeds, cultivating young plants and caring for them to maturity. Every plant has its individual characteristics which furnish unlimited subjects for study. Life is not complete without having had the privilege of personally caring for a few plants, whether it is forty acres of corn, a mountainside of pine trees, or a lone geranium on a window ledge.

when we have periods of several weeks of sunny weather with low air humidity, the soil around plants may become so dry that the roots cannot replace the moisture that is evaporated from their tops. Then we have damage that we will call "winterkill."

Heaviness or lightness of soils, steepness of slopes, various exposures, and seasons of the year will all affect the frequency of watering, but it is NEVER time to completely stop watering.

After receiving no water for five months it is also bad for plants to suddenly start to water them several times a week, for this induces them to grow only shallow roots which cannot withstand the severe weather sure to come in fall.

Pre-Watering

Some of our best horticulturists believe that we should consider more often the advisability of soaking the soil BEFORE planting. Many would think that this would be a waste of water, but actually it is the most efficient use of water and promotes better growth of newly transplanted trees or newly seeded lawns. Most of the ornamental plants that we grow here came from areas where there was naturally sufficient subsoil moisture, and when we plant those things here and then just "water them in" the surrounding dry soil sucks up this little applied water like a blotter and the plant that it is intended for suffers.

It is good practice to dig the holes for all trees, shrubs and other plants some time before planting and fill them with water, if necessary several times, until the surrounding soil is thoroughly wet. Then very little water will be required to settle the soil when the plant is put into the ground. Prewatering a lawn area just before seeding will not only fill the subsoil with water so the new seed will not dry out so fast, but it will settle the loose soil so that a roller is not needed.

ROSES HAVE THORNS

And peaches have fuzz. Corn must be husked and catalpa trees drop their bloom on the walk.

The low shrubs that look so well now—leadplant, dwarf peashrub and bush cinquefoil—look like dead tumbleweeds in winter. The quick-growing trees like poplars, willows and Chinese elm are short lived and practically weeds.

Dandelions and plantain grow vigorously in poorly made or cared for lawns, while the bluegrass is sickly. Petunias grow easily and quickly, while peonies take many years to produce their gorgeous flowers.

Oaks must be very carefully planted in good soil and cared for many years before they are the massive sturdy trees that we all admire. Mountain ash, with their brilliant display of fruit, and linden with their symmetrical spread of limbs, are difficult to start.

We must pay for what we get when we deal with nature. If we do not want to work we must take cheap things. The really fine things are only for those who are willing to study and sweat for them.

The mark of culture and stability may be seen in a community by observing the better and more permanent plants that are grown, just as well as by inspecting the banks and libraries.

Let's Cooperate with Nature

LEARNING proper methods of watering and preparing the soil to help introduced plants acclimate themselves will increase the list of things we can successfully grow in this Rocky Mountain country. There are other special practices which tend to make these desirable plants feel at home and happy.

Mulching is Nature's way of protecting the soil surface. Each autumn falling leaves gradually accumulate in a layer of partly decayed vegetable matter—to help hold the moisture, prevent runoff in severe storms, and keep the soil surface from packing. This natural mulching also prevents excessive changes in soil temperature and, as it decays, furnishes valuable plant food.

We cannot always let nature take its course in laying down mulch, so we should try to approximate this effect by cultural practices. One of the best mulching materials is peat, though it lacks fertilizing value. Manure has been much used as a mulch but it must be carefully handled to avoid burning or over-fertilization. Because fresh manure is richer in chemical value, it always must be used with care, and for many uses, well-rotted manure is safer. Leaf mold, taken from the forest or made in compost

It is especially important in this Rocky Mountain Area to save every bit of waste vegetable material to make into valuable humus compost. This can be done in a few months in pit, pile or pen if the right methods are used.

COLOR IN SUMMER

It is well to be careful of combinations of just two or three colors, especially those "funny" colors like magenta and lavender, but a con-glomeration of all colors is always good. The unplanned combination of colors in wildflowers on the hills is always attractive and a similar mixture in the garden is satisfying.

---

piles, is very valuable, both for surface application and working into the soil. Every gardener should have some out-of-the-way place where a pit, pile, or pen to make compost is available. This humus, which our Rocky Mountain soils lack, should be preserved whenever possible.

Many other materials may be used as mulches if they are handled right. In areas where such things are available as byproducts, peanut hulls, ground corncobs, shredded bark and chopped straw are often used. Sawdust may also be used, but, as it breaks down very slowly and ties up the surrounding nitrogen until it is broken down, it is important to use about 2% ammonium sulphate or some such form of nitrogen with it.

Cultivation or stirring the surface of the soil when it becomes suitably dry after rain or irrigation has been a standard practice of gardeners for many years. It is still important, but more to destroy competing weeds than to make a "dust mulch" as was once thought necessary.

Aeration, by hand or power tools, is coming to be a standard practice where soils are compacted and do not "take" water readily, such as an old lawn planted in heavy soil. While this is strictly an emergency measure it will do some temporary good where it is impossible to make over a lawn and properly prepare the soil.

Another special practice for the Rocky Mountain area is to provide protection from the severe northwest wind or from the equally severe southwest sun. Some of our less hardy trees, shrubs, vines, and evergreens may be successfully grown in this area if they have a little extra protection during the first few years. It is this matter of weather protection which makes it possible for many of these tender things to grow on the east side of a building when they don't seem to survive in other locations.

Shading for a few years the trunk of such tender-barked trees as Linden, Hard Maple, and Mountainash with coarse wrapping or boards set up on the southwest side will often allow them to get established. A lath or burlap screen on the southwest side of a tender evergreen like the White Pine or White Fir may also mean the difference between a healthy plant and one which just doesn't seem to get along.

Hilling up hybrid tea roses is now an accepted practice in the Rocky Mountain states. Other similar plants might well benefit from the same treatment. Some difficult plants like the tuberous begonias may be successfully grown when the soil, watering, and shading are carefully done with an additional application of humidity by occasional overhead sprays. One of the reasons some plants will grow in what looks like poor mountain soil and yet will not be happy in the heavier soil of our irrigated areas is that they must have better drainage. Some of these plants may prefer a little rain every few days but cannot stand "wet feet" and soggy soil which goes with it. Here it should be stated that to approximate natural drainage in our gardens doesn't mean throwing a hand-full of sand or a few rocks or tin cans in the bottom of a hole dug to plant a tree. Real effective drainage must go further than that. Generous amounts of humus worked into the soil deeply will help the drainage problems. Careful layout of the garden slope to allow excessive rainfall to drain off is another good practice. In some cases a few tile will relieve the situation. However, where the soil is inclined to be wet and heavy, the best practice is to plant only those things which will tolerate these conditions.

217

Protection for Exotic Plants

UP TO the present time, we, in the Rocky Mountain Plains area, have not learned to use but very few of the native plants that have adapted themselves to our climate through the centuries. Probably 95% of the ornamental plants that we commonly use are those that we have become accustomed to in the East, or other areas where there is more precipitation, more humidity in the air, an acid soil and comparatively "regular" weather. Here these introduced plants suffer from our dry air, especially in winter, from lack of moisture in the soil, from the direct sun, untempered by clouds or fog, by a generally alkaline soil and most especially from the unpredictable weather in fall and spring. We may have nice, sunny, fall weather up to Christmas, then a few weeks of severe weather, weeks of sunny weather through February and March and snow in May. One of the most important lessons that the gardener in this area must learn is to provide protection to the introduced plants against these difficult conditions which the plant is not accustomed to.

Natural fall weather does not always condition these introduced plants to successfully go through the winter. If possible the irrigation should be reduced in fall (August and September), to allow woody plants to ripen up so there is no soft, new growth to be easily killed when sudden, severe weather strikes later.

Then, after there is no chance of further growth (usually when the leaves begin to fall) it is very important that everything be soaked down deep, to the farthest roots. Even when a woody plant is dormant there is some circulation of water through it, and our very dry air and hot sun may suck out more moisture than can be replaced unless there is moist soil around the roots. If there are periods of open warm weather during winter, when the ground is not frozen, it is important to check the moisture in the soil and if it is not sufficient give everything another soaking. This may be necessary several times during many of our winters.

This especially hot sun and dry air may also tend to dry up the bark of some trees with especially tender bark such as Mountainash, Linden and Cherries. Wrapping with some porous material like burlap or old screen wire will often prevent this damage. There may be purchased special paper for wrapping trees. Partly tender shrubs or small evergreens which have no natural protection of trees or buildings may be benefitted by a screen of burlap or lath. In many new gardens much winter damage may be avoided by erecting windbreaks to break the force of the northwest winds, until plants become established or regular shrub screens can grow to effective size.

A protective mulch on the ground around perennials, shrubs and trees will often prevent much winter damage. This mulch will help to hold moisture in the soil, help to prevent rapid changes in temperature of the surface soil and keep plants from assuming spring has arrived when one of the frequent warm periods happen during the winter months. Contrary to general thought, mulches are chiefly to keep plants cold rather than keep them warm, and it is usually much more important to have them in place after the New Years than before. They should be left in place until permanent spring has really arrived. It is general practice to mound up hybrid tea roses when they go dormant in fall and leave this protection on until new growth starts in spring.

Many of the nice, but partly tender plants from the East may be grown here if given a little additional shade. A lath house would be a valuable addition to any garden. In this the nice things like Lilies, Clematis, Eastern wildflowers and ferns could be kept happy. More ornamental pergolas or the northeast side of buildings could be used.

Remember that most of our "winter-kill" is not from the cold but the warm, dry, winter air, and from the unpredictable and sudden changes in weather which fool the plants into starting growth before the proper time.

Hardiness

JUST what do we mean when we refer to a plant as "Hardy" or not "Hardy?" To some this may mean simply the plant's ability to withstand cold, and their charts showing plants hardy in various areas of our country indicate only the average length of the growing season, or the average days from the last frost of spring until the first frost of fall.

In this Rocky Mountain Plains area there are other factors that determine a plant's ability to survive and thrive. First of all there is the amount of water that it can have in the soil for the processes of plant growth and the amount of humidity in the air to supplement this soil moisture and prevent excessive evaporation from the above-surface parts of the plant.

The average amount of sunshine and cloud-free days will make a great deal of difference in how well certain plants, especially the broad-leaf evergreens, will survive.

Then, the amount of precipitation usually expected in an area usually affects the character of the soil. In an area of great rainfall the soil is inclined to be acid while soils in areas of small rainfall are usually alkaline to some degree.

Texture and composition of soil will encourage some types of plants and discourage others. Well drained soils or poorly drained soils affect the growth of various plants.

While the location north and south will usually affect the length of growing season, other factors will also modify this so that straight lines east and west will not define the areas of certain length of growing season. Altitude will also affect this and ocean currents along the coast will warm or cool for many miles inshore.

Protection of nearby cliffs or locations in deep, narrow valleys will often vary growing conditions to approximate several thousand feet in elevation or several hundred miles farther south.

To determine plant growth areas, especially in this western country of ours, ALL these factors must be considered.

Recommended reading:

OUR GREEN WORLD, Rutherford Platt.
FLOWERING EARTH, Donald Culross Peattie, Pub. by Putnam.
THE GREEN EARTH, Rickett, Pub. by The Jacques Cattell Press.
PLANT GROWTH, Yocum, Pub. by The Jacques Cattell Press.
COLLEGE BOTANY, Fuller and Tippo, Pub. by Henry Holt & Co.

ANTS AND APHIS

We might say that all ants have a sweet tooth, but ants do not have teeth. Anyway they like sweet things, and that habit gives them a reputation for doing damage, that they do not deserve.

They are seen crawling over peony buds in the spring, and people think that surely they must be eating the buds, while actually they are simply gathering the sweet sap that covers the buds and are doing the peony no harm.

They may be seen crawling up and down shrubs, trees or flowers; and the assumption is that they must be damaging the plants, while actually they are herding and milking their "cows." These cows are aphis, or plant lice which give off a sweetish fluid from two glands on their back.

The ants only damage the plants indirectly, as they winter some of these aphis over in their underground nests and "plant" them on the ends of twigs of the proper plants when growth starts in spring. These aphis then multiply very rapidly and soon furnish the ants with plenty of sweet "milk" and at the same time suck enough sap out of their host plant to seriously weaken it. On the other hand if we humans are watchful we may use this habit of the ants to our advantage, as when we see the ants busy on a plant the chances are that the plant has aphis on it, and we should get our spray guns and go after them. This is another interesting example of the interdependence of various parts of this intricate and interesting plan of nature.

Even the Bugs Act Differently

TO THE average gardener the control of insects seems a very complicated procedure—there is such a variety of insects which at times become a pest, such a long list of plants affected, and worst of all, the number of insecticides is becoming greater and much more complicated every year. It almost takes an expert in botany, entomology and chemistry to keep up with all the latest developments. There is an increasing tendency to use regularly the all-purpose sprays and dusts which are made with the thought that they will, in a single application, control all the common insect pests. This may be a desirable procedure in the case of valuable plants which are regularly damaged by several insects, but these all-purpose insecticides may often do more harm than good in the long run by also killing off beneficial insects. It is better to learn a little of the identification, habits and controls of the principal insects that commonly feed on the plants in the garden or house and then treat for just this trouble.

In addition to the general problems of insect control there comes the problem of adapting known procedures to fit our climate which most often affects insects and their control differently than in other sections of the United States.

Manufacturers are often so enthusiastic for their own insecticides that they disregard other similar products which may be equally effective. We will refer to most insecticides by their chemical name and the gardener may check this with the particular brand name which he finds most convenient to purchase.

Also listed are the principal insects which harm plants in the ornamental garden and those that infest house plants. Insect pests of fruit and vegetables have been rather carefully treated by the Agricultural colleges and we will only mention a few of the most common. Some of the ornamental plants which are usually bothered with one or several pests will be listed along with principal insecticides. Your garden should be checked weekly for signs of the first damage done by insects, and the necessary measures taken before too much damage is done or a great population of insects built up.

SHALLOW vs. DEEP ROOTS

Every gardener should be aware of the definite plant characteristics connected with deep and shallow roots. The shallow-rooted trees are usually quick-growing and short-lived. They transplant easily, require only shallow soil and leaf out early in the spring. They are mainly "weed" trees such as poplars, willows, boxelder and Siberian elm.

The really good trees are almost all deep-rooted. They are slow-growing, hard to transplant and are very conservative about leafing out in the spring. The very deep rooted trees include the Black Walnut, Buckeye, Kentucky Coffeetree and the Oaks. Fairly deep rooted and good trees include the Elms, Maples, Honeylocust, Hackberry and Catalpa.

We should learn to plant more of the deep-rooted plants adapted to the Rocky Mountains.

Plants Commonly Subject to Disease or Insect Pests in the Rocky Mountain Area

AFRICAN VIOLETS: Mealybug, spidermites, nematodes.

ALDER: Leaf miners.

ALYSSUM, Sweet: Fleabeetles.

AMARYLLIS: Thrip.

APPLES: Coddling moth, fireblight, spidermites, borer.

ASH: Oystershell scale, borers.

ASPEN: Oystershell and cottonwood scale, borers.

ASTERS, CHINA: Wilt, yellows and other diseases, blister beetle, aphids.

AZALEA, Potted Florists' Plants: Mealybug.

BACHELOR BUTTONS: Aphids.

BARBERRY: Chlorosis, webworm.

BEANS: Bean beetle, fleabeetle, rust.

BEGONIAS: Mealybug, whitefly.

BIRCH: Aphids, borers.

BOXELDER: Boxelder bugs, leafrollers, aphids.

BUCKEYE: Cottony-maple scale, leaf blotch.

CACTUS: Mealybug.

CABBAGE: Cabbage worm, grubworm, aphid, maggot.

CALENDULA: Bean aphids.

CARAGANA: Blister beetles, spidermites, grasshoppers.

CARNATION: Thrips and many other diseases and insects.

CEDAR or JUNIPER: Cedar-hawthorn rust, aphids, spidermites, bagworms.

CHERRY: Leafslugs, cherry fruitworm.

CHOKECHERRY: Webworms, tent caterpillars.

CHRYSANTHEMUM: Spidermites, midge, cyclamen mite.

CINQUEFOIL or POTENTILLA: Spidermites, midge, cyclamen mite.

COLEUS: Mealybugs, whiteflies.

COLUTEA, BLADDERSENNA: Blisterbeetles, spidermites.

COLUMBINE: Aphids, columbine borer, mildew.

CORN, SWEET: Earworm.

COTONEASTER: Oystershell and other scale, spidermites.

CLEMATIS: Spidermites.

COTTONWOOD: Cottonwood and oystershell scale, caterpillars, slime flux.

CURRANT: Currant worm, aphids.

CYCLAMEN: Cyclamen mites, nematodes.

DAHLIA: Aphids, spidermites, powdery mildew.

DELPHINIUM: Aphids, crown rot, blacks.

DOGWOOD: Oystershell scale, spring and fall aphids.

DOUGLAS FIR: Aphids.

ELM: European elm scale, Dutch elm disease, aphids, slime flux, spidermites, scolytus beetle, snout beetle, appletree borer.

EUONYMUS: Spring and fall aphids, euonymus scale, crown gall.

FIR: Aphids.

FORGETMENOT: Fleabeetles.

FLOWERING QUINCE: Chlorosis.

FUCHSIA: Whitefly, spidermites, mealybugs.

GERANIUM: Whitefly, mealybug, cyclamen mites.

GLADIOLUS: Thrips, various diseases.

GLOXINIA: Thrips.

GOLDENGLOW: Aphids, mildew.

GOLDENROD: Aphids.

GOOSEBERRY: Caterpillars, maggots.

GRAPES: Leafhoppers, mildew.

HACKBERRY: Nipple gall, witchesbroom.

HAWTHORN: Cedar-hawthorn rust, fireblight, leafslug, aphids, maple scale.

HOLLYHOCK: Rust, spidermites.

HONEYLOCUST: Cottony-maple scale, borers, spidermites, leaf midge.

HORSECHESTNUT: Cottony-maple scale.

HYDRANGEA, Potted Florists: Spidermites.

IMPATIENS, Sultana: Mealybug.

IVY, ENGELMANN and BOSTON: Leafhopper.

IVY, ENGLISH: Scale.

JUNIPER: Cedar-hawthorn rust, aphids, spidermites, bagworms.

LAWN GRASS: Fairy-ring fungus, ants, mildew.

LILACS: Oystershell scale, leafminer, mildew, borers, spidermites, citrus mite.

LILY: Mosaic disease, aphids.

LINDEN: Cottony-maple scale, sun-scald.

LOCUST, BLACK and PINK: Locust borer.

MAPLE: Cottony-maple scale, chlorosis, borers.

MOUNTAINASH: Sunscald, big bear beetle, fireblight.

NASTURTIUMS: Aphids, fleabeetle.

NINEBARK: Chlorosis.

OAK: Chlorosis, caterpillars.

ONION: Thrips.
PANSIES, VIOLAS: Spidermites, slugs.
PEAS: Aphids, spidermites.
PEACH: Borer, tarnished plant bug, aphids.
PEONIES: Ants, mosaic.
PHLOX: Spidermites, mildew, rust.
PLUM: Curculio, aphids.
PINE: Tipmoth, aphids, scale, spidermites.
POPLAR: Canker, borers.
PRIVET: Thrips.
PRUNUS: Leafslugs.
PUSSY WILLOW: Canker.
RASPBERRY: Spidermites, cane borer.
ROSES: Aphids, leafhoppers, leafslugs, snout beetle, mildew, blackspot, cutter bees, rust, rose midge.
SANDCHERRY: Spidermites.
SNAPDRAGON: Rust.
SNOWBALL: Spring and fall aphids.

SNOWBERRY: Blister beetles.
SPIREA: Aphids.
SPRUCE: Aphids, spidermites, pine scale, gall aphids.
SQUASH: Squash bugs, maggots.
STRAWBERRY: Millipedes, red stele and root rot, cyclamen mite, root aphids.
SWEET PEAS: Spidermites, aphids, mildew.
SYCAMORE: Canker stain, chlorosis, anthracnose.
TAMARISK: Spidermites, leafhoppers.
THIMBLEBERRY: Spidermites.
TOMATO: Psyllids, tomato worm, whitefly, blight, wilt.
VERBENA: Blister beetle.
WILLOW: Aphids, oystershell scale.
WALNUT: Aphids.
ZINNIA: Mildew, blister beetle.

Common Insects and Specific Controls

ANTS. Chlordane in some form and under various brand names has been so effective that it has gradually taken the place of most former controls. Usually the ants do not harm plants much directly, but they protect and encourage aphids which do a great deal of harm to a large variety of plants. Lindane and dieldrin are other materials which have been extensively and effectively used.

APHIDS. The aphids, or plant lice are soft-bodied insects which live by inserting their sharp beaks into a plant and sucking its sap. They multiply very rapidly when conditions are favorable, and may attack most kinds of growing plants at certain times. The activities of ants often indicate the presence of aphids, as ants enjoy the sweet "honeydew" given off by aphids. The ornamental trees on which they are most commonly found are Birch, Elm, Boxelder, Hawthorn, Willow and Walnut. Common ornamental shrubs on which they often are found in damaging numbers are: Spirea, Dogwood, Snowball and Eunonymus. On the last three they build up a large population just before the leaves fall and lay eggs which hatch early in the spring. These very early aphids roll themselves in the leaves and seriously deform the plant but are almost impossible to kill at this time. They should be sprayed when they appear in late fall, or with a dormant oil spray in fall or spring. Of the ornamental evergreens the most seriously damaged are the Pine, Fir, Spruce and Colorado Juniper (*Juniperus scopulorum*). These must be watched all through the summer to catch the aphids before they do serious damage. A great many garden flowers and house plants are regularly infested with aphids, the large red aphids on goldenrod and goldenglow seeming almost like a part of the plant. Control is easy, if it is remembered that they must be hit with spray to kill them. They are soft bodied, and so are killed by a contact poison. The most common insecticide used is nicotine sulphate usually sold under the name of Black Leaf 40. This should be used when temperatures are 80° or over, as much of its effectiveness is from the fumes. The normal dose is 1 to 1½ teaspoons per gallon of water. It is usually most effective when used in connection with a good grade of soap chips. Preparations of Rotenone and Pyrethrum are also commonly used. DDT and Chlordane will kill some species, and

Aphids

other new insecticides are being introduced. There is some danger of burning from the use of Chlordane on a few plants. Malathion is effective against most aphids and is also a good miticide and general insecticide. These preparations should all be used according to directions of the manufacturer. Poisonous dust may also be used. It is important to repeat any treatment in a week or ten days to catch those which have hatched from eggs since the previous spray. The aphids which cause the disfiguring galls on blue spruce have a different life history from the common run of aphids. When the galls or "cones" on the spruce ripen, they release the adult aphids which fly to the nearest Douglasfir tree. Here they feed on the surface of the needle in the ordinary manner. Later some of the young may fly back to the spruces and lay eggs. These eggs lay dormant over winter on the spruce buds, and then in spring, hatch and lay eggs, which hatch and are enclosed by the new growth of the tips. Here they spend their life, with food and lodging supplied, until the gall ripens and starts the cycle over again. Some benefit can be gained by picking these galls off before they ripen or spraying the tree just before new growth starts with 10% lime-sulphur. Spruce and Douglasfir should not be planted close together.

BAGWORMS. A few Bagworms have been found in this area on junipers. All shipped in specimens should be watched closely for signs of Bagworms which should be immediately destroyed. One treatment is to pick off all that are visible; another recommends the spraying with 3 or 4 level tablespoons of arsenate of lead to a gallon of water, adding one teaspoon of nicotine sulphate. Some of the newer insecticides such as Lindane, Parathion or Vapotone are now reported to be more effective.

BEETLES. This term covers a great many insects, but as all of them are chewing insects, the control generally consists of spraying with a stomach poison such as arsenate of lead or one of the new, more powerful insecticides such as DDT, Lindane or Methoxychlor.

BLISTER BEETLES. This insect, which commonly attacks plants of the pea family, may be prevented from damaging the plants by protecting with a stomach poison such as Cryolite, DDT, Chlordane or Dieldrin.

BORERS. These insects may require varying treatment, depending on how they work. Those most serious in this area include: Bronzed Birch Borer, Honey-locust Borer and Flatheaded Appletree Borer, Lilac Borer.

BORER, BRONZED BIRCH. This borer is rapidly becoming a serious menace to Birch Trees in Denver. It has wiped out birches in some eastern communities. Difficult to detect until much damage is done. Dying limbs or swelled ridges in limbs indicate its presence. Keeping up the vigor of trees will help to combat this pest. To thoroughly control this, there must be community-wide efforts.

It may also be controlled by spraying with 1% Technical DDT emulsion in May or June and again in summer. A closely related insect also works occasionally in Honeylocust and Bolleana Poplar.

BORER, HONEYLOCUST. This is very similar in appearance to the Birch Borer, but all indications now are that they may not be as serious in the Honeylocust. Controls similar to Birch Borer may be used.

BORER, FLATHEADED APPLETREE. This insect works in newly transplanted trees or those which are not growing vigorously from any reason. They make large irregular galleries under the bark or in the wood. They usually do most of their work on the warm southwest side of trees or the upper side of large horizontal limbs. They are most common in elm trees but may be found in almost any shade or fruit tree when conditions are suitable.

Control consists largely of prevention. Keep trees growing vigorously, and wrap the trunks of newly transplanted elm trees with wire screen for a couple of years. Prevent sudden exposure of trees that have been heavily shaded. When borers are first discovered they may be cut out or killed with a wire.

BOXELDER BUG. The boxelder bug lives most of its life on the boxelder trees and there does comparatively little damage. When fall comes they try to get into houses and are found swarming over south-facing foundations. The red parts of their body readily identify them. In spring they crowl from their hibernating places to the trees and lay eggs which produce many more bugs for another season.

Control consists of removing the trees if possible, or spraying those bugs that gain entrance to houses with household sprays, and those outdoors on buildings with kerosene. When on plants they may be killed with sprays of pyrethrum, nicotine thiocynate or similar sprays at about double ordinary strength. 1% DDT, Dieldrin, Lindane and Chlordane have also been found to be very effective. Do not use household sprays on plants.

BUGS. Another rather broad term, but generally referring to beetles which are chewing insects and controlled with stomach poison.

CATERPILLARS or WORMS. (Including the larval forms of many beetles and moths). There are a great variety of worms or caterpillars which feed on a great variety of trees and other plants. In Denver they have only occasionally become serious, as the natural predators usually keep them in check. The tent caterpillars can become a nuisance as they are not so easily gotten at; however, any chewing insect such as caterpillars and beetles may be controlled with a stomach poison. Arsenate of lead, 3 lbs. to 100 gallons of water, has been used for a long time. Now the new DDT, chlordane and dieldrin poisons are taking their place as they are less poisonous to animals and they have, when properly applied, with special spreaders, a long residual effect.

CORN EARWORMS. DDT has given control when sprayed on first silks.

COLORADO POTATO BEETLE. DDT has been effectively used for control.

CURCULIOS. Includes a large family of Snout Beetles feeding in both the larval and adult stage on a variety of plants. We are most concerned with the damage to cherries, plums and roses. These are beetles with a snout much like an elephant's trunk with which they bore holes in rose buds and do other damage. They are very destructive, but are hard to find as they work mostly early or late in the

Snout Beetle or Rose Curculio

day. No completely effective control has been developed, but spraying periodically with the all-purpose sprays or dusts may help to keep them under control. As they insert their snout into the plant to feed they are seldom affected by stomach poisons applied to the surface, and as they are not soft-bodied, they are not affected by contact sprays. Hand picking in the early morning and a careful sanitation program have been found to be very effective, and 1 to 2% DDT spray with Chlordane will help to control them. Two sprayings of arsenate of lead, 1 tablespoon per gallon, one at petal fall and one ten days later has been standard control on plums and cherries, but Malathion or DDT would probably be much more effective.

CUTWORMS. There are surface feeding types of cutworms, climbing and underground. The surface workers are most effectively controlled by paper collars around the valuable plants when they are small, the climbers are killed by scattering poison bait of various mixtures and the subterranean kinds are destroyed by grub-proofing with arsenate of lead, applied 10 pounds, mixed with a bushel of soil or sand, broadcast over 1,000 square feet of ground and immediately watered in. A commonly used bait is made by mixing 1 ounce of Paris green, zinc arsenite or sodium fluosilicate, 1¼ pounds of bran, 4 ounces molasses and

Cutworm

½ pint of water. Scatter at sundown. This is very poisonous and must be thoroughly scattered or covered with boards or screen to keep from animals and birds. Lindane, Dieldrin, DDT, and Chlordane have also been used.

EARTHWORMS. The organic gardening cultists almost worship the earthworm as a "maker" of good soil, but when the large kind called "night crawlers" appear in great numbers in a lawn almost every home owner is anxious to be rid of them. One of the safest, cheapest and most effective controls is to broadcast one-half to one pound of arsenate of lead (You will probably have to mix this with sand, soil or peat to scatter it evenly) over 100 square feet of infested lawn and water in thoroughly at once. Do not give this treatment during the time robins are feeding their young as it may kill them to be fed the poisoned worms. Chlordane or Dieldrin may also be used.

EARWIGS. Of more harm to nerves than plants, usually, but earwigs may become a nuisance. Control with bait scattered thinly around hiding places. One formula consists of six pounds wheat bran mixed with ½ pound sodium fluosilicate and moistened with 1 pint fish oil. DDT and chlordane may also be effectively used.

ELM BARK BEETLES. Three bark beetles are sometimes found in Elm trees. The smaller European Elm Bark Beetles (Scolytus multistriatus) is the main vector of the Dutch Elm Disease, and has increased rapidly in Colorado the last few years, until there are at present thousands of beetles and hundreds of trees affected. As they are only successful in breeding in recently dead wood, the removal of this kind of wood, either in the tree or in the wood pile, is the most effective control. Spraying with the approved 2% DDT emulsion will prevent their feeding on Elm trees for as long as three months. Dead wood in trees should be removed and burned. Logs in dumps or wood yards may be sprayed with 2% DDT in fuel oil, or burned.

The Native Elm Bark Beetle (Hylurgapinus rufipes) is only occasionally found. The galleries of this beetle are similar to those of the Scolytus beetle, but the main gallery is across the grain of the wood, rather than with it. It seems to be an insect of only secondary damage. Removing weak or dead limbs will ordinarily keep this borer under control.

The Black Elm Snout Beetle (Magdalis barbita) works under much the same conditions as the Native Elm Bark Beetle, and controls are about the same. These beetle galleries are under the bark in irregular patterns.

FLEA BEETLES. DDT, Lindane and Dieldrin have been effective in control.

FLEAHOPPERS. This insect feeds on many vegetables and a few ornamentals, but can be controlled by sprays of nicotine sulphate and soap, pyrethrum or malathion.

FLIES. Common house flies have been most effectively controlled by sprays of DDT, but this material has recently been ruled out as dangerous or ineffective for certain uses and methoxychlor or lindane substituted.

GALLS. Galls are common on some species of willow, cottonwood, roses and many other plants but about the only one serious enough for concern at the present time, in this area, is the Nipple Gall (Eriophyes) on Hackberry. This may be controlled by spraying with DDT or one of the newer similar compounds, soon after the leaves are formed. Raking up and burning or composting affected leaves may help to prevent spread of this insect. The gall midge affecting the new leaflets of Honeylocust may be controlled by spraying with a contact spray as the leaves are developing.

GRUBS. In lawn, may be controlled with Chlordane or Dieldrin.

GRASSHOPPERS. Grasshoppers may feed when hungry on almost any plant, but when there is plenty of food they may develop definite preferences; for instance, they may almost destroy iris without seriously damaging other plants. They are more abundant in some years than others and seem to prefer dry, hot weather. Insecticides containing chlordane, toxaphene or lindane have recently been found to be very effective in their control. The usual treatment has been a poisoned bait scattered at sunrise in spring when the first small 'hoppers appear. A recommended bait consists of bran, 1½ pounds; molasses, ¼ pint; sodium fluosilicate or Paris green, one ounce; water, 1 pint. In most counties, grasshopper bait, ready-mixed is available through the County Agent's office. Chlordane is now found to be very effective and safe to handle.

Grasshopper

LEAF CUTTER BEE. Cuts neat circles from the leaves of roses. As they do not stop to feed on the roses, the control is difficult. Learn to appreciate their artistic work and forget them.

LEAFHOPPERS. Leafhoppers are most destructive to rose, grape or ivy plants but may attack many others. They cause a fading and lifeless appearance to leaves when they are numerous. The young are soft-bodied and may be controlled much

Leafhopper

like aphids, but the adult are winged insects and may be controlled with a coverage of some such stomach poison as arsenate of lead. Repeated applications of either insecticide is necessary to control those that hatch later. DDT, Lindane, Malathion and TEPP have also been effectively used.

LEAF MINERS. The larvae of these insects develop as a small white worm between the upper and the lower surface of the leaves. When numerous enough they may almost defoliate the plants. We are most concerned with their damage to Lilacs and the Native Alder. They may be controlled with applications of nicotine sulphate at double the usual strength when

Lilac Leaf Miner

they first appear, or by one of the new insecticides such as DDT or Chlordane which have a residual effect. Pratts D-X

used with linso soap, mixed according to manufacturer's directions, has been reported to be very effective when used as the insects first start feeding.

LEAF ROLLERS. Several insects may roll the leaves around themselves to give protection. These are commonly worms and because of this protection, are difficult to kill. A dormant spray before the leaves appear may help to control them or a stomach poison applied with considerable force. Removing fallen leaves will sometimes help. Some leaves may be rolled by infestations of aphids which require a contact spray.

MAGGOTS. In onions may be controlled with Chlordane.

MEALYBUGS. These are chiefly found on house plants such as coleus, cactus and ivy. Washing the leaves of susceptible plants frequently will keep them in check or they may be killed by touching each with a toothpick with a little cotton moistened in alcohol on it. Volck oil spray at 1-50 solution is sometimes effective. Wash off with water a few hours later. Do not use alcohol on African Violets. Malathion should also be effective.

MILLIPEDES. These are usually harmless scavengers, but may enter strawberries, which touch the soil, and scare the eaters. Control by mulching to keep strawberries off the soil, or bait with poison bran or raw potato smeared with Paris green, or some other stomach poison.

MITES. There are many mites attacking a variety of plants, but most of them we will mention under the head of "Spidermites" and they are even more frequently called "red spider," though many are not red. The cyclamen mite is the most common of the regular mites bothering cultivated plants. Hard forces of water on both sides of the leaves, frequent washing of the leaves, setting in dry saucer of Naphthalene flakes, and spraying with some of the new insecticides like Lindane, Endrin, TEPP or Vapotone have been reported effective.

MITE, THE CITRUS RUST. In the last few years this mite has been found on the upper surfaces of lilac leaves in great numbers. They give a browning effect like frost would give to the leaves. Nicotine or Vapotone has been reported as giving control but the treatment must be repeated. Malathion should be more effective.

NEMATODES. These are tiny insects usually working in the soil and may affect many garden or house plants. In gardens and greenhouse, soil sterilization by tear gas or steam is effective while with pot plants the best treatment is probably to start new cuttings in new soil.

PINE TIP MOTH. This small moth lays eggs on the tips of small pine trees in early spring just before the new growth starts. These hatch and the larvæ bore down through the tips, destroying them. The larvæ then drops to the ground and pupates in a mass of material just under the surface of the soil on the trunk of the tree. Other kinds may have more than one brood or may pupate in other places.

Picking the damaged tips off before the larvæ emerges may help to control them. Spraying with arsenate of lead just before new growth starts and in a week or two later has been used as a control, but the most effective thing yet found is a spray of 1% DDT emulsion as new growth starts about May 1-10. These insects pupate around the trunk, just under the ground, and may be found there in fall and scraped off.

PSYLLIDS. We are chiefly concerned with their damage to potatoes and tomatoes. Tomatoes could hardly be grown, in the last few years, without dusting or spraying with sulphur or DDT every ten days.

SCALE. Scale insects might be referred to as modified aphids—they move around for only a few hours in their lifetime. Most of the adult life of the females is spent in one location, with their sharp beak piercing the bark of a plant to suck its sap, and a protecting scale covering them. At the time the young hatch, they grow legs which they use for a short time to carry themselves to a new location on the plant, then these legs are shed and the protecting scale grown. At this crawler stage they may be killed by a contact spray such as used for other aphids.

At other times the common control is a dormant spray of 6% miscible oil or lime-sulphur 5% to 10%. Dormant sprays are applied during that period when the leaves are off or the growth (in the case of evergreens) has ripened. In recent months it has been found that some scale insects may be controlled by a suitable DDT emulsion.

The Oystershell scale commonly attacks ash, willow and cottonwood trees, dogwood, lilac and cotoneaster shrubs. Oystershell scales do not usually move as far as other types and so form dense masses on limbs until that limb is killed. They have a hard shell and usually require a stronger solution to kill them. A 6% to 9% dormant oil has been good control.

SCALE, EUROPEAN ELM. This is our most common pest on American Elm and will attack Siberian Elm on occasion. There are few American or European Elm in the area which are not more or less seriously infested. Careful spraying with high powered sprayers and a solution at proper strength is necessary. A high pressure of water may dislodge some of the scale in late spring, as they are on the underside of the lower limbs in preference, and in late spring they are not as firmly attached. A 6% dormant spray of oil emulsion, malathion or ½% DDT emulsion before crawlers hatch has given good control.

Cottony maple scale are much larger than the two preceding kinds. They prefer soft maple trees but may be found on Honeylocust and Linden trees, Grape, Snowball, Snowberry or other plants. In the spring when the cottony egg masses are under each scale they are very conspicuous. They do a great deal of damage and spread rapidly and widely. The regular miscible oil, 5%-6%, and lime sulphur sprays are effective when properly applied. No effective summer spray program has been developed.

SCALE, PINE. White, round and about the size of the head of a pin, they attack chiefly Pine and Spruce. They may become plentiful enough to do a great deal of damage to evergreens. The usual control is a dormant lime sulphur spray (10%).

SCALE, COTTONWOOD. The cottonwood scale is much similar to the Pine scale, but usually larger and found attacking poplars. They are easily controlled if sprayed in time with a suitable dormant spray. Volck oil spray has been used safely and effectively to eradicate scale on house plants.

SLUGS AND SNAILS. Small shell-less snails are most destructive to the leaves of Cherry, Pear, Plum, Hawthorn, Cotoneaster, Roses and similar plants. The adult lays tiny eggs on leaves, which develop rapidly and may do a great deal of damage. They eat the green from between the veins of leaves, sometimes almost defoliating the trees.

The control is easy but the treatment must be done promptly when the slugs first appear. As they are soft bodied they may be killed with a contact spray, as they also chew they may be controlled with application of a stomach poison and as they are slimy creatures they may be destroyed by throwing ashes or dust on them.

Slugs thrive in gardens where there is shade, excessive watering and much sur-

Leaf Slug

face trash. When once established they are difficult to eradicate and may do much damage to ornamentals and vegetables. The prepared snail pellets and bait are partially effective and chlordane or methoxychlor will kill them if they come in contact with it. One effective method is to spray a board with chlordane and turn it over with just enough room for them to crawl under. The chlordane will then come in contact with them and kill them.

SOD WEBWORMS. (Lawn Moths.) Generally easy to control with Chlordane or Dieldrin.

SOW BUGS OR PILLBUGS. These little gray bugs are common in damp dark places, under boards, pots or refuse. They feed on roots or tender shoots of plants and may do considerable damage if allowed to become numerous. Removing their hiding places, keeping the surface

of the ground drier and setting out poison bait, or a poisoned raw potato are the usual controls. A common formula for Sowbug bait is 1 part Paris green, 9 parts sugar (or part flour or corn meal). This must be applied under boards or in places where animals and birds cannot reach it. Chlordane, Dieldrin and DDT are now effectively used.

SPIDER. Black widow and others. Chlordane, Malathion or Dieldrin have been successfully used.

SPIDERMITES. Usually referred to as red spiders, but mites may be greenish or yellowish. They are of the spider family rather than the other six-legged true insects, and are difficult to control because they do not chew as the beetles and worms, nor are they soft-bodied as the aphid. These pests are very small, so are seldom seen unless special effort is made to locate them. Tapping a suspected twig over a white piece of paper may disclose tiny red or brown dots moving, which are the red spiders. Their time of greatest activity is during the hot days of late summer, but a few specimens may be found on infested plants almost any time of year. They multiply rapidly and live by sucking the sap from their host plant. They may attack a great variety of plants but are most conspicuous for their damage to Colorado Juniper, Blue Spruce, Currant, Bush Cinquefoil, Perennial Phlox, Hollyhocks, Apples, Elms, Thimbleberries, Begonias and other plants. Plants infested with them show a brown-

Red Spiders or Spidermites

ing and dirty look on the under side of the leaves, or, in the case of evergreens, a gradual dying of needles from the inside of the plant toward the outside. Sulphur in some form has long been used in the control of red spiders and is still effective. It is most efficient when applied between 75 and 90 degrees temperature. Many new insecticides, or rather miticides, have

Sowbugs or Pillbugs

229

been recently introduced which are more effective but are dangerous to use. Some have recommended a periodical spraying all summer with a mixture of wettable sulphur, pyrethrum and nicotine sulphate to keep spiders and other evergreen pests under control. The pre-growth lime-sulphur spray is probably the best all around spider control, as it will have considerable residual effect. Care should be taken in using wettable sulphur or lime-sulphur around painted surfaces as it will leave a stain. A hard force of cold water applied frequently helps to keep them under control, but cannot be expected to completely eliminate them. Malathion, Aramite, Dimite, Ovatran and Kelthane are newer miticides and very effective for the control of some species.

RED CLOVER MITES. These may become a nuisance in winter by crawling up the south side of homes, in the cracks around windows and all over the house. They probably do no damage except to nerves, but no one seems to like them. They may be effectively controlled by wiping a kerosene soaked rag over the windowsills where they enter, or placing a small line of grease in their paths. Spraying with kerosene when found outside, or contact sprays repeated may discourage them. The new, powerful insecticides, such as Parathion will kill them but are too dangerous for general use. The miticides mentioned above will give some control with Kelthane especially effective.

SPRINGTAILS. Springtails are tiny white insects seen springing into the air when potted plants are watered. They are practically harmless but disagreeable, and may be killed by pouring an ordinary dilution of nicotine sulphate through the soil of the pot.

SQUASH BUGS. These are seriously damaging squash and related vines. Sabidilla dust or lindane has been used effectively to control them.

THRIPS. Thrips are tiny black or yellow insects which often damage gladiolus, onions, privet and some house plants such as gloxinia and amaryllis. They are seldom seen as they move very fast and hide much of the time in the spaces between leaves. Evidence of their damage is faded areas on leaves and faded or distorted blooms. They are difficult to control when they become numerous. Prevention is usually more effective. Gladiolus bulbs should be treated with DDT or naphthalene flakes when in storage, and they should be planted in ground where no glads or onions have previously been grown. Dipping the bulbs in a 1% DDT solution for a few minutes some time before planting is effective. When thrips have become numerous on gladiolus or privet the accepted spray has been two teaspoons tartar emetic, four teaspoons brown sugar

Thrips

to a gallon of water. Other sprays which seem to be effective include lindane, dieldrin and DDT. These materials should be applied in early morning, late afternoons or on cloudy days when the insects are out in the open feeding.

WEBWORMS. Being chewing insects, Webworms are controlled by stomach poisons, but may be hard to reach because of the enclosing web. Sometimes are burned with a torch on a pole, when in trees, or clipped out with a long pruner and burned.

WHITEFLIES. These may become numerous around greenhouse or garden plants. Controlled partially by frequent sprays of nicotine sulphate and soap, rotenone, DDT or volck.

WORMS. "Worms" is another word for caterpillars, and they may be controlled by stomach poisons, especially DDT.

The new insecticides are more powerful and effective than any of the old products, and they may also be more dangerous. It is fine to be able to positively kill off some insect pest that is becoming a problem but for each bad insect destroyed there may also be ten harmless or beneficial ones killed. Insects are closely tied up with all the biological processes, and once the fine balance that has been developed over the centuries has been broken, anything may happen.

When we once get Nature out of balance then we must continually develop more and more powerful treatments to be able to survive.

We Have Disease Problems, Too

THIS list will not attempt to give all the diseases which may affect ornamental plants in the Rocky Mountain area; only those which are common or more serious will be mentioned with practical controls given.

The disorders of plants that we classify as diseases may be caused by a fungus growth of some sort, by bacteria, by the ultramicroscopic viruses or by physiological causes. Fungus growths may be illustrated by the mildew of roses, the Cedar-hawthorn rust or the cankers of poplars. Bacterial wilt of Carnations might be an example of a disease caused by bacteria, and Mosiac of lilies a virus disease. Physiological causes would be illustrated by chlorosis which might be caused by a lack or an oversupply of minerals or water.

While the conditions over this area may be very favorable for the rapid build up of insect pests, luckily these same conditions of hot sun and dry air are unfavorable to the rapid spread of many diseases common in other areas. Black spot of roses, for instance, is not nearly the serious disease here as it is in more moist climates.

Several things may be done, sanitation being the first, to control those diseases which may become serious. Some diseases are spread by spores which are held over in diseased leaves or stems of plants. Careful cleaning and burning of refuse that is known to be affected will limit the chances of spreading such disease. Quarantining newly acquired plants from older stocks until they have proven themselves clean will eliminate much infection. The breeding of disease resistant plants seems to be the answer to such threats as the Snapdragon rust and Aster yellows.

Spraying with such fungicides as sulphur, bordeaux mixture, lime-sulphur and the newer materials such as Fermate, Dithane, Captan, and Zerlate should be considered as a preventive, rather than a cure for already badly damaged plants. These materials used as sprays or dusts are intended to kill the spores of fungus diseases when they light on susceptible plants.

SPORTS

Not of the tennis, fishing or baseball variety, a "sport" in horticulture is a variation from true type or a break from the regular habit of a plant. Something happens to the chromosomes in the plant allowing it to vary from the characters which have continued to be handed down for generations.

Most sports are fixed and constant when propagated from grafts or cuttings. Thus, our named fruit varieties are largely sports and will be the same wherever found. On the other hand, the Austrian Copper Rose is a sport which seems to be unable to make up its mind whether it wants to stay red or go back to its original yellow. Often one-half of the petal or half a bloom, or even half the bush will "go back" to yellow while the remainder stays red.

Why millions of plants will continue to propagate themselves true to type and then one will vary, is one of the mysteries of Nature.

Common Diseases and Their Treatment

BLIGHT OR CANKER. This disease affects several kinds of trees and there appears to be more than one form, but the most destructive kind affects Bolleana poplars of all ages and kills smaller limbs or eventually the whole tree. In most parts of Denver there are so many of these trees giving off spores of the diseases that any Bolleana which is not growing vigorously or which has unprotected wounds may become infected.

Control consists in keeping trees growing vigorously, avoiding wounds, or properly protecting them, and, early in the progress of the disease, in cutting out infected parts and disinfecting. As Poplars live very largely on water, trees which have been started with good soil and plenty of water, and then have been neglected are the most susceptible. When trees have a considerable percentage of blighted limbs, it is seldom worth spending money on them. Even young, apparently healthy poplars are so likely to be attacked by this disease that they are seldom worth treating.

CANKER STAIN DISEASE. This disease attacks Planetrees or Sycamores. It is not very common and can infect the tree only through cuts or abrasions of the bark. Children, linemen, or tree trimmers are the usual causes of spreading the disease. The effects of the disease are shriveled places on the bark and discolored wood.

Control consists of preventing spread of the disease through tools or even common tree paint. All tools and brushes used in working on Sycamores which might have this disease should be disinfected before and after each cut.

CEDAR-HAWTHORN RUST. This disease is similar to the Cedar-apple rust of the East, but attacks the native Colorado Juniper and has, as alternate host, some Hawthorns. There may be some other species of Juniper which are attacked by this same disease, and it is possible that some other alternate hosts may develop, but at present these are the two most important plants affected. The small or large galls attached to twigs of the Junipers will enlarge into horned orange colored gelatinous masses following the first warm rain of spring. A few days later these galls will have dried up and will be discharging spores which the wind will carry to Hawthorn trees. The Downy Hawthorn seems to be the most susceptible while the small, smooth-leaved species like oxycantha are least affected.

Soon after the spores light on Hawthorn leaves they cause orange spots to grow. These gradually get larger until they may almost cover the leaf and prevent the natural manufacture of food for the tree. Usually in July these infected spots will spread through the leaf and protruding spore bodies will form on the under side. These will ripen and produce spores which the wind must carry back to the Junipers to complete the cycle. On the Junipers again the spores will spend about eighteen months until they have made a little growth and are prepared to start the process all over again.

Previously all control has been aimed at removing all adjacent Junipers or Hawthorns, whichever were less numerous or valuable; and in spraying to kill the spores AFTER they light on either the Junipers or Hawthorn. Now we are learning to kill the spores on the originating plant, BEFORE they fly out. On the Junipers this is a Bordeaux 180 spray before the galls reach their gelatinous state; and on the Hawthorn a spray of Fermate in July.

BORDEAUX 180 FORMULA:

Copper sulfate	12 pounds
Lime (fresh hydrated)	12 pounds
Mono-calcium arsenite	2 pounds
Zinc arsenite	8 pounds
Soybean flour (sticker)	1 pound
Water	100 gallons

CARNATION RUST. One of the many diseases sometimes found on carnations; it may be controlled by sprays of Sulphur, Fermate or Bordeaux.

CHLOROSIS. Chlorosis is a deficiency disease. It may be brought about by lack of certain necessary chemicals in the soil, or through the inability of the tree to obtain these chemicals, because of the excess of other chemicals, or soggy soil, or other difficulties.

Soft Maple trees are most often affected, also Pin Oak, and in many of these cases the lack is iron. Many shrubs will also become affected, Flowering Quince,

Spirea, Ninebark, Roses and Barberry being especially sensitive.

Control usually consists in supplying the lacking chemical to the tree. This has been accomplished by injections in the tree, by spraying the leaves, or application in the soil. The most practical method seems to be to apply chemicals or mixtures of chemicals in bar holes, punched in the soil under the spread of the tree. These holes are usually spaced about two feet apart and may be 18 inches, more or less, deep. Iron sulphate is most often effective, but sometimes aluminum sulphate will give results, especially in the case of Oaks. Iron chelate or sequestrene will often give quick results when other things fail. A complete fertilizer is often used, straight or mixed with peat or sand. Our soil, which often contains excessive amounts of alkali or added amounts of lime is largely responsible for this condition. A trench dug around a tree and filled with manure will usually give very good results. To apply direct to tree, drill ½-inch holes 1½ to 2 inches deep, depending on size of tree, 6 inches apart around base. Fill hole with Ferric citrate, covering hole with wound dressing.

DUTCH ELM DISEASE. Control consists almost entirely in eradicating the bark beetle which is responsible for spreading it. This beetle may carry spores of the disease on or in its body from the tree in which it was hatched to any other tree. When they first fly from their home tree they will feed on the small twigs of any Elm available within a short distance or even miles. After feeding a few days they then hunt for a suitable tree in which to lay their eggs. A recently dead limb or trunk of American Elm is preferred, but if no suitable place is available they may attempt to enter healthy trees. Healthy trees will usually repel them, but after repeated attempts they will weaken the tree and kill it. They also feed and breed occasionally in Siberian Elm.

Control consists in removing and burning all possible material in which they might breed, in spraying valuable trees with the recommended DDT emulsion in May and July, and in better care of trees through watering, fertilizing or trimming.

FIRE-BLIGHT. A disease which attacks Apple trees and other trees in the family such as Hawthorns and Mountainash. The damage may be limited to the dying of a few small twigs, may kill back a great majority of the twigs, or may attack the bark near the base of limbs. It is most serious following a wet spring. Spores of the disease may fly through the air from uncared-for trees in the neighborhood and infect trees which may be well cared for; also may be spread by insects and animals. The infection seems to take place largely at about the time of blooming.

Treatment may consist of removing all infected wood 6 inches below the infected point in fall or winter, or spraying with zinc chloride or Dithane when in 10% bloom and again ten days later. Tools should be disinfected with a good disinfectant after each cut, and all wood removed should be burned. 1-1000 Bichloride of Mercury is most generally used. Some benefit may be had from spraying with Bordeaux when the trees are in bloom. There is no known positive cure or prevention, but keeping up the vigor of the trees will help. Recently encouraging results have been had with the proper use of Agrimyacin.

MILDEW. Powdery gray fungus most common on Roses, Phlox, Delphinium, and Chrysanthemum, mildew can be controlled by spraying or dusting with sulphur or copper fungicides or other fungicides if the plants are not too far gone.

MOSAIC. This is a virus disease most dangerous to lilies. Some kinds such as the common Easter Lily act as carriers of the disease and will infect other lilies close by while they may remain undamaged. The disease is spread by aphids also. One control is to avoid planting lilies of unknown qualities in the same area with established lilies.

SLIME FLUX OR WETWOOD OF ELMS, POPLARS (and other trees). Attention is called to this condition by leaking places from old wounds and cracks. The dried sap may form discolored places down the trunk of the tree. This sap is usually sour smelling. Additional presence of the disease may be determined by borings into the heartwood of the tree. When this disease is present the heartwood will smell foul, and at times in the spring an actual pressure of sap will force a stream from the hole.

There is no positive cure known, though certain sulpha drugs are known to kill the infection if they can be brought into contact with it. Sometimes boring drain holes and inserting drain pipes will prevent its spread.

Apparently the disease enters through improperly treated wounds in the upper part of the tree. There is a theory that it is encouraged by overwatering of the soil, such as might happen in the case of trees in lawns. Fertilization, spraying for scale, or any other procedure that will increase the health of the trees will help them to combat this disease.

SUN-SCALD. Many fine trees brought into Colorado from the East or other areas of cloudier climate, are seriously damaged here by sun-scald or winter-burn when they are young. Mountainash, Linden, Sugar Maple, Cherry and some Oaks are especially tender.

Wrapping with some loose cloth like burlap, or with ordinary screen wire will usually break the sun sufficiently to prevent damage. Shading with a board set up on the southwest side of the tree, or a lath screen will help. When sunken areas on the southwest side of small tree trunks appear, following an open winter, it is usually an indication of sun-scald. These places will heal over quicker if they are carefully traced out in a streamline form and the exposed wood sterilized with Bichloride of Mercury solution (1 tablet dissolved in a little water and added to a few ounces of 70% alcohol) and then painted with a good tree paint.

YELLOWS OF ASTERS. This disease is spread by a leafhopper, so the most effective control has been to cover plantings of asters with wire screen or cheesecloth to keep out the leafhoppers. All affected plants should be pulled and burned as soon as they show the characteristic yellowing. As the same disease overwinters on many weeds, another control is to keep adjoining weeds cleaned out.

COMMONLY USED INSECTICIDES AND FUNGICIDES

To be mixed and applied according to manufacturer's directions.

CONTACT SPRAY OR DUST
Nicotine sulphate (Blackleaf 40)
Pyrethrum, in many brand names
Rotonone, straight or in mixtures
Lethane, thyocynate
Tartar emetic, Potassium antimonyltartrate
Hellebore, from rhizomes of Veratrum
Fish oil
Summer oil
Malathion

STOMACH POISON
Metaldehyde
Arsenate of lead
Arsenite of zinc
Calcium arsenate
Sabadilla, powdered seed of S.A. plant

GENERAL OR DUAL-PURPOSE INSECTICIDES
DDT, Dichloro-diphenyl-trichloro-ethane
Chlordane
HETP, Hexaethyl-tetraphosphate
TEPP, Tetraethyl-pyrophosphate
(Vapotone)
BHC, Pure gamma isomer of benzene hex-achloride, Lindane (Isotox)
Toxaphene, chlorinated camphene
Cryolite, Sodium fluoaluminate
Dieldrin or Aldrin
Nicotine bentonite

Methoxychlor
DN 111, a dinitro compound
Naphthalene flakes
Parathion, an organic phosphate
PDB, Paridichlorobenzene
Benzene hexachloride

FUNGICIDES (for control of plant diseases)
Sulphur, usually the wettable kind
Lime-sulphur
Dinitro compounds
Bordeaux mixture
Puratized, an organic mercury
Fermate, Ferric dimethyl dithocarbamate
Sulphicide (non-staining)
Bichloride of Mercury, Corrosive sublimate
Captan
Dithane Z-78
Karathane

DORMANT SPRAYS
(For control of scale insects and eggs or immature forms of aphids, spidermites or other insects, used when all leaves are off.)
Scalecide
Sunoco oil
Dendrol
Elegetol, Sodium dinitro-o-cresolate
Volck, white oil emulson
Lime-sulphur solution (1 gallon of liquid lime-sulphur is the equivalent of 4 pounds dry lime-sulphur)

Suggestions on Spraying

THERE is no such thing as a spray which is a cure or preventive for *all* plant pests, and diseases. The only way to get good results from spraying is to become familiar with the various common kinds of pests and the treatment for each.

We will mention here some of the groups of insects most frequently found. The most common class of plant pests is the aphid or plant louse. They are usually small and green, but may be larger and red or black. They do not chew the leaves but simply insert their sharp beaks in the plant and suck its sap; consequently, they cannot be killed by a stomach poison. Since they are soft-bodied insects they can be killed by a contact poison. Nicotine-sulphate or "Black leaf 40" has been one of the usual treatments. Pyrethrum, Rotenone, Pratts D-X, Malathion and many other materials are also used. These, of course, can only be effective if the spray or dust hits each insect at the time of application.

Scale insects of various kinds might be called simply "lazy lice." After hatching and moulting a few times they stick their beak into the plant and remain there for the balance of the season. They, however, protect themselves with a hard shell, making an ordinary contact spray ineffective. The most effective treatment for them is an oil-emulsion spray when the leaves are off (or Lime-sulphur in the case of evergreens), as a spray strong enough to be effective in killing them when the leaves are on is also liable to kill the leaves. When found in small numbers they may be brushed off with a stiff brush.

Worms, beetles, and other leaf-eating insects are usually controlled with a stomach poison such as arsenate of lead or all purpose material like DDT or Methoxychlor. Naturally this can only be effective when the plant is completely covered so that the insect cannot take a bite without getting some of the poison.

Slugs, the slimy snail-like insects which skeletonize the leaves of cherry, plum, and cotoneaster, are easily controlled if discovered in time, by an application of stomach poison, contact poison, or dusting with lime, ashes or common dust.

The tiny red spiders such as are found on the under side of the leaves of hollyhocks, junipers and chrysanthemums in hot dry weather may be held in check simply with a frequent application of a *strong* force of water, although applications such as sulphur, lime sulphur or a miticide such as malathion, dimite or aramite, will always be more effective.

The leaf hoppers found on woodbine and white mealy bugs found on house plants are also partly controlled by this same cold water cure if used before they get too bad. Malathion or Dieldrin are usually effective.

Leaf miners such as are becoming more common in lilac leaves are difficult to control, as they are covered by the leaf surface; but strong applications of nicotine may help and materials such as DDT and D-X have been used quite effectively.

The various diseases, blights, mildews and rusts which fortunately are not so common here, require specialized treatment and cannot be controlled with any one spray.

Proper soil, moisture, sunshine and other conditions usually play a larger part in the health of a plant than diseases and pests, and a vigorously growing plant can withstand the attacks with much less damage.

So, don't waste your time and money just "spraying," but know what you are spraying for and what chemical is proper to use, and then, when and how to apply it.

SAFETY IN SPRAYING

Every year sees the introduction of new and more powerful chemicals. Many of these materials have been used only a short time and their effects on plants, birds, animals, humans and soil is not fully known. Handling these powerful chemicals by the average gardener is comparable to a layman writing his own medical prescriptions. Much of this work should be left to the experts, and even they do not as yet know all the answers.

Safety in handling these spray or dust materials requires a consideration of their possible effect on birds, or pets or the human operators; their possibility of burning plants through being incompatible with previous or future sprays, of their being used on sensitive foliage; and their ability to stain painted surfaces or concrete.

When some of the new, powerful sprays like Parathion, Vapotone, Dieldrin, TEPP or DDT are to be used, great care should be taken that feeding dishes for pets, children's toys and bird feeding stations are covered or removed from the area. Operators should regularly use masks, rubber gloves or respirators with some of these.

Many of the insecticides and fungicides now used are not compatible with others, and are likely to cause severe foliage burning if used soon before or after the use of some of the other chemicals. Lime-sulphur or wettable sulphur is especially dangerous in connection with an oil or soap spray. Rotenone, Pyrethrum and Arsenate of lead are incompatible with certain other chemicals.

Lime-sulphur will stain white paint or concrete and wettable sulphur will sometimes do the same. Surfaces likely to be hit by drifting spray should be covered with tarps. Dormant oil sprays used for scale control on deciduous trees will frequently burn seriously, or kill, evergreen trees which may be hit by it. Where evergreens are near deciduous trees being sprayed with oil they should either be completely covered or washed thoroughly both before and after being hit.

Recommended reading:
THE GARDENER'S BUG BOOK, Cynthia Westcott, Pub. by Doubleday.
INSECT PESTS OF NORTH AMERICA, Essig.
THE PLANT DOCTOR, Cynthia Westcott, Pub. by Lippincott.
DISEASES OF ORNAMENTAL PLANTS, J. L. Forsberg, Colorado State University.
FIELD MANUAL OF FOREST AND SHADE TREE DISEASES, W. D. Thomas, Jr., Pub. by Colorado State University.

I like people who are simple, straightforward and plain. Maybe that is why I find so many interesting people in gardens and hiking in the mountains. People who love flowers and trees and mountains are nice people, regardless of what they do throughout the week to earn a living. There is a common bond and interest in the growing things of Nature.

Animal Pests in Gardens

I LIKE dogs. I also like gardens. In the city it is difficult to cultivate both loves—unless one of them is completely fenced in.

Who would want to restrict the pleasure that a dog gets from burying choice bones, and who would question the dog's judgment in burying them in the nice loose soil which was dug up yesterday afternoon and planted to radishes. But that sort of thing just does not go with good gardening.

Probably the greatest damage done by male dogs is to lower limbs of evergreens, and by female dogs is burned spots in the lawn.

Some dogs can be trained by patient owners to respect growing plants but this is the exception. There are several products on the market which are supposed to repel dogs by their odor. These seldom are effective for long. Large dogs certainly have no place in the city for they cannot be successfully penned up in a small space and certainly should not roam at will to bother neighbors.

Cats offer less of a problem in a garden.

Sometimes gophers, mice or rabbits will do considerable damage to a garden, but this is usually in places on the edge of undeveloped country. There are now products sold which will usually control these animals.

Most birds are encouraged to make your garden their home but occasionally, robins will become a nuisance at cherry time, or the less desirable birds like magpies, sparrows and starlings will do more harm than good. Trapping is about the only safe way to control them in this case.

The young of the human animals are probably the most destructive of all, and as they cannot be trapped, penned up or poisoned the only treatment is patient training and an early development of a feeling of ownership in the garden.

TREES DON'T LAST FOREVER

One difficult lesson that a gardener has to learn sooner or later is that the beautiful effects he creates with plant material do not last forever. Trees and shrubs will outgrow their effectiveness; others will live their life and die. Pictures painted with living plants are never static; they are ever changing.

The cute little spruce planted in the front yard this year may have grown so large in 15 years as to completely spoil the desired effect. In the older sections of some cities you can see in most every yard trees or shrubs which have outgrown their usefulness and should be replaced with small material. A fine old Juniper tree which might be worth $200 in the right place may be worse than worthless in the wrong situation.

To those who enjoy growing things this continuous changing should be recognized in their planning. It should not be a discouraging factor; but just one of the things that makes gardening interesting.

Weeds We Always Have With Us

WEEDS we have always had and always will have with us. It is natural for weeds to come up in vacant places. This is a valuable provision of nature, which helps to prevent erosion and often covers unsightly rubbish. Cultivated plants have largely been selected for particularly desirable qualities such as large bloom, brilliant color, etc., with no regard for other qualities. On the other hand, plants which we call weeds have been naturally selected by the difficulties of survival—ability to resist drouth, to seed readily, and thrive in poor soil. The plants which we cultivate in our gardens often lack vitality and ability to compete with more vigorous and primitive plants. Thus we must continually protect the useful plants and fight the weeds.

The time to combat weeds is when they are very small and can be readily eradicated. If the battle is started too late, it can develop into a difficult job and the enemy may have seriously damaged the valuable plants by crowding and robbing them of nourishment. Plants grown in good soil and properly cared for are better able to compete with weeds. Every gardener knows that weeds around plants in bare soil can be easily cultivated out. It is the weeds among grass and dense planting that require special treatment.

Many chemical weed killers have appeared on the market in recent years. Each has its advantages and disadvantages. In most general use at the present time has been the compound 2,4-D, sold under a variety of trade names. It has proven its worth as a killer of dandelions, plantain, and some of the other broad-leaved weeds in lawns. In general, though, it is not always the case that broad-leaved plants are killed by 2,4-D as there are many common weeds which apparently are not affected. Up to the present time there has been much damage by 2,4-D because of careless application. Failure to consider that there is a certain amount of "drift" when the powerful chemical is being applied has ruined many especially susceptible nearby plants.

The most common cause of damage to valuable plants is the attempt to use a sprayer for other spraying purposes after it has been used for 2,4-D. It is almost impossible for the average gardener to completely clean out a sprayer once used for 2,4-D, since it is reported that as little as one part of 2,4-D in a million is enough to damage certain plants. It is an undisputed fact that careless use of this material by air and ground equipment has killed valuable shade trees and native shrubs along some of our scenic highways.

Crab grass killers have come and gone. Some of them seem to be fairly successful, others just mediocre, still others worthless. The two most popular on the market at the present time appear to be PAX and SCUTL. Reports on PAX at the present time are about evenly divided as to effectiveness and failure. Used when and as directed, PAX appears to do some good and it is recognized as comparatively harmless to valuable things. SCUTL is too new to have a complete report, but present indications are promising.

Arsenate of lead or potassium cyanate are the active chemicals in some of these products and may often be bought under their chemical name for much less cost if one wants to handle them carefully.

Much has been written recently about the advantages of certain preparations that will prevent the sprouting of weed seeds. Properly used these will prevent weeds starting but will not damage growing plants. Sodium 2,4-Dichlorophenoxyethyl Sulphate or Crag Herbicide is one popular kind. 3-amino-1,2,4-triazole (Amizol) or under the trade name of Weedazol is a non-selective herbicide which kills by destroying the chlorophyll in plants. It is effective against many difficult plants and is not as dangerous to handle as some.

Di Sodium Monomethyl Arsonate, under several brand names such as Sodar and Dimet seems to offer great promise in the control of crabgrass, both in the pre-emergence stage and as young plants.

Recent experiments indicate that some of the weed killers leave a residue in the soil which seriously interferes with germination of seeds planted weeks later. Thus every gardener should be extremely careful what he uses and religiously follow the progress reports on the use of these powerful new chemicals.

For killing woody plants, a sodium sulfamate preparation called AMMATE has been used safely and effectively and seems to be practically harmless to the soil. When used in the dry form, a tablespoon of AMMATE placed on the stump of cut brush or in notches around the base of a tree has been known to completely kill the plant. It is sometimes used effectively as a spray, but care should be taken to avoid any drift to evergreens, which are reported to be susceptible to damage.

Another relatively new chemical, 2 4 5-T, has given very effective kill on woody plants. In some cases, a half and half mixture of 2 4 5-T and 2,4-D has been used. Here again every precaution should be taken to protect susceptible plants which you do not want killed.

PLANT DOCTORS

Sugar pills allegedly administered by some doctors to patients who think they are ill may often give as good results as more specific treatments, and no good doctor can ignore the fact that a person's mind does influence his health. But, this psychology doesn't work with plants because they don't have minds which might influence their welfare.

One of the most frequent questions asked horticulturists is "Won't some one spray control all pests?" That's it. Some panacea or cure-all is what many gardeners want—something to compare with the human doctor's sugar pills. There are certain new insecticides and fungicides which can be applied to plants subject to attacks of various insects or diseases which may prevent these insects or diseases from damaging the plants later, but under most conditions it is only practical to spray a plant with some specific chemical designed to control a specific pest.

People who demand this cure-all sugar pill treatment only encourage quack plant doctors. Gardeners should strive to learn enough about their plants and pests so they will have an idea of which treatments are proper and which may be expected to do some real good.

Some of the older common treatments such as kerosene, borax, and salt will kill plants, but these products also sterilize the soil. Usually no other plant will grow in the spot where they have been used, often for several years. Our knowledge of the effectiveness of these powerful new weed killers is increased as the years go by, and we will undoubtedly see introduction of new and better products on the market. They must all be used with care and under the specific direction of the manufacturer who produces them.

The best control for crabgrass is still prevention. A good program for crabgrass infested lawns would be to first use one of the good seed killers so that there could at least be a fresh start. This would be sometime between fall, when all seed would be ripened, and the last of May when the seed would sprout. Then, through April and May, so treat the lawn by careful watering, fertilization and aerating, if necessary, that a good, dense stand of Bluegrass would be grown. Mow this high and leave the clippings lie so as to cover the bare soil between grass plants completely. Crabgrass being an annual dies completely each fall and must have a location when sun shines on bare soil about the first of June to germinate the seed. If some grass comes through this treatment it may often be killed by holding off on water for a couple of weeks about the first of June which will make the Bluegrass look bad, but seldom kills it. If some still persists an application of Di-met, when still small, will often get it.

Recommended reading:

COLORADO WEEDS, Thornton and Durrell, Bulletin No. 403, Revised, Colorado State University, Fort Collins, Colo.

JUST WEEDS, E. R. Spencer, Pub. by Chas. Scribner's Sons.

FOOD FACTORIES

Man builds large factories to process foods and thinks that he is pretty smart, but nature has been operating billions on billions of food factories since before the time of man.

How many realize that all our food, most of our clothing and most of our building material comes from plants, and all these plants depend on the transformation of crude elements into food through the action of the sun on the chlorophyl (green matter) in plant leaves?

Sure, some of this food is processed by cattle and sheep before we eat it, but it all originated in the grass and plants from the earth. Even the food of the Eskimo, which appears to be all meat, comes originally from small aquatic plants which are eaten by tiny sea animals, and they in turn by larger creatures, until it comes to man.

Cotton comes direct from the plant, and wool, again processed by the sheep, comes from the plants eaten by the sheep. All the lumber in our houses was formed cell by cell in this same way by the trees.

If we could pick out the most important operation in the world it would probably be this process of photosynthesis by which various inanimate materials are transformed into materials necessary to the life of man.

15 Common Weeds of the Rocky Mountains

LAMBS-QUARTERS. When young is a more ▶ palatable green than spinach. Seeds readily, so is found everywhere. Easily eradicated from lawns by regular mowing.

◀ DANDELION. When found in mountain meadows it is called "Taraxicum officinale," but when found in lawns it is called x?!!xx. With the coming of 2,4-D it may be easily eliminated. Public lawn enemy No. 1.

YARROW. In a lawn it may establish itself ▶ as an almost complete mat. Is found as a native plant from the plains to the tops of the highest mountains. Eliminated by cultivation or spraying.

◀ COMMON PLANTAIN. Public lawn enemy No. 2. Usually found in poor soil, or overwatered, shady lawns. May now be eliminated with 2,4-D sprays.

WILD MORNING GLORY. One of the most ▶ difficult weeds to eliminate as it spreads from underground runners. May now be destroyed with 2,4-D.

◀ COMMON MALLOW. Common, indeed, in most new lawns. Hugs low to the ground and chokes out good grass. Easily dug, as it has just one long tap-root.

PROSTRATE PIGWEED. Common, especially ▶ in dry places. Seeds readily, but easily destroyed when young, by cultivation.

◀ MEXICAN FIREWEED (Kochia). Almost as generally distributed as the Russian Thistle. Also easy to eliminate if gone after when it is small.

WILD LETTUCE. Another weed which is much ▶ better than spinach when young. We will have to teach a lot of people to eat it, however, before it becomes extinct as it is a liberal seeder. Easily destroyed by cultivation or mowing.

◀ RUSSIAN THISTLE. It evidently likes America. Widely distributed all over the West because of its "tumbling" habit when the seeds are ripe. Easily destroyed when young, by clean cultivation.

CRABGRASS. "Suddenly it's fall" when the  first cold nights make the crabgrass in a lawn stand out prominently. An annual, but seeds freely, and these produce new plants in June. Several new chemical preparations have been developed in recent years which will kill both the crabgrass and the seed without seriously damaging bluegrass.

 MOUSE-EAR CHICKWEED. Rather pretty, little, notched, five-petalled, white flowers. Persistent in lawns, but can be controlled by the use of the modern weed killers. Your canary will enjoy eating it if you do not.

CREEPING BELLFLOWER. The cancer of the  garden. Spreads by underground roots which are very difficult to destroy. Not affected by one spraying of 2,4-D. Innocently spread from one garden to another by gifts from neighbors because of its beautiful blue flowers. About the only control is frequent cultivation or sifting ALL the roots out from the area it occupies.

 PEPPERGRASS. One of the many common weeds of the Mustard family. Seeds freely and spreads rapidly, but easily eliminated by cultivation or mowing, as it is an annual.

PURSLANE. Very persistent little plant because 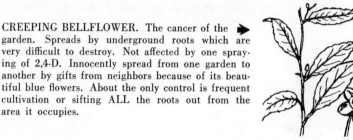 its leaves are so succulent that it can lie out all day in the sun without roots and still take root and grow if later covered up. Also forms seeds when very young. Another good salad plant.

JUST WALKING

It adds to the pleasure of walking if there are definite objectives. Walking in the mountains can be much more enjoyable than walking on a city sidewalk.

It also adds to the physical benefits if the walking is done where the air is fresh and the ground is soft underfoot.

But walking at any time and in any place is a fine exercise. A vigorous walk will relax a weary mind.

It is so easy to ride everywhere we go that walking is becoming a lost art. In planning city and mountain park developments definite consideration is given walks and trails, yet few really use these trails.

Try getting up early some morning and walking a mile down the center of one of our fine parkways, or do the same in the evening.

When you go to the hills on Sunday try walking across a cutoff or down a stream while some one drives around to pick you up. Walking alone is fun.

Why and How to Trim Trees

NO TRIMMING or pruning of a tree should be done unless there is a real reason for it. The practice of pruning fruit trees is for the purpose of opening them up or thinning the limbs so they will produce larger and better fruit. On the other hand, most of the pruning or trimming needed on ornamental plants is to improve their health and better their shape. While a peach tree properly pruned may be anything but beautiful, ornamental trees must be cared for with their greatest beauty constantly in mind. Furthermore, the natural shape of the tree and growth habits must be maintained whenever possible.

Large deciduous trees receive the most attention because they are more conspicuous and require considerable equipment to trim them properly. Few people are agile enough to safely climb around in a tall tree to do their own work. Every home owner, however, should know enough of the principles in tree care so he may supervise others or at least know when he is getting a good job by commercial tree men.

Let's consider the reasons for trimming a tree:

First, trimming is done to improve or maintain desirable shape, symmetrical or natural, by—

1. Removing too-low or too-high limbs.
2. Cutting back lopsided trees.
3. Removing limbs which interfere with buildings, wires, or other valuable trees.

Second, trimming is done to build up a sturdy framework of limbs by—

1. Cutting out bad crotches when small.
2. Shortening back too-heavy limbs or thinning to reduce weight and minimize storm damage.
3. Removing duplicate, weak, rubbing, or misplaced limbs.
4. Removing dead limbs so the scar can heal quickly.

Trees planted too close together can not find sufficient nourishment for their roots or sunlight for their tops. They become distorted and diseased.

Rough stubs like these can not heal and decay soon runs down into the tree.

The home owner who is considering tree trimming should always keep in mind that in shaping a tree he cannot add a limb to fill a vacancy. All he can do is cut back the limbs which are too long and let the shorter ones overtake them.

Treatment of former scars, removal of dead stubs, and shaping, trimming, or filling partly decayed holes is often of more importance in tree care than the removal of live limbs. In every operation, the gardener should have in mind ways to shape the wound so new growth will start as soon as possible. This usually means to so streamline the wound that the sap flowing by can deposit new material and begin the healing process. Painting tree wounds is not as important in the Rocky Mountain area as in the more moist climates. Some of the larger cuts, however, of two inches or more, where there is danger of decay before natural healing takes place, should be painted. A prepared tree paint, or asphalt roof paint, because of its flexibility, is satisfactory.

Good arborists now make a practice of disinfecting all cuts of considerable size, as a preventative of decay.

Bracing of tree limbs is sometimes necessary where crotches are in danger of breaking or splitting from storm damage. On the smaller limbs, screw eyes connected with clothesline wire are very effective. Larger limbs and trunks of trees require bolts at the split and cable wire in the crotch to remove the strain. The latter is a technical operation which requires experience and study for each particular job.

When removing large heavy limbs, it is usually considered safest to first remove the bulk of the weight. Then the final cut can be made close up to avoid splitting and peeling down. It will be necessary to lower large limbs carefully with a rope and it is always safest to make an under-cut to avoid splitting down and disfiguring the tree.

Most trees can be trimmed at any time which is convenient, but they are easier to work on in the winter when the leaves are gone. Wounds will heal over sooner if made just before the new growth starts in the spring.

Some trees, such as maple, birch, and walnut, should only be trimmed while in leaf, because they sometimes have a tendency to "bleed" excessively.

Much tree trimming is necessitated by neglect or improper treatment. It is much more important to give trees the proper care when small than spend a great deal of time correcting mistakes later. Some of the things gardeners should consider to avoid such mistakes include:

1. Buy only healthy well-shaped trees with a liberal amount of roots.
2. Be sure they are transplanted carefully and promptly while the roots are still fresh.
3. Do not expect vigorous, healthy trees planted on poor soil. If soil conditions are not favorable take special care in fertilization and mulching.
4. Be sure the tree is a suitable variety for the situation which exists, such as shade, moisture, protection, and soil.
5. Do not plant too close together. Allow for ultimate proper development.
6. Inspect frequently for disease and insect pests and treat before serious damage is done.
7. Water thoroughly rather than frequently. It is the water which gets down to the growing roots which counts.

Some of the signs of poor trimming include limbs left unnecessarily long; "topping" or removal of upper limbs larger than one inch in diameter, without a special reason; thinning just to make brush, with no particular reason; leaving dead stubs and decayed spots without cleaning out or draining.

Most evergreen trees require little trimming as their chief beauty is their natural shape. In the case of dead or broken limbs from any cause the same rules apply to them as to deciduous trees. If evergreens have been planted which are likely to become too large for their situation they should be regularly pinched back BEFORE they become too large. This practice of pinching or shearing the "candles" may keep a naturally large tree within bounds for many years, and in the process it may make it denser and more beautiful.

Trees which naturally grow tall should never be planted under wires.	*Conflicting limbs should be removed when they are small.*

Properly made open cavity which is healing quickly.   *What happens when foreign objects are fastened to trees.*

Junipers may require regular shearing to keep them formal looking, where this is appropriate. This shearing can be done at any time during their growing period. It is sometimes dangerous to cut into an evergreen's limbs farther than the present year's growth or to shear them very severely after the growing season is over. The natural top should not be cut from a spruce or juniper unless it is absolutely necessary as this will spoil its natural growth-habit.

Recommended reading:

PRUNING HARDY FRUIT PLANTS, U.S.D.A. Bul. 1870.

MAINTENANCE OF SHADE AND ORNAMENTAL TREES, P. P. Pirone, Oxford Press.

TREE EXPERTS MANUAL, Fenska, Pub. by DeLaMare.

TRIMMING TREES AND SHRUBS, E. P. Felt, Pub. by Orange Judd Pub. Co.

CARE OF ORNAMENTAL TREES AND SHRUBS, U.S.D.A. Bul. 1826.

LET THE CHILDREN ENJOY GARDENING

When Johnnie must mow the lawn as punishment and Mary must weed the flowers because Mother doesn't want to do it herself, they cannot be expected to develop a love for gardening. Fortunate, indeed, are the children whose wise parents let them help with the attractive garden tasks, calling attention to the sprouting seeds, the unfolding flowers and scattering fruit. When shown the wonderful partnership that gardeners have with Nature, they can't help but share their parents' enthusiasm for working in the soil.

Any person who has not developed a feeling for trees and flowers has missed something which prevents him from enjoying a full and satisfying life. It takes time to stop and show these interesting things to the youngsters, but where could time be better spent?

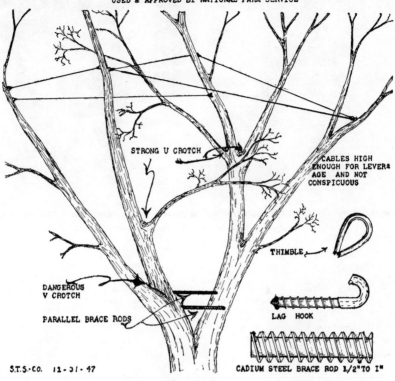

TRIANGULAR CABLING & BRACING SYSTEMS AS INSTALLED BY SWINGLE TREE SURGEONS
USED & APPROVED BY NATIONAL PARK SERVICE

STRONG U CROTCH

CABLES HIGH ENOUGH FOR LEVERAGE AND NOT CONSPICUOUS

THIMBLE

DANGEROUS V CROTCH

PARALLEL BRACE RODS

LAG HOOK

S.T.S-CO. 12-31-47

CADIUM STEEL BRACE ROD 1/2"TO 1"

Trees with weak crotches, heavy limbs or storm damage may be saved with proper bracing and cabling.

Trees topped like this,   **look like this, next year.**

247

How to properly trim or "streamline" a rough bark wound in a tree so the
sap can flow by readily and heal it.

Well shaped, healthy trees like this Little-leaf Linden at the Civic Center,
Denver, are the result of proper care.

There's a Right Way to Trim Shrubs

TRIMMING shrubs is a simple matter if a few general rules are observed. Each kind of shrub has its own peculiar requirements, but in every case the trimming should be done with the idea in mind to preserve the natural shape and habits as much as possible.

One general rule is to only do any considerable cutting on shrubs right after they have bloomed. The reason for this is that it gives the plant 11 months or so to grow new blooming wood and so the least bloom possible is lost.

Another general rule is to gradually take out a few large stems, clear to the ground, each year when a shrub becomes overgrown. Thus, in a few years time an entirely new shrub may be had, and still there will be little bloom lost.

A few examples of particular technique on some familiar shrubs may serve as examples that can be modified to fit others.

The most common pruning job seen on a lilac would be where ALL the lower stems, suckers and limbs had been cut off to a height of several feet and then the top given a GI haircut. This spoils all natural beauty and eliminates the chance of blooming for several years. A better way would be to leave on the more vigorous sprouts and lower limbs and thin out a few of the taller stems.

A Bridal Wreath Spirea should only have the older, half-dead stems cut off, clear to the ground. Shearing this shrub destroys much of its natural arching beauty. Flowering almonds and Garland spireas may, however, be benefitted by a light shearing right after bloom each year. This tends to keep them low and dense.

Each shrub has a character of its own, and this should be maintained when it is trimmed.

Lopping and scraggly as well as broken and dead stems may be cut at any time to keep shrubs looking neat.

The good gardeners will enjoy keeping the pruning shears in their pocket continually so that they may do a little necessary trimming whenever it is noticed. The indication of a good trim job is that the casual observer will not be able to see that it HAS been trimmed.

Good gardens, we learn, are the result of good design, good plants and good maintenance, and, of the latter, NEATNESS is the most important. Gardens may lack much in the other good qualities and still be attractive if they are kept neat, and trimming is a most important part of neatness.

Trimming is necessary not only to woody plants but to perennials and lawns and all other growing things. Trimming off seed heads as they dry up and stems of perennials when they are mature helps keep an attractive garden. Much lawn edging is unnecessary if gardens are properly planned but where this has not been done edging and shearing are very important.

Formal hedges, of course, are a special problem of their own. The important thing with them is to *shear frequently* so that little growth is lost and they will become denser with every cutting. If a plant is designed to be formally sheared, be sure to keep it that way and if a plant is intended to be informal do not let it look as though it had been sheared at all. The half-way between job may look pretty awful.

Every gardener should learn something about the growth of a tree, how the sap flows, where the live cambium layer is located, the function of the roots and leaves. If he understands these principles, he will understand the reasons back of these trimming rules.

ROSES AND THORNS

The law of survival has evolved plants and animals in such a way that they are attractive to their kind but unattractive to those who would prey upon them. The thorns on roses and cactus plants protect them from those that would destroy them and allow them to remain to produce beautiful blooms. As plants and animals ascend the scale of evolution they often develop these protective devices and gradually seem to lose the quality of producing progeny in such great numbers. Compare mice with horses or tumble weeds with hawthorns.

Here all natural beauty has been lost by unnecessary trimming.

Learn How to Plant

Here are Important Rules for Every Gardener

THE growing of good ornamental plants is probably dependent *at least half* on their being properly planted, and yet this operation is the one that is most often done hurriedly or improperly.

Planting in Other Areas

In many parts of the United States the planting of trees and shrubs is a very simple procedure. All that is necessary is that you dig a hole, set in the tree or shrub, and let nature take its course.

Planting Peculiarities in the Rocky Mountain Area

In this *Rocky Mountain Area* we have several conditions which make proper planting more difficult. Soils in general are alkaline, the ground is often dry when the planting is done and there is small chance of newly set things getting natural precipitation enough to keep them growing. The most difficult situation of all is the especially hot sun and dry air, which many of the plants from other climates cannot tolerate.

Plan First

The most common mistake made in planting is to buy a few things that look good at the nursery and take them home and then try to figure where to plant them. Under these circumstances they are usually planted in the wrong place for their best effect and are most often put in the ground in the quickest way possible.

The right way is to have planned well in advance for the things needed and then buy only plants that will fit these plans and create the effects desired! Ultimate height should be the first consideration, then such things as bloom, fall color, fruit, and winter effect. Plants must be selected which will tolerate the conditions found in the place where they are to be set; such as shade, bright sun, wind, heavy soil or competing tree roots.

Planning all the details of a planting is good winter garden work, then when spring comes and the frost is out of the ground all attention can be given to the actual work in the soil. Put these plans on paper so that you will remember them.

The Main Planting Season: Spring

The main planting season in this area is in the spring between the time the frost is gone from the soil and the time that the leaves start to grow. This season may start anywhere between February first and April first and usually ends the middle of May. Except for some particular plants which do better if moved later all things may be moved as soon as the frost is out of the soil.

The Fall Planting Season

There is usually a fall planting season from about the middle of October to the middle of December, which depends on season and weather. Many of the evergreens, slow-growing trees and shrubs with difficult roots are not as safely moved in fall as spring. They may set through the winter with our hot sun shining on them and sucking out their moisture and be in poor condition in spring when the weather becomes favorable for new

251

growth. Each nurseryman has special preferences as to planting in the fall so if he is willing to take the risk, let him be the judge. There is always too much to do in spring and anything that can be safely done in the fall is just that much out of the way.

Preparing the Soil First

Too often ornamental plants are planted in soil around a new home without doing anything to improve it. When every house had a basement this usually meant planting in the lifeless soil from the bottom of the basement. The garden was doomed from the beginning.

Take time to prospect all over new grounds and if very poor spots of soil or deposits of plaster and rubbish are found, remove them and bring in good soil to replace it. This may cost money and delay the planting but it is the most important step in making a good garden. Even with reasonably good soil, there should be some work put on working it up rather deeply and adding manure, leafmold or peat.

Soils vary in texture and quality, so no general rules can be made, but it is certain that ANY soil will be benefitted by deep loosening and a thorough mixture of humus with it. Humus added to a light, sandy soil will enable it to hold more water and plant food and humus added to a heavy, clay soil will break it up and allow better drainage and allow the plant roots to penetrate it better. Adding sand to a clay soil or clay to a sandy soil can sometimes be done if a great enough proportion is used and if it is THOROUGHLY mixed to a sufficient depth. The same amount of time and money for adding humus will usually do more good.

Humus or organic matter may be manure (cow, horse or sheep) it may be peatmoss, leaf mold or it may be composted plant material. Fresh manure has also more chemical value while peatmoss has little or none. Peat may profitably be added to most soils up to 35% while fresh manure must be used cautiously to avoid burning the new roots of plants.

Digging the Holes

With your plan in mind it is good practice to dig the holes for the things that you intend to get that day or the next. Dig them plenty large, especially at the bottom, where the roots will want to spread; and remember that the harder the holes are to dig the larger they should be. You can loosen up the hard soil easier than the new roots can. If poor soil or subsoil is encountered in digging these holes throw it out and fill back with good topsoil when the plants are put in.

Backfilling

New plants like to be set in *good soil*—soil with humus in it, but they cannot tolerate great quantities of rich fertilizer, either organic or chemical. Up to a third in bulk of peat can profitably be mixed with most any soil, as it has little chemical value, and smaller quantities of leafmold or well-rotted manure can be used, depending on the age and chemical strength of the material. It would be good practice to prepare the soil for planting many months in advance, if possible.

Get Good Stock

Don't let the pretty colored pictures and glowing stories of nurseries from far distant places fool you into getting things which are not adapted to our climate. Even species of plants which are adapted here may be poorly grown or badly packed so that they arrive more dead than alive. Don't fall for "bargain" plants. The only way to economize in buying plants is to get small sizes. These small plants will usually move easier, start growing sooner and will cost considerably less. If you must have large plants, see that they are moved with a good proportion of roots or balled. This is expensive work at best.

Your local nurseryman is more likely to have the plants that are adapted to your conditions and he will be able to get them to you in fresh, live condition. Many nursery plants are dug in the fall and stored in cellars until planting time in spring. This process can be done so that the plants are in good condition when delivered to you, but there is plenty of chance for careless handling and you should see that the plants you get are not dried up or damaged from handling. The larger sized trees and shrubs are much better when moved directly and promptly from the nursery to your home.

If You Dig Yourself

If you have stock given you, that you must dig yourself, you should dig carefully so that you will get all the roots possible and protect these roots from sun and wind until they can be put back into the soil again.

No definite rule can be made for the amount of roots necessary on each kind and size of plant to assure its growing vigorously. Root systems of plants vary in character and ability to start new growth. In general, slow-growing trees and other slow growing plants have deep roots and are difficult to transplant, especially when they are of any considerable size. Fast-growing things usually have shallow roots and are comparatively easy to move. Walnuts represent the deep-rooted things and willows the shallow. A shade tree might require a two-foot spread of roots for each inch trunk diameter, while shrubs and perennials might need a root spread of half their height.

It is good economy to move trees and shrubs when they are small—trees under two inches in diameter and shrubs under three feet high. Smaller things are more easily handled and there is likely to be a larger proportion of roots with them. Young plants usually take hold more quickly after being moved, and usually they are cheaper. Often a small plant will move so much better that it will catch up with the larger things within a couple of years.

Care of Stock Before Planting

When the plants are delivered before the ground is ready to plant them, they must be cared for carefully so that they will not become dried out. If they are small plants or are carefully packed in some moist material they may lay several days without harming them. Open the tops so that air can circulate around the tops, but leave the roots covered, and be sure that the material around the roots is moist. Set the package in the shade. If plants must lay for several days, or if they are large it is best to "heel" them in the soil. To avoid digging a large hole they may be laid on their sides and just enough soil thrown over them to keep the roots from drying out. Water as necessary to keep moist. If stems of plants appear shriveled, cover them completely with moist soil for a few days. Often roses will be benefitted by this treatment.

Protect the Roots

After all these preparations, then comes the actual planting—the place where many start. Bring out your plants and look over their roots. Make fresh cuts with a sharp knife or shears where there are mangled ends or dead tips. A good clean cut will encourage roots to start. Keep all roots covered while preparing to plant.

The Actual Planting

With the holes dug in the proper places and sufficiently large, and suitable soil available to backfill, you are ready to plant your stock.

This is best done by two people so that one can hold the plant, spread out its roots and see that the soil fills around them. Throw in the first few shovels of soil very carefully—just sift it in, so that the roots are not thrown all out of shape or matted together. Put the best soil in first. When the hole is almost full of loose soil work the hose, with the nozzle off, down to the bottom of the hole and turn on the water. Let the soil settle from the bottom up and there will be no air pockets. When the soil has settled and the water begins to show on the surface turn it off, check the plant for depth and position and fill in the balance of the soil. If hose water is not available the same effect can be had by watering from a pail if a spade is used to work a passageway down to the bottom of the hole. Unless there is no water available and the soil is already moist do not tramp or pack the soil. Watering and tramping both are likely to form "bridges" of soil with air pockets underneath.

If the surrounding soil is very dry, it will soak up the water like a blotter, so another soaking should be given within a few days.

This, of course, will have to be given from the surface, and it is a good practice to leave a low dyke of soil around the original hole to hold water while it soaks away. After these initial waterings, the condition of the soil should be checked every ten days to two weeks, and whenever it is dry, another watering should be given. A thorough watering every two weeks will generally be more effective than daily sprinklings of the surface. Most plants require a certain amount of air in the soil, as well as water, and this is impossible when the soil is kept too soggy.

Depth to Set

Plant all things at about the depth that they grew in the nursery. This can usually be told by the difference in color and texture at the natural ground level.

Planting Shade Trees

Careful planning should be done before planting shade trees. Decide what effects or results are needed from trees and then find out from your nurseryman what trees will give these effects. Space them properly so that they will have room to grow without interfering with other trees, buildings or overhead wires. Find out how large your tree is likely to grow before you plant it.

Moving Large Trees with a Ball of Earth

Large trees can be safely moved if proper care is given to the digging and handling. It is a job requiring proper equipment and experience. A ball of earth of the proper size must be dug around the roots and this ball must be wrapped and bound and then handled so that it gets back into the new hole in sound condition.

If poor soil is encountered in digging the new hole it is important to remove much of this and replace with good soil so that the new feed roots from the ball may easily become established. For particular trees like oaks it is helpful to add peat to the soil and to take steps to counteract excess alkaline conditions.

Large trees cannot be moved cheaply for they must be handled carefully. When the work is done properly there is no reason why they should not soon recover and grow.

Transplanting Shrubs

After the hole has been dug to sufficient depth and width, place each plant in the hole separately allowing sufficient room for a little root expansion. Top-soil that was put in a separate pile should be placed deepest in the hole. It contains the most plant food and humus and will give the roots something to feed on as they begin to penetrate the surrounding soil area. The subsoil which is added next should be mixed with a little leaf mold or peat moss and should have an addition of one-half cup of superphosphate per cubic foot of soil. (A bushel basket of soil usually is about one and a quarter cubic feet.)

In planning a shrub, attention must be paid to the ultimate size and spread of that plant.

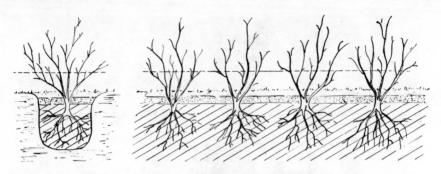

Hedges

Hedges are usually planted by digging a trench the distance of the hedge and setting the plants at intervals in the trench. By carefully lining up the trench and setting all the plants a uniform distance from one edge a straight line is assured.

Roses

Roses are planted much as other shrubs, but should be cut back to about 8 inches and hilled up with soil almost to the top of the stems until the new growth starts. Pick a spot with about two-thirds sun for best results.

Plant graft or bud slightly below ground level. Dig holes large enough to receive roots in natural position. Re-water once a week or 10 days. Remove mound of soil gradually over a ten day period, as soon as new growth starts.

If plants are dried out when received cover them with moist soil for a few days or soak in water for a few hours to replace lost moisture.

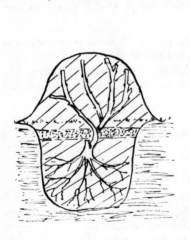

Evergreens

Transplanting evergreens is a specialized job. Their roots do not tolerate being dried out for even a few minutes, so the general practice is to move them B&B (balled and burlapped). This balling is a particular job, the important thing being to keep the ball of soil around the roots solid and undisturbed until it is back in its final hole.

256

Balled stock should be handled carefully, and always by the ball and not the top. Prepare the holes to receive balled evergreens so that there is plenty of room to set the ball and work it around in position. Usually a hole about a foot greater in diameter than the ball will do. The soil in the bottom of the hole should be loosened up some but the depth of the hole should be carefully measured so that when the ball is lowered in it will set at the same depth that the tree grew originally. Then carefully plumb the tree and pack some soil under the edges of the ball so that it will stand solid. Backfill and water then much as for deciduous stock.

Evergreens that are delivered to your home with the roots balled and burlapped should be planted without removing the burlap. It is however advisable after the plant is set to cut the top string near the crown of the plant which may girdle the plant before it rots.

Perennials

Most perennials are handled with some soil remaining on their roots. These clumps can be planted much as would the larger things, watering in carefully. Small bare-root perennials and annuals should be set with a shovel or trowel, spreading the roots out as naturally as possible and carefully watering in. Sometimes a little shade from a shingle or newspaper will allow these bare-root plants to become established quicker.

Bulbs and Such

Dahlia roots must be carefully handled to avoid breaking the "neck" where all the new sprouts originate. Gladiolus bulbs may be planted 6 inches deep when put in early or a little more shallow when set late in the season. If set deep they can be planted before danger of frost is over. Cannas are easy to plant but are tender and should not be put out until frost danger is over—probably June first. There are many species of lilies requiring varying treatment, so the only way to get them in properly is to study the requirements for each kind.

The fall-planted or Dutch bulbs should generally be planted about 50% deeper than the usual directions for the East. Tulips usually do best when planted about a foot deep.

Fruits and Berries

Fruit trees and berries may be handled much as would ornamental trees or shrubs.

Cut back at least ½ of top as shown. Have lowest branch pointing to Southwest for a trunk shade. Plant top of graft just below ground level. Remove crowded branches at trunk, with a smooth flush cut.

Grapes

Plant just above second bud. Trim top to 3 or 4 strong buds on each cane.

Plants Requiring Special Treatment

Some slow-growing trees require special treatment to assure their growth. Birch are safely moved for about a week in spring just when the new buds break into green. At this time they may be safely moved bare root, but at any other time they require a large ball of soil. When Hackberry, Hawthorn, Honeylocust, Oaks and other slow-growing trees are transplanted, they may set dormant half the summer before breaking out in leaf. Success can be assured with these difficult trees by digging with plenty of roots, keeping the roots from drying out, using much peatmoss around the roots in planting, keeping the soil moist, and frequently sprinkling over the top.

Care After They are in the Ground

These new plants must be considered much like babies of any kind— they need a little extra attention until they become established with new roots and tops. It is a good idea to check the moisture content of the soil around them about every two weeks for the first year. Unless you are sure that the soil is moist down to their farthest roots, give them another soaking. The only way that you can tell how long it takes to soak down far enough in your soil is to experiment and check the actual conditions a few times. Do not assume that if a little water is good for them, a lot is better. Many new plants are killed by this "kindness" of continually keeping the soil around their new roots soggy. Water thoroughly but infrequently.

For the first year it will often be found convenient to leave low dikes and bowls around the new plants to facilitate thorough watering.

Protection from Sun

Some protection from the wind and sun will be appreciated by many of the better plants. Mountainash, Linden, Hard Maple, Wild Cherry, Walnut and Buckeye trees will appreciate being wrapped or their trunks shaded for a few months or even years. White Pine, White Fir or Arborvitae would benefit by having a lath or burlap shade set on the southwest.

Protection from Wind

Tall trees should be braced for some time until the ground settles and the new roots take hold. Be careful to pad the wires used for bracing, where they are attached to the tree, and move them frequently as the tree grows.

Cutting Back

Trees and shrubs that have not been pruned by the nurseryman before they were delivered should be pruned and trained somewhat, to make up for the loss of roots in transplanting. Shrubs are usually cut back one-third to one-half. On trees, many of the smaller branches are removed, narrow crotches are eliminated and only wide-angle crotch branches are kept for the development of a good scaffold for the trees.

Most all newly transplanted woody plants will make a better growth the first year if they are carefully thinned or cut back. This allows the roots to become established before they have a large top to support. This trimming can at the same time be done in such a way as to encourage the plant to shape itself in the form desired. A hedge should be cut away down to encourage it to branch freely while a tree may be thinned or the individual limbs cut back to encourage it to grow tall. Evergreens, other balled or potted plants and very small plants usually need no trimming.

One method is to cut back tops about one half either at marks or at dotted line, or, remove the stems at ground level as indicated by zig-zag lines.

There are so many different kinds of soil and so many variations in climate in the Rocky Mountain area that each section will find, with experience, those planting practices which are most successful under local conditions. Nurserymen are developing the practice of growing plants in pots so that they may be moved safely at any time. This practice will, of necessity, be restricted to small plants. Some of the perennials, however, like Iris and Shasta Daisies, can be safely moved at almost any time except when they are in bloom or have much tender growth. Chrysanthemums are often moved even in bloom, if taken with a good ball of soil. Transplanting is one garden practice where a good green thumb is an asset.

We read much lately of various methods or preparations designed to make transplanting easier and safer. Some of these things have merit and some are still in the experimental stage or actually "quack" practices. Nothing takes the place of good care and the observance of the ordinary precautions that have been practiced for generations. Plant hormones designed to ease the shock of transplanting and encouraging the early growth of new roots are often very valuable. These may be called "Transplantone" or some such name. Certain waxes or plastics are designed for spraying plants to limit the evaporation of water from them until the new roots become established. These are sometimes successfully used in moving balled evergreens or trees in full leaf or very large trees. The use of these materials is a rather particular job and generally left to experts.

Some good nurserymen and tree men will spray the leaves of newly moved trees with a mild liquid fertilizer to give them a quick boost until the natural growth begins. Products like Rapidgro or Heller-gro are used. Carefully done according to directions this may be a good practice.

These same concentrated fertilizers or the common dry "complete" products are sometimes given the new tree through bar holes or root feeders. This work should be carefully done.

Drainage

Drainage is one of the important considerations in gardening, yet few people seem to even know what is meant by proper drainage. Directions for planting roses or bulbs will recommend putting a handful of sand, a few tin cans or some pebbles at the base of a plant. This may make the gardeners feel as though they had done their duty, but this is not drainage. Many fine plants of the mountains cannot be successfully grown at lower altitudes because of lack of drainage. These plants may get a good rain almost every day where they grow naturally yet the water never stands around them, for the soil is made up of coarse particles and it is on a slope so that water cannot stand.

It is often forgotten that many plants need a certain amount of air in the soil around them as well as water, and excessive water prohibits the entrance of air.

Drainage does not consist of a few coarse things around the base of a plant but must in some way loosen up the soil so that excess water can drain out.

Just preparing the soil for its best physical character with peat, manure, compost or some such material will go a long ways towards securing drainage. It would take a lot of sand or gravel and this thoroughly mixed with the soil to give adequate drainage. Avoidance of low spots and prevention of floodwaters from neighbors' property or down spouts will help a great deal. Sometimes it will be necessary to put in tile which lead out to a lower level.

Some few plants tolerate soggy and heavy soil, but most of the nice ornamentals prefer and appreciate well drained soil.

MULCHING

Contrary to popular opinion mulching is not done to keep the plants warm. Rather it is done to keep the plants cold, or to prevent sudden changes in soil temperature. A mulch of leafmold is the natural way of preparing a plant for winter. Peatmoss, straw, barnyard manure and even sawdust can be used effectively by home gardeners. Mulching is practiced by gardeners everywhere, but here in the Rocky Mountains where we must protect our plants from extreme temperature changes and a hot winter sun, it is even more important.

It's Fun to Start New Plants

PROPAGATION of plants is becoming more and more regarded as a job for specialists. The everyday home gardener has generally turned to buying his plants already started rather than gamble with propagation practices. The more we learn about plants, the more we realize that each plant has peculiar requirements with which to propagate itself, and a complete knowledge of various techniques should be left to the experts. Still, one of the great thrills of working with plants is to be able to start them ourselves, though we might be able to buy them cheaper. Then there are such plants as the large-seeded annuals, both in vegetables and flowers, which are so easy to start that most anyone can propagate them successfully. Other desirable plants may be started by seeding under favorable conditions, by cuttings (slips), by layering, grafts, and budding. We will not go into detail as to the best method of starting each plant, because there are any number of good books available which can tell of that special phase of gardening more completely.

It should be recognized, however, that the propagation of most plants is more difficult in a dry climate such as we have in this area. Especially the very small-seeded plants grown here require seeding in flats or beds where moisture, temperature, and sunlight can be regulated to simulate natural conditions best suited to the seedlings. It should be remembered that seeds once moistened must be kept from drying out until they are well sprouted. On the other hand, few seedlings can tolerate a wet, soggy soil. To strike the proper balance of moisture conditions best suited to the various plants is where a "green thumb" is valuable. Most seed packets will give the particular directions for proper care of its contents and these directions should be carefully followed.

SEEDS

At this time of year we are all interested in seed catalogs. The colored pictures of ripe fruit, vegetables and flowers fascinate us. But when the small package of seed comes, we are a little disappointed. There is no resemblance in the tiny seed to the plant we wish to grow.

What a wonderful thing a seed is when we stop to think about it. Here in the tiny shell is the start of a new plant which will have all the characteristics of the plant from which it came. We now know of the microscopic chromosomes and genes which transmit accurately every detail of a plant's characteristics to its offspring.

Annual plants which die each fall have no other way of perpetuating their kind.

The tiny concentrated bit of life may have many ingenious ways of traveling and spreading its kind to new spots of soil. Some may have wings or silken parachutes to catch the wind. Some may be light enough to be carried like dust in the air and some may be carried by birds and animals.

Each has its own method of keeping its particular kind of life going and finding favorable new places for growth.

The mysterious germ of life in a seed continually reminds us of the unknown possibilities of life and purpose in the universe.

Those who have had gardening experience realize that some plants do not start readily from seed, while other highly-developed plants, even though started from seed, do not produce true to type. Thus it is sometimes necessary to use some method of starting these plants from parts of old, established plants by cuttings, layers, grafts, or buds. These are all rather technical processes and should usually be left to the experts.

There are some house plants such as geraniums, begonias, sultanas, and philodendrons which are rather easy to start from cuttings in water, moist sand, or vermiculite. A few gardeners can be proud of the fact that they have green enough thumbs to get rose "slips" to root under a fruit jar in the garden. Occasionally low-branching shrubs may be started by layers—weighting down a limb and covering with soil until it starts roots of its own, then removing it. Most of the ivies and other vines will root readily by this method.

When it comes to grafting and budding plants, the techniques can be learned by the average gardener, but it is generally regarded as something to play with rather than a practical method of propagating your own plants. Most all roses and fruit trees are grafted or budded and, in recent years, a great many of our better evergreens are grafted from plants which have especially desirable qualities.

For those who would still like to try the propagation of a few favored plants it might be well to give a few general suggestions.

Seeds of the tender annuals that are generally planted out in the open after danger of frost should be started indoors from 4 to 8 weeks before time to plant out. If started too early the plants will become weak and spindly before they are planted in the open and if started too late they may be too small to handle safely. A small shallow box or flat pan with drainage will be suitable for this job. The soil should be made loose by the addition of a good proportion of sand and peat or leaf mold. Seeds must be kept moist but not too wet until they sprout, then they should have full sun, careful watering and a temperature of around 65° daytimes and 50° at night.

Cuttings of the easily rooted things can be started in boxes or pots of clean sand, peat, vermiculite or perlite if they are kept properly moist. One of the greatest problems in rooting many kinds of cuttings is the evaporation of water from the stem while it has no roots to replenish it. This is corrected by the use of the new mist techniques. Bottom heat is supplied by the experts to assist in rooting the more difficult things. The use of the root promoting hormones is very generally practiced though this does not mean that the application of this material will form roots on cuttings unless all the old established practices are also used. Some woody plants can be started by soft wood cuttings taken in early summer when the new growth is just firm enough to handle, while many other shrubs or trees can be best started by cuttings (about the size of a pencil) taken about January, put down in a cool place in moist sand to callus until May, and then planted out in a moist shady spot.

The much advertised method of rooting cuttings "in place" by wrapping stems of growing plants with moist moss covered with plastic has not always been successful when used by inexperienced people.

The Wonders of Plant Growth

A GARDENER'S most important material is the plants with which he works. But how many gardeners know the complicated, yet simple, story of how all plants grow, and their importance to animal life. Scientists differ as to the exact details and even the best of them can go only so far into the plan of life which governs the growth of plants. Yet, there are some fundamental facts which every gardener should learn so he may know why he should use certain practices to make plants grow.

Actually most of the gardening practices were developed by the trial and error process and methods which have been successfully passed down from generation to generation by word of mouth. Serious study on plant life and scientific experiments to determine the best practices have been developed in recent years. Not only is it necessary to understand plant growth to be able to use results of scientific experiments, but it makes gardening much more fun when the gardener knows what is happening to the plant under different conditions.

Basically, plants, like animals, are composed of cells. While most of the animal cells are living, only a small proportion of cells in some woody plants are actually still filled with living protoplasm. The buds and cam-

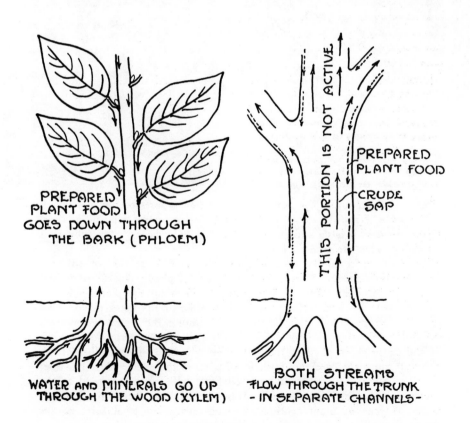

PREPARED PLANT FOOD GOES DOWN THROUGH THE BARK (PHLOEM)

WATER AND MINERALS GO UP THROUGH THE WOOD (XYLEM)

THIS PORTION IS NOT ACTIVE

PREPARED PLANT FOOD

CRUDE SAP

BOTH STREAMS FLOW THROUGH THE TRUNK – IN SEPARATE CHANNELS –

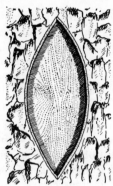
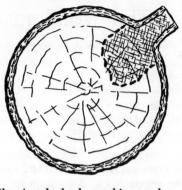

Showing the bark, cambium and wood
areas, with decay beginning as a result
of unhealable stubs left.

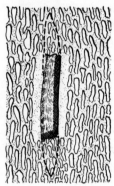
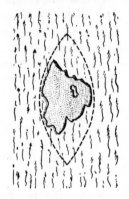

A wound in a tree properly pointed
up or streamlined and healing
over quickly.
When a wound is not pointed up so
the sap can easily flow by, it can not
heal quickly or possibly not at all.

bium layer just under the bark may be the only parts of the tree which are capable of growth. Most of the heartwood of a tree may be as dead as the wood in a table and even the sapwood may be acting simply as a plumbing system to transport sap.

Trees have circulatory systems almost comparable to that of animals, but with fundamental differences. The roots of plants absorb water and some minerals from the soil and transport them up the plants into the leaves, where the wonderful process of photosynthesis takes place. This process may be roughly explained as combining the water taken from the soil with carbon dioxide from the air through the action of the sun on the green chlorophyll in the leaf. The "digested" food is then transported through the cambium layer to all parts of the plant where it is used to form new cells. Some cells may be bark cells, some may add to the roots, some to the inner wood and some form new leaves so that still more food can be manufactured. We can only guess what force causes sap to flow upward against the natural pull of gravity. Furthermore we cannot even guess what causes the action of the sun on chlorophyll to create new energy in the form of edible sugars out of the minerals, carbon dioxide in the air and water from the soil. We only know that it happens and that practically all energy in the world comes from this process in plants. Even coal and oil and gas, on which we depend for heat and energy originate from plants which had first obtained it through this wonderful process. All animal foods comes from plants because animals cannot use raw elements directly.

Much of human effort seems to be directed toward burning up this accumulated energy, burning as we breathe, as we operate our cars or heat our cities. If it were not for the continual manufacturing process of plants all available animal food would be quickly exhausted.

When we realize how fundamental plants really are, we gain a new appreciation of them. Somehow, it brings us close to nature when we work among plants, even though our main interest in them may be because of their beauty.

Many plants are only growing actively during certain seasons and then become dormant at other times. We know these plants as deciduous, because they shed their leaves in the fall. The annuals live only one season and hold over their germ of life in the seeds until the next year. In the case of annuals, the tiny germ is enclosed in the seed along with a supply of digested food so it can start new growth again when the temperature, light, and moisture conditions are suitable. Then it can begin the same process of obtaining food from the air.

The old story that Jack Frost caused leaves to fall in the autumn is not necessarily true. We know it is a combination of temperature and length of day and probably some other factors which cause the active growth of the plant to stop and leaves to detach themselves and fall. Evergreens slow up or stop growth at certain seasons, even though they retain their leaves.

During growth and during dormant periods, woody plants are continually transpiring water from their leaves or stems and this causes circulation of sap at all times. While both the crude materials and water flowing up the tree from the roots and the transformed food flowing back to all parts of the tree are commonly called "sap," it is well understood that these are two very different materials and that they travel in separate "plumbing systems."

Each part of a plant is designed for a particular purpose. The roots anchor the plant and collect water and minerals necessary for plant growth. Roots may vary in size, habits or even color as much as the above-ground parts of the plant, but generally only the nurseryman who digs these plants has an opportunity to learn plants' differences in root habit. Much can be learned of the requirements of plants in our peculiar area when the root habit of the native plants are studied. All of the plants growing naturally in our areas of limited rainfall have provisions to accommodate themselves to little soil moisture. Some, like the clovers, have very deep roots which go far in search of subsoil moisture, some have large, fleshy roots like the Yuccas which can store large quantities of water when the infrequent rains do come, and some are able to complete their yearly cycle of sprout, form leaves, flowers and fruit from the water taken from one rain. The plants that we bring in as familiar ornamentals from moister climates mostly have finer roots which require more frequent rains to grow properly.

The buds on a plant are the only places where new growth of stems and leaves can form, and in the case of woody plants survive through the winter to be ready for forming new growth next year. Any thing that damages the buds on a plant may prevent it from making further growth even though the existing wood may not be damaged.

The bark, especially on woody plants, is largely designed to protect the inner wood and the cambium layer where the life-giving sap flows. One thing that we learn here is that the bark of many nice plants in the east is not heavy enough to insulate the vital parts of the tree from our hot, drying air and the plant "winter-burns."

When the function of leaves is understood it makes plain many of our common garden practices. After all, plants are "soup" eaters and cannot obtain necessary minerals and nourishment from the soil unless they are in solution. We can understand why a limb should be cut off flush with the trunk of a tree so the flowing sap can easily add new cells and form a new growth over the wound. We can understand why soils are more valuable when they are "friable" or loose and full of humus. It gives us an idea why many hardy plants of the East "winter burn" here in our hot, dry winter weather.

When we understand some of these basic principles of plant growth, it is easier to know why we must keep the soil around plant roots moist.

Leaving the foliage on tulips until it naturally ripens makes sense, and watering lawns less frequently and more thoroughly can be understood to encourage deeper rooting.

The factors then that are necessary for plant growth include sunshine, temperature, water, air, soil and necessary chemicals or elements found in these mediums. Each plant requires a slightly different combination of these influences and it is the job of the good gardener to learn these preferences. Thus they develop the coveted "green thumb." All of the traditional garden practices make sense when we understand how a plant grows.

Little Bobby, 8, and Trudy Ann, 5, were getting acquainted with the new little brother, fresh from the hospital. Mother and Daddy were telling of their plans for the new little life. Little Bobby spoke up and said, "When he gets old enough I'm going to teach him to read." Trudy Ann looked at him a while and then said, "I'm going to teach him to kiss."

The more I thought of it the more I was inclined to think that Trudy really had something there. We all need to learn the things that make it possible to compete for our living with our fellows, but I wonder sometimes if we forget that other part of our life; learning to love—learning to see and appreciate all the fine things around us—learning to appreciate people, and sunsets, and flowers and snowcapped peaks. Maybe in our struggle for learning we should stop occasionally and learn to kiss.

Garden Tools

THE OLD saying that "A good workman is known by his tools," is true in gardening as other crafts. A few well selected tools may satisfy the average gardener but there are an endless number of gadgets which may do specialized jobs or make the garden chores easier or more interesting. A hoe, shovel, rake, clippers, trowel, lawnmower and edging shears are minimum equipment.

I prefer a long-handled irrigating type shovel in the small No. 1 size and straight blade. This saves the back and can be used to dig trees, shovel dirt or spade equally well. For edging lawns or moving sod a square bladed, old-fashioned spade is very useful, and for working up hard soil or digging bulbs a spading fork is very handy. If the man of the house wants to encourage his wife to get some of the benefits of garden work he should make her a present of one of those new ladies-size garden shovels. There are also special long handled gadgets for digging round holes to plant bulbs.

The regular garden rake can still be used for a variety of jobs, but its principal use is to rake up trash, level gravel areas and break up garden soil that has been spaded. The dandelion rake is not as popular as formerly for there are now many more effective ways to control dandelions and crabgrass. For removing loose leaves and trash from a lawn without removing the valuable mulch from the surface of the soil a bamboo or similar rake of metal is very useful. Now one may buy rubber-finger rakes that do a similar job.

The garden hoe is still a valuable tool for breaking soil crust and eliminating weeds. Now they may be had in many widths and shapes to suit every purpose and person. Cultivators with several tines may be preferred by some.

Tools for pruning are a must for every good gardener and leading the list would be a good pair of hand clippers. When one finds a kind that he likes they are usually carried in the pocket whenever working in the garden to clip a broken limb, cut back a wayward sprout or remove a dead stem. This tool is almost the sign of a good gardener. The old shears type is being replaced by the clip-cut type in the affections of many, for they are easier on the hand and do a good job if kept sharp. Specialized types may be had, such as the rose cutter that grasps the cut rose and avoids scratching the hands when picking up a cut rose. For those with extensive large shrubbery borders the long handled pruners will allow cutting large limbs with ease. Sooner or later most gardeners will want a tree pruning saw for their own even though the bulk of the tree pruning is done by professionals. A long pruner to reach stray limbs high in a tree will be added to the equipment if many trees are in the yard.

Keeping hedges neat requires still more equipment. Ordinary hedge shears are inexpensive but do require considerable "elbowgrease" to operate. Various power hedge trimmers are available which cut the monotony of this job. A hedge to be really effective requires frequent trimming.

The most expensive tool in the average garden is the lawnmower. Here there may be a great variation in choice. The old hand mower is still a good investment, and it pays to get a good make to begin with and have it adjusted and sharpened when necessary. The power mowers are becoming more and more popular, for they do cut considerably the work of maintaining a good lawn. Here again it pays to get a good one in the first place. The reel type still does a better job on most lawns, but if there is also some weed cutting to be done many now prefer the rotary type even though most of them do not leave as neat a lawn. The possibility of getting a power mower that will also take attachments for snow plowing, spreading fertilizer, leaf-mulching or cultivating is also an inducement for getting this type of equipment. These valuable machines should not be bought on a price basis alone, but it is well to check with your older neighbors before buying to see which kind has done the best job and stood up the longest without expensive repairs.

Grass edgers now can also be had in a great variety. The old hand clippers were time and patience killers, so now many kinds of mechanical and power outfits are available. These power machines may be had in electric or gasoline powered. The electric are light and compact but many do not like the nuisance of the ever-present cord. Gasoline engines are now so refined that they operate with little trouble or fuss.

For those who only have few weeds and no power weed cutter there are golf-club-style weed cutters that develop the golf muscles as they efficiently mow the weeds.

The old-fashioned garden trowel is still an important tool, and now may be had in a great variety of sizes and shapes.

Kipling said that "Half a gardener's work is done upon his knees," and realizing this some like to wear knee pads. There are also gloves made especially for garden work which protect the hands and still allow free action.

A garden wheelbarrow or cart is indispensable, for there is always trash and soil and fertilizer to move. Many prefer to have their own fertilizer spreader and grass seeder. These may now be had in small hand outfits with a crank to turn, that do a good job in a small garden.

An important part of any gardener's equipment is the sprayers and dusters for controlling pests. The simplest thing is the "Flit" type sprayer that is effective for small jobs but is tiresome to work. A two or three gallon knapsack type pressure sprayer is most effective for the average garden. In these the concentration of material and pressure can be accurately controlled and a uniform coverage of material made. For larger estates the small power sprayer may be effective. For the lazy gardener there are many types of varying effectiveness for attaching to the hose.

More and more gardeners are preferring dusting to spraying. While this method may be slightly less effective, especially in windy weather, it certainly is handier, eliminating the fuss of mixing liquid preparations. Again these dusters may be had in the small push types or more effective crank models, and now of course most dusts come in pump-gun applicators which may be expensive and inefficient but mighty handy.

Garden hose might be included with the necessary tools. This is now sold in plastic types which are light and come in attractive colors. With their advantages there are also disadvantages. They are stiff and kinky when cold, they are often too small to carry a suitable volume of water and they are generally difficult to repair when damaged. Many gardeners are going back to a well made rubber hose.

Sprinklers now come in such a variety as to be bewildering. In general a sprinkler is most efficient when it throws a small volume of water in comparatively large drops low to the ground. Those that throw a fine mist, high in the air, or in such a volume that they may not be left long in one spot will lose much water from evaporation and run-off. Those that revolve or may be adjusted to swing back and forth in any part of a circle are often good and some claim to spray rectangles and squares. The old twin spray is generally a water waster, but there are places yet where the fan spray is needed. The perforated plastic hoses are popular, but as usually used are water wasters and would be much more effective if turned upside down and used as soakers. Regular canvas and plastic soakers are very useful to thoroughly soak areas where surface sprinklers would waste water. More and more the underground sprinkler systems are being installed. They surely cut down on the work of watering the lawn if they are properly engineered. For the old beds and new seedings and planters there may still be need for the old sprinkling can.

Aerators operated by hand like a spading fork or larger power outfits are valuable tools where the lawn has been put in improperly or has become so compacted on the surface since, that it refuses to "take" water, air or fertilizer as it should.

Good gardeners will surround themselves with good tools to fit the size and requirements of their particular garden. Remember that good tools are necessary to do good jobs.

ALL IS NOT GOLD

Certainly some of the new seed and nursery catalogs that flood the mails in the spring glitter like gold. It is well, however, to stop and notice where they are from before sending too much money for some of these things that are so attractively displayed. Magnolias and Flowering Dogwood may be described as "perfectly hardy" where the catalog is published, but they are certainly not here in the Rocky Mountains. Unless you have had much experience with Rocky Mountain gardening, the only safe thing to do is to depend upon the advice of some local seedsman or horticulturist whom you know is familiar with plants in your area.

This should not discourage adventurous people who like to try new things. If it were not for them we would still be planting two or three kinds of trees and a half dozen shrubs in this Rocky Mountain country. But those of local experience can usually advise what things are hopeless and what stand some chance of survival under favorable conditions. So enjoy the colorful catalogs to your heart's content, but don't believe that all you read applies here, just because you saw it in print.

A Garden Notebook Is Important

ONE of the interesting things about gardening is that most of the work must be done by faith. The bulb which produces the beautiful tulip in the spring must be planted the previous fall when it is a dry, apparently lifeless thing. Tiny seeds which produce the brilliant petunia or zinnia during the summer must be put in the ground early in the spring. The shade tree must be transplanted when it is out of leaf and a mere skeleton. Plants that are to become beautiful perennials in season are transplanted when they have no growth above the ground.

Some of us have good enough memories to remember just what these things look like when they are in their fullest glory. However, to intelligently plan out plantings to fit the space that is needed, the average person finds it a much safer practice to make notes during the growing season and to make use of them during the planting and remodeling when things are dormant. Thus a garden notebook is an important part of a good gardener's equipment.

As you walk in your garden today, make a note of that clump of Shasta Daisies in the center of your rear border which is crowding out the nice new Dianthus set out last spring. You can't do anything about moving the Shasta Daisies now, but next spring when they are dormant, they can easily be divided. Make a note to get another plant of privet next spring to fill out that thin place in the hedge where the mailman walks through. Note the name of that new flower blooming next door and find out where it can be obtained.

Along with this garden recording system, your plan of garden labels should also be developed. Next spring when you go out to divide the Shasta Daisy, there will be no tops to show where the Dianthus plant you are trying to protect is located. With a permanent but inconspicuous label, you can mark the spot now. Perhaps a good friend wants a division from one of your new Iris plants. Will you be able to remember which was which when they are out of bloom? Label them when they are in bloom with something which will stay put and be legible, though not too conspicuous.

The garden records serve other purposes. Suppose you find your zinnias were put in too late this year to get the most bloom. Will you remember just when you planted them and be able to make adjustments accordingly?

Put it down in your garden notebook.

You find a new bug in your garden this summer and after several attempts to kill him, you find an insecticide which will do the job. When the bug shows up a year or two from now, will you remember the formula and where you were able to buy it?

Put it down in your garden notebook.

Then, your new Oak tree becomes chlorotic in the spring and you inquire about what chemical to use in correcting this deficiency. It worked, but will you remember just what you used and how much and where you applied it? A year from now these things may not be so clearly in mind.

Put it down in your garden notebook.

Possibly you will find that when you have kept this garden notebook a few months you will have accumulated much material which will be too bulky. You also may have accumulated several articles from magazines and pictures of your specialty. You will want to start a scrap book. One scrap book usually calls for another, as new interests are developed. Though you may not refer to them a great deal, just the process of assembling and preserving this material will impress it on your mind and improve your memory.

Some gardeners continue this accumulation of garden books, magazines, bulletins, and garden notes until they have given over a whole room to them. Few of us have the time, patience, and ability to go that far, but a shelf or drawer might well be given over to garden literature.

Your pleasure in gardening will definitely be increased by the habit of keeping garden records and accumulating a reference library of garden literature.

MY GARDEN

Unless my palm may press the soil,
Unless my hand may pull the weed,
Unless my brow be damp with toil,
The garden is not mine indeed.
    —Chinese Proverb.

BEAUTY vs. UTILITY

One of the best definitions of landscape architecture is, "the arrangement of the land to combine the greatest amount of beauty with the maximum utility." Practicing these principles would benefit a small garden or a large estate. Too often only one of these ideas is considered in laying out land for human use, in which case we lose important values. There are those who consider conservation only from the beauty angle, and others who give no consideration to beauty in their efforts to squeeze the last dollar of profit from a project.

271

Call Each Plant by Its Correct Name

WHEN we realize there are nearly half a million different kinds of plants, it becomes apparent there must be some systematic method of naming them. Before the middle of the Eighteenth Century, much of the meager literature on plants was very confusing, with names assigned to fit the fancy of various individuals. It is interesting to note that most of the plants with accepted names were those with some real or imagined medicinal value.

It was about this time that the great Swedish botanist Linnaeus attempted to bring order out of confusion and devised a system of genera and species based on similarity of flowers and seed. Above the genera were the groupings of families and order and below the species were varieties.

Today a plant textbook published in Sweden, England, or Germany may not be understood by those who speak other languages, but the plant names given are the same as those used all over the world.

The beginning gardener may think scientific names are hard to remember and unnecessary. One does not have to garden long, however, until he comes to have an appreciation for the scientific, or botanical, names. While common names are necessary and useful, they often just grow like "Topsy" and have no meaning to anyone but those in the particular community where they are developed. For example, there are several very different plants called Bachelor's Button, or Dusty Miller, in various communities. Pansies or Dogwood, or Linden trees are called by many common names.

The botanical name is also valuable to indicate certain relationships. Who would suspect that the Staghorn Sumac, Poison Ivy, Skunk Brush, and Smoke Tree were related, if they did not know they were all in the Rhus genus due to the similarity of bloom and fruit? It is interesting to know of the relationship between wild and cultivated species in the same genus, whether they are called Penstemon, Golden Glow, or Maple.

Only recently has there been an organized effort to standardize the common names. Now the book "Standardized Plant Names" is available in all good libraries and nurserymen, seedsmen, and gardeners are gradually making their use of common names conform to it. It is true that when the name adopted does not correspond to what we have previously learned it is difficult to adjust our writing and speaking of this plant, but gardeners should make a practice of following standardized plant names whenever possible.

GARDENERS AND CENTS

To most of the green thumb kind of gardeners, money does not mean much. They work for the love of it. They enjoy the feel and odor of soil. They thrill to the sight of expanding new buds and appreciate the harvest of fruit and flowers. Having worked with fundamental things, they can never be happy away from growing plants. Most of them feel as Henry Field, the noted Iowa seedsman, once put it: "We might sell fruit or grain at a reasonable price, but we would much rather give away flowers and shade trees."

Glossary of Horticultural Terms

Commonly Used Horticultural Terms Which
May Not Be Understood

Acidity: In reference to soil indicates a soil having a pH rating below 7. Usually found in soils with much humus and good drainage.

Adventitious Buds: Those which come in unusual places and usually only develop when the regular buds are destroyed.

Alkalinity: The opposite of acidity. A pH of above 7, usually found in soils lacking in humus or poorly drained.

Alpines: Plants from the mountains, usually dwarf. Used in rock gardens.

Annual: A plant that lives its whole life, from seed, to seed again, in one season.

B. & B.: Balled and Burlapped. Evergreens are usually sold with balls of earth around them, held in place with burlap.

Biennial: Plants that grow from seed one year (usually in fall), live through one winter, flower and seed the next year and then die.

Bulb: The living part of a plant in its resting stage (usually underground). All surviving underground parts are often referred to as bulbs, but true bulbs are only those made up of scales like an onion or Easterlily. Other forms of underground parts may be called rhizomes, corms, or tubers, depending on their construction.

Bulbil or bulblet: Small young bulbs.

Coniferous: Cone bearing, such as the Spruce, Pine and Fir. These trees are usually called evergreens, but the Larch is coniferous though it sheds its leaves each fall.

Corm: A solid bulb-like underground part of a plant. Often called bulb. Gladiolus and Crocus are examples of corms.

Cormel and cormlet: Small young bulbs from the larger bulb or above ground in the leaf axils.

Crown: The part of a plant at about the ground level where new growth starts. Above this point are the stems and below are the roots. This point is usually distinguishable by the color or texture of the plant.

Cutting: Sometimes called slips. In actual practice this is usually a small section cut from the tip of shoots, which is rooted to start a new plant.

Deciduous: Dropping their leaves or fruit at maturity, usually each fall.

Dioecious Plants: Those where the flowers are either stamens or pistils but are on different plants. Cottonwoods are good examples.

Division: Separation of a plant having both roots and top which is used to start a new plant. Shasta Daisies and Fall Asters are examples of plants usually propagated by division.

Dormant: Not growing. Deciduous plants usually indicate this period by dropping their leaves and evergreens by making no new growth.

Drainage: A condition of the soil which allows water to flow through it freely. Especially important in heavy soils. A few tin cans, or rocks in the bottom of a hole does not always give the necessary drainage.

Ecology: The relation of plants to their environment and each other. Columbines and Aspens are always found in moist places and Rabbitbrush and Yucca in dry sunny places.

Evergreen: Holding its leaves overwinter when the deciduous plants have dropped theirs. Most of the coniferous trees like Pine, Fir and Spruce are evergreens, but the Larch is deciduous and there may be many broad-leaved evergreens.

Exotic: Might be used in referring to a plant brought in from some other place.

Fastigiate: Means closely parallel, usually referring to a tall slim growing tree.

Friable: Used in reference to soil it indicates a soil that is easily crumbled because of a good proportion of sand or humus.

Fungicide: A chemical used to control undesirable fungus diseases in plants.

273

Genus: The first word of the scientific name of a plant. It refers to the group of plants under that head such as Campanula for Bellflower and Aquilegia for Columbine. After this generic name comes the specific name for each different plant in that group.

Glaucous: Refers to a "bloom," usually gray, that may rub off, such as on a cabbage leaf or plum.

Grafting: A process of propagating plants where a small stem of a desired species is fastened to a seedling root-stock so that they grow together and produce fruit or flowers of a definite type.

Hardy: A much abused word, but usually refers to the ability of a plant to stand severe cold. May also be used to refer to a plant that will survive drouth, hot sun or wind.

Herbaceous: With no overwintering parts above ground. Most of the perennials are herbaceous.

Heeling in: Temporarily covering with soil until plants can be planted in their permanent location.

Humus: Partly decomposed vegetable matter in soil.

Hybrid: Plants resulting from crosses of unlike but similar plants.

Indigenous: Used in referring to a native plant.

Monecious Plants: Those which have flowers with the stamens and pistils in different flowers but on the same plant.

Mulch: A covering of leaves, peat, sawdust, straw or other materials to maintain soil moisture, prevent rapid changes in soil temperature or eliminate cultivation.

Naturalize: To establish plants in an environment where they will continue to propagate themselves unaided as would wild or native plants.

Node: The point on a stem where a leaf originates.

Perennial: A plant whose top dies each fall but whose root lives three years or more.

Perfect: Referring to a flower, means that both stamens and pistils are contained in the same flower.

pH: A symbol to indicate acidity or alkalinity of soil. pH 7 is the neutral point and smaller figures indicate acidity and larger alkalinity. Most of our area soil runs from 7 to 9.

Pistillate: Refers to the female part of a flower which produces the fruit.

Pruning: Usually connected with shaping, thinning, or regulating the growth of fruit trees. A well pruned peach tree may not be beautiful. See Trimming.

Rhizome: A thickened underground root stock such as Iris.

Shrub: A plant with several woody stems above ground and usually of small size.

sp.: Following the generic name of a plant indicates that several or undetermined species are included.

Sport: An unusual variation from the normal growth of a plant, such as when a plant with normally white flowers produces pink ones. Many of our fine flowers and fruits have originated that way.

Staminate: Refers to the male part of a flower, which produces the pollen to fertilize the female flower.

Succulent: A class of plants containing those from many genus, all of which have thickish, juicy stems or leaves and are able to tolerate dry conditions. Sedums and Sempervivums are examples.

Suckering: Usually referring to a plant that sends out underground parts that form new plants around the original. Wild Roses and Chokecherries are good example:

Sub-soil: Soil lying under the "top soil." This may be down a few inches or feet. Sub-soil normally contains little humus but may have valuable minerals.

Tender: Used as the opposite of hardy. May refer to susceptibility to damage by cold, drouth or other causes.

Tree: A woody plant with usually only one stem and growing tall.

Trimming: Usually referring to cutting back growth from ornamental plants to increase their beauty or health. In general use is interchangeable with pruning.

Tuber: A short congested part of a plant, usually the underground part that survives when the top dies down in fall.

Gardening by the Month

January ... THE MONTH TO MAKE GARDEN PLANS

WHAT gardening chores could there be in January, you ask? Of course, the ground is frozen up and the plants are dormant. January should be the big planning month—the time when you surround yourselves with seed catalogs, gardening magazines and horticultural books and let your minds wander to the big things that you will do in gardening in this fresh new year.

GOOD FROM THE COLD

My Mother always used to tell me, when some childish tragedy had happened, "There's no great loss without some small gain," and then we would hunt around to find the small gain, and forget the loss.

The severe weather at this time of year may cause some gardeners to become restless and resent being confined to the house, but "bad" weather for humans may be good for the plants outdoors. If plants are damaged, usually harmful insects are also destroyed and in the end there is more gain than loss.

NOW that leaves are gone from the deciduous trees and shrubs you can appreciate the coniferous evergreens and the few broadleaf evergreens that survive our hot winter sun. Plan to use a good proportion of them in further planning. Notice also how much more interesting gardens are that have been planned for interest in ground pattern and changes in elevation.

❧ During some of the stormy days get out all those clippings that you have hoarded around the place and classify them ready to paste in a scrapbook. Most good garden magazines have a few things that are of lasting value and to which you may want to refer later. However, you will never find them when they are wanted if you must look thru stacks of unclassified material.

❧ When the warm days do come and the ground can be worked there is little time to plan, so now you should make your plans definite enough so that you can concentrate on carrying them out later with the minimum of wasted time.

❧ You have often wished as you plant the seed or pick the fruit, that you knew more about these plants—where they came from, how they grew, what relation they bore to other plants, how many kinds were included in one family or what their cultural preferences were. Now is the time to study these things.

❧ Take notes as you study. Even though you never refer to these notes, you will find that it helps to remember desirable facts. When you have decided on some addition or change in your garden, work it out in detail on paper so that you will not forget.

❧ We usually have our coldest weather in January, so our chief outside chores may be to prevent snow damage. Bracing trees or tying up shrubs and low evergreens may prevent some snow damage. If the ground is not frozen and there are a few warm days it would be worthwhile to check the moisture in the soil around your plants. The space south of a building or south facing slopes will dry out first.

WINTER COLOR

With good design and proper planning for winter color, gardens may be attractive in spite of the cold and snow.

This is the time of year we most appreciate all the fine coniferous evergreens that do so well in the Rocky Mountain area—Pines, Spruce, Firs, Junipers of every size and shape. A few small broadleaf evergreens such as English Ivy, Mahonia and Euonymus also help make little spots of green in the winter.

Then there are the deciduous trees and shrubs with their various colored bark, stems and berries, like the native red-twig Dogwood, the Golden Weeping Willows, Japanese Barberries and several kinds of Cotoneasters.

Winter is the time to become intimately acquainted with all the trees and shrubs in the garden. Good gardeners will learn to recognize the many differences and characteristics which are apparent when the plants are neither in bloom or in full leaf.

A S YOU get the flood of beautiful seed and nursery catalogs from other areas learn to discount their wonderful stories and pictures. You may learn from local gardeners and nurserymen the plants that are likely to grow here and which things might possibly look like the pictures. Remember that our climatic and soil conditions are different and order your plants with that in mind.

We do not have to be nudists to learn to appreciate the sunshine—to let it into our homes at the proper times and to so design our homes that it is easy to get from indoors to the garden outside. We may also design our gardens so that there is not too much sunshine during the heat of the day, so we may enjoy this wonderful climate of ours the greatest number of days in the year.

FEBRUARY is an unpredictable month. Some years the weather may warm up early in the month, the frost may leave the ground and transplanting of woody plants may begin. Other years may bring the most disagreeable days of the winter in February. All good gardeners will be prepared to start outdoor work if conditions are favorable and be content to plan and dream indoors if the month is unfavorable. Don't be fooled by a few promising days and uncover the perennials or take the shade off the tender plants. Turn your back on this impulse for you can be sure that there will be more cold weather before spring is really here.

❧ As a traveller prepares for a long trip, it would be well now to check all your equipment and be sure that all is in readiness for the year's garden work. While you are waiting, bring in a few twigs of the early flowering shrubs, put them in water in a warm room, and get a preview of the grand display to come later. Forsythia tops the list, and Plums, Pussy-willow or Spirea are sometimes effective.

❧ Plans should now all be definitely made, the necessary plants for new work or remodeling ordered. As short let-ups come in the weather the garden may be cleaned up, manure brought in and possibly some warm spots spaded up. Look for the first unfolding leaves of the Bush Honeysuckle, the tips of Tulips showing through on the south side and the first Crocus bloom. Any of these first signs of spring encourage the real gardener.

❧ One of the most important spray operations of the season is the dormant spray which can be done anytime now that the weather stays above forty for a few hours, the wind is not too strong and the new leaves have not opened.

❧ There may be work to do now on the tops of plants even though the ground is frozen. This is usually the best time to prune grapes. Shrubs may have been misshapen by weight of snow or tree limbs may have been broken. This pruning may be done any time now that the weather is fair enough.

❧ Inspect the bulbs and such which were stored last fall. Dahlias are especially particular as to drying out or becoming too warm. Glad bulbs should be treated for thrip if it has not been done before. It may be time to get the Tuberous Begonias started in flats. If you like the fun of seeing new plants start, you should plant a few things in flats indoors and watch them sprout and grow.

SPRING CLEANING

When those premature warm sunny days that come in the spring give everyone the urge to get out in the garden, you can work off your surplus energy by cleaning up the place. Without removing all the leaves, peat moss, compost or manure which is so valuable on the ground, you can make the place look much better. Utilize your energy by doing such constructive things as cleaning out the weeds and papers blown in by the winter winds, perhaps raking around the walks and lawn and removing the dead stems of such things as hollyhocks and goldenrods.

A S THERE are days when the frost is out of the ground and it is not too wet it will be a good job to start preparing the soil for spring's new plants. Dig in manure, peat and compost, throw out impossible rubbish, and loosen the soil deep so that air, water and freezing can mellow it. Remember that half the success of a garden depends on the quality of the soil.

❧ Some like to pot up their tuberous begonia bulbs in peat now. This will assure that they have good growth and are ready to go right to blooming when they are set outside the first of June.

❧ If you are lucky you may have flowers blooming now—the Christmas Rose, Heleborus Niger. If you do not have a plant make a note now to plant one next season.

❧ Properly planned gardens should be interesting now, even when covered with snow. If yours is not, it would be a good investment to call in a competent landscape architect and have him show you how it can be made attractive every month in the year.

MARCH is traditionally the time for wind, rain, snow and "bad" weather. Remember tho, bad weather as we humans view it, may be good for the garden. Additional moisture may mean better plant growth later and continued cold weather will retard early plants, so that you will be assured of good bloom later. While it is disagreeable outside you will have an excellent chance to catch up on all the little indoor chores, like ordering your seeds, planning the remodeling and studying up on new bug killers.

❧ If you are becoming impatient for spring to arrive take a trip to the lower hills and hunt for the first signs of wild flowers on the sunny south slopes. The Oregon Grape, Early Candytuft, Storksbill and Spring Beauty should be showing up.

❧ The middle of March is the time to plant Sweet Peas, seeds of the self-seeding annuals such as Larkspur, Calendulas, Cosmos, Bachelor Buttons and Marigolds, providing the ground is unfrozen.

❧ It may be that some nurserymen will get impatient and rush the season a little, sending the plants that you have ordered while it is unfit to plant them. If this happens, it is a good idea to open the packages so that the tops may get air but cover the roots with moist material so that they will not dry out. It is not a good practice to leave plants in water for long, but roses, for instance, may be covered completely with moist peat, soil or sand for a few days if they appear to be dried out when received. Often these things may be temporarily "heeled in" in a spot of unfrozen soil, at the south of the house.

❧ This is the time to plant woody material such as trees, evergreens, shrubs, roses and vines. Your plans should have been made and orders in before this so that all attention can be given now to getting the plants back into the soil promptly and properly. The ground should be warming up a little now so that lawns may be planted. The grass planted now will not grow much until the soil is fairly warm, but when planted late in the spring it will require closer attention to prevent baking.

❧ It adds greatly to your enjoyment if you do a little playing at least with propagation—by seeds, cuttings, grafts, buds or layers. Start a few tomato and zinnia plants in a box on the windowsill, experiment a little by making a few simple grafts and prepare some cuttings for setting out when it is warm. If you do not know how to do this, look at the process illustrated in some of the many books on propagation.

❧ You have probably learned over the years to identify the plants that you work with by their bloom. Now is a good time to notice the woody plants and learn to distinguish between them by their bark, twig color, buds, remains of last year's leaves and fruit, their general shape, and, as the transplanting begins, from their roots of varying habit and color.

Probably the greatest good comes from our gardening efforts because we are annually having our faith renewed in the rightness of everything as we see seeds and twigs break forth in new leaves.

T HE PAPERS will soon tell you that it is time to "begin" watering. In other words after having the hose locked up in the garage since the first of last October now you should begin to water things three times a week. This practice is not only wasteful of water but is the worst possible thing that you can do to your lawn and garden plants. Most of our ornamental plants come from climates where they receive enough rain and snow to keep the ground around their roots moist at *all* times and we should learn to simulate those conditions as nearly as possible here. Too frequent, shallow waterings, now, will cause the roots to seek moisture in the upper few inches of soil and when the hot weather of July and August comes, such plants cannot thrive as deep-rooted plants will.

❧ If you enjoy seeing new plants grow, it is time now to start a few annuals indoors. A box or pot in a sunny window will do.

❧ Remember that our Springs are very erratic here, and don't uncover the roses or take winter protection off perennials and trees, when a few warm days come at this time of year.

APRIL is called the "in-between" month in gardening. It's not quite spring, but there is evidence that winter may be losing its grip. Again may we caution: don't get in too big a hurry, a few warm days do not mean that summer is here.

❧ Properly preparing soil for planting is probably the first and most important gardening chore for this month. Grass, trees, shrubs or flowers planted in good soil will thrive so much better than those planted in poor soil that much of the later spraying and fertilizing will be eliminated.

❧ All our Rocky Mountain soil needs humus to improve its texture and plant-food value. Both heavy clay soil and light sandy soil will be benefited by mixing peat, manure, leaf-mold or other organic material with it before planting. Soil which contains much lime, plaster or lifeless subsoil should be removed and replaced with good soil. During periods of good weather do the necessary remodeling of your borders. At this time you will appreciate the full and detailed notes that you made last summer when the flowers were in bloom. If you plan on new plants of rhubarb, peonies, asparagus or bleeding hearts, they should be planted early.

❧ Almost any of the trees and shrubs may now be pruned with the exception of Maple, Birch and Walnut. Do not do more than emergency work on early blooming shrubs if flowers are wanted this year. Extensive work on shrubs is best done right after blooming time.

❧ Start now the habit of inspecting your upright Junipers for signs of aphids about once a week. If let go until a large population of insects is built up, a great deal of damage may be done. About the time of the first warm rain is when the galls expand on the Junipers, making them look as though full of orange bloom. Learn the best ways to control this Cedar-Hawthorn gall.

❧ If you have a Dogwood bush in your yard go out now and look in the crotches where small twigs branch off and see if these areas are covered with tiny jet black spots. These will be the immature forms of aphids which will come to life at the first flow of sap and begin to feed on the newly opening leaves. The new leaves will immediately roll around the aphids so that hitting them with a killing spray is impossible. You should get them now with a dormant spray of lime-sulphur or miscible oil.

❧ While you are examining your shrubs look at your Lilacs, Cotoneasters, and Dogwoods for signs of oystershell scale. These are tiny insects covered with a scale that looks like a very small oystershell. Treat with a spray of lime-sulphur or miscible oil.

❧ And while you are looking for scale on the shrubs, examine your trees for signs of scale. If you have American Elm you are fairly sure to find them covered with the European Elm Scale. There may be some on the Chinese or other species of Elm also. These scale appear as small gray spots along the cracks on the under side of limbs starting from the lower part of the tree. The cottony maple scale may also be on your Maples, Elm, Honeylocust, Linden or other trees and shrubs. These appear as larger spots with a base of white cottony material. Control is also a dormant oil spray.

All good gardeners get their greatest thrill out of the first flowers of spring. If you have planted crocus, snowdrops and such last fall, you will have some color in your own garden, but if not go to the warm, south slopes in the foothills and hunt for the first wildflower. It will do you good and make a better gardener of you.

Towards the last of this month many like to take the chance of killing frosts being over and put out the tender annuals. One old rule here, is, "wait until after Decoration Day."

Birch trees that have been back-ordered from earlier plantings may safely be planted about the first week of this month, just as the buds begin to break.

If your lawn and garden needs fertilizer and you are using the most economical form such as ammonium sulphate or urea, the first of May is the earliest time to apply it. As it lasts about six weeks, the middle of June and first of August would be the other two dates to fertilize.

TRANSPLANTING of trees, shrubs and evergreens should usually be completed by the middle of the month, as this is the time when the leaves are beginning to unfold. Many perennials can still be safely moved if taken up with a shovel of soil. Tender annuals are usually left until about Decoration Day, to avoid those late freezes. The tendency of some nursery firms is to provide more and more things in pots which can be set out at any time—something you might want to consider.

❧ Keep a close watch now for the first signs of insect damage. The sucking insects — aphids — are most likely to appear at any time after the weather warms up. Ants seen running up and down plants often indicate that there are aphids present which the ants are "milking". While the ants seldom do much damage, they may encourage the aphids. Killing either the ants or the aphids will tend to discourage both insects. Watch your Spirea, Juniper trees and Spruce for signs of insect infestation. An ounce of prevention now may save a lot of damage later.

❧ Some weed killers may be used on the lawns this month. Be sure to use them according to directions and avoid letting any of the chemical get on desirable plants. Avoid the practice of using the sprayer for other purposes.

❧ Don't cut all the leaves from tulips after they bloom unless you do not care for flowers next year, for they require these leaves to develop energy in the bulbs to produce next year's flowers.

❧ Unless natural rainfall has been more than usual, it is time to begin to check all plants for sign of drought and give them enough water to reach to their farthest roots. Remember that the larger the plant the larger the roots and the more water needed so soak them thoroughly until the soil is wet down where the roots are growing. Generally it is a good rule to water thoroughly and not so often.

❧ Cultivation is the start of the summer's war on weeds. Cultivate no deeper than is necessary to destroy them. The weeds are much easier killed soon after they come up than they are after they become established. Mulching with leaves, grass clippings, peat or sawdust is taking the place of cultivation in many places.

RAIN

There is nothing quite so good for our growing plants as a slow, soaking rain. When I wake up in the night and hear the eaves gently dripping water, I roll over with a sigh of relief and realize that Nature is doing my work for today. Every plant is getting a good drink, and how much better Nature does it than I with all my hoses, sprinklers and irrigation ditches! Rain falls on the just and the unjust, on the grass and the dandelions, on the wildflowers and the newly-sown rows of radish seed. So common it is that we take it for granted. Yet, let's not forget how wonderful a provision Nature makes for our welfare by collecting this moisture, distributing it thru the atmosphere and dropping it in fine particles on the land, for the thirsty plants to use.

WATERING

How a person goes about watering his garden, trees, shrubs and lawn is a good indication of the knowledge he has of a growing plant's requirements. A person with a green thumb does not keep plants saturated, nor does he permit drought to wither the foliage. The correct method falls in between these two extremes. Most roots are benefited by the entrance of oxygen into the soil by withholding water for a week or ten days, then giving a thorough soaking. There are exceptions to this rule. Some vegetation will not tolerate a dry period. Some trees will do better on a longer interval between waterings, especially Birch, Cherry, Linden and Oak. But keep in mind, you are not watering the roots of a large tree, by sprinkling for ten minutes. It may require four hours or more to soak down two or three feet.

We repeat: "Overwatering is caused by the frequency not the quantity of water." Until you know from experience, you should dig down occasionally near the roots (but not touching) to ascertain the moisture content of the soil. When you find the soil too dry to form a ball, when squeezed in the hand, it needs water, if it makes a moist ball, hold off on the watering. The surface soil should be cultivated to conserve moisture, or better still have a surface mulch of grass clippings or other organic material. Do not worry about the dryness of the top inch or so of ground.

FINISH planting out tender annuals early this month. Clumps of perennials may be planted at this time if they are not too nearly in bloom. Some of the nurserymen carry roses, various perennials and even a few shrubs and vines in pots which may be planted out at any time.

❧ Shrubs which have bloomed may be pruned now. Do not shear back the Bridal Wreath Spirea and such naturally arching habit shrubs. Flowering Almond and the early Garland Spirea should be sheared back to keep them from becoming thin below as they grow older.

❧ Do not remove all the suckers from around Lilac bushes. Leave a few of the most vigorous to form new growth to cover the bare stems of older growth. Some of these very old stems may be taken out down to the ground each year if a young vigorous looking bush is wanted.

❧ As the new plants begin to grow the weeds begin to grow even faster, for they were there first. A little work when the weeds are very small will do more good than much work later. At the same time that weeds are eliminated the surface of the soil around trees, shrubs, perennials and annuals can be broken where it has become compacted from watering or tramping. Where there is no chance to damage valuable plants the 2,4-D weed killers may often be used to advantage, but this material is dangerous if it drifts on to good plants.

❧ June is the month when insects may take a heavy toll. Here, as with weeds, "a spray in time" is worth more than the later attempts to eliminate them after they have done considerable damage. Continue habit of checking the Spirea, Spruce, Delphinium and Juniper for aphids. Be on guard, especially with the evergreens, for the damage done usually does not show up until weeks after the insects have come and gone. If there are caterpillars, beetles or other chewing insects damaging the plants they should be controlled with a stomach poison such as arsenate of lead or one of the new insecticides like DDT or chlordane.

❧ If the garden has had normal watering up to June it should be in good shape. Start now training the plants for the hot weather to come, by watering them thoroughly each time but less often. Newly transplanted things will need a little extra attention.

❧ If fertilizers and mulches have been applied as needed early in the season, little need be done now. Later, when trees, lawns and flowers slow up they may be given a little "shot" of some quick-acting fertilizer.

❧ Lawns should be in their prime now if they have been properly cared for up to this time. If you will watch for the tiny, triangular seed-leaves of the crabgrass, early this month, it may be eliminated by digging or by drying up the lawn for a few days. Let all the clippings fall that will disappear among the remaining grass stems.

❧ Plants which are not growing vigorously may now be given a little stimulation, remembering that many of the chemical fertilizers are quick acting and of short benefit while the organic fertilizers are slower, but longer lasting.

MOUNTAIN GARDENS

While I am in our Colorado mountains I do not like to have my attention so fixed on reaching the top of the mountain or making a certain number of runs down the ski hill or catching another trout, that I can not stop and enjoy the work of the Master Landscape Architect, about me.

Be it in full leaf of mid-summer, brilliant fall color, the first greening-up of spring or when everything is covered with snow — there are examples of the beautiful effects created by nature.

Little open parks carpeted with grass, studded with bright bloom and surrounded with evergreen trees will be seen around the bend in the trail from beautifully planted rock gardens.

We may learn much from these natural gardens which may be used in our city grounds. Many of these native plants may be used in our gardens to better advantage than those from areas of very different climate.

At the most all that we can do is try to copy in our gardens some of the effects that we see naturally in the hills.

THE BIGGEST garden job in July is usually pest control. All-purpose sprays and dusts are fine for the really busy or lazy gardener, but all the real gardeners will want to learn how to recognize the damage done by the ordinary insects and what the best control is for them. Unnecessary sprays may kill many beneficial predators of the harmful insects. There are many new insecticides on the market now which are very effective when properly used but they may do much damage if not used in the right way.

❦ If you have not already started a garden diary, do so at once, now that it is fresh in your mind. All the little improvements that would be desirable in your garden, next fall or spring at planting time, you will have forgotten. There may be clashing color combinations, or tall plants hiding short ones or rampant growers crowding out the nicer but weaker things. Make a note now of all these desirable improvements.

❦ Begin your hedge trimming program early. The beauty of a hedge depends very much on the frequency with which it is trimmed. If you are starting a small hedge, cut it back quite severely at first and shear it every time there are two or three inches of new growth.

❦ Watch for the first formation of the disfiguring galls on the tips of spruce limbs. Pick these off and burn them as soon as they are noticed. After they have turned brown is too late to do more than improve the looks of the trees.

❦ Some of your plants may now be showing signs of chlorosis. This is a deficiency disease which affects the green coloring matter in the leaves causing them to become pale or yellowish. Barberry, Ninebark, Flowering Quince and Soft Maples are most subject to this disease. Excess alkali, gypsum, plaster or lime in the soil might cause this, or even overwatering can produce much the same effect. Treatment with manure, iron sulphate, aluminum sulphate or sulphur might correct the soil condition.

❦ Proper watering at this time of year is most important. In general we usually water more often than necessary and not thoroughly enough. Learn that the soil for grass should be soaked to a depth of at least six inches, for perennials and annuals at least a foot, for most shrubs at least two feet, and trees, three or four feet. The only way that you can know when the soil is sufficiently wet is to dig in and see. Sandy soils would require more frequent waterings than heavy clay soils. Be careful about watering roses late in the evening. Water standing on rose leaves overnight might cause mildew.

❦ Cut off faded blooms and keep the garden looking neat. Some emergency trimming may now be done to shrubs which have bloomed. Tulips may now be entirely dormant and the bulbs may be moved to new locations if necessary or desirable.

❦ Weeds should be kept down now so that they will not go to seed and produce more plants next year. Mulching or cultivating will keep the weeds eliminated.

❦ Any necessary trimming to trees or shrubs may be done now as well as any time.

August ... FIGHT THE HEAT AND DROUGHT

W HY are gardeners and Nature lovers generally healthier both physi-
cally and mentally, than the average?

There are, it seems to me, several reasons. The working out of doors
in the fresh air and sunshine certainly helps. In the case of the vegetable
gardener, his fresh products add to a healthy diet.

Certainly there is something calming and soothing to distracted nerves
in working with Nature's plants, whether in the mountains or in a little
garden. Having definite objectives helps to keep a person going when
otherwise he might join the "chronic grunters" and become really sick.
Working with the beauty of the wild flowers in the mountains and the
trees and lawns of the city can not help but reflect itself in actual physical
and mental well-being.

If using the soluble nitrogen fertilizers, the first of this month should
usually be the last application for the year.

Notice how much the fall fruits on the ornamental shrubs contribute to
the beauty of the garden. Plan for more fruiting shrubs, both for their
beauty and their attraction for birds.

AUGUST is usually hot and dry. Plants which have been properly trained by careful and thorough watering will survive this critical period, but those which have been pampered with daily, shallow watering are sure to suffer. Toward the last of the month, it would be proper to begin to hold off the water a little on the woody plants so that they might begin to ripen up their wood ready for the frosts next month.

❦ Do not let down in your war on garden insects and diseases. The large red aphids are likely to be on your Goldenglow and Goldenrod. Perennial Phlox may be losing their lower leaves. Dust with sulphur to control both rust and red spiders. Aphids may be sucking the life out of your Delphinium, Columbine or Spirea bushes.

❦ Your tulips are completely dormant now. Some of the old top may still be present to show where they were. If they bloomed well this spring they should be left alone. If they are weak and appear to have divided into many small bulbs, it is time to dig and divide them. They do not need to be kept out of the ground until fall, but may be replanted at once. Put them in about ten inches deep in a partly shaded place, for best results.

❦ Now is the time to move Oriental Poppies, if that should be desirable. They are dormant now, but will begin new growth in September. Even a small piece of root will often start a new plant. Plant them in large masses where they may be seen at a distance.

❦ With the routine garden work letting up a little, now is the time to do those things that were neglected earlier—level up the flagstone walk, nail back that loose panel on the fence, patch the crack in the pool, paint the trellis, trim the dead out of that old Lilac or edge the borders.

❦ Try saving a few seeds of your really nice flowers. You can start them in boxes in the house next April. Sit down now and make a record of the successes and failures of your plants up to date. This will be invaluable to you next January when you are planning your new garden.

❦ This is the time that your garden looks empty and colorless unless you have planned in advance for the heat loving things to fill in the gap between the early and late flowers. Even the best planned perennial border needs a few of the summer annuals to fill in at this difficult time. Petunias, Zinnias, Calendulas, Marigolds and Four-O'Clocks are all common flowers, but they enjoy this heat and require little care.

❦ A garden may be beautiful because of its good plan, its good plants, its good maintenance, or better yet because of all three of these things. Neatness is the one thing that costs little and makes a great deal of difference. Take off the old bloom stalks and the plants that are entirely thru for the year. Trim back the rampant things that are lopping over the walks, but do not cut off green, growing stems unless you are willing to forgo bloom the next year. Many plants, especially the bulbs like tulips, must store up energy for the next season's bloom by their growth after this year's bloom.

DO SOMETHING DIFFERENT

It is so easy to get into a regular routine of doing things, and the deeper the rut the harder it is to get out. Nothing is more deadly and soul-killing.

If you would keep young in mind and body regardless of your date of birth, try doing something different every day.

If you always have toast and eggs for breakfast, try some pancakes and sausage sometime. If you always sleep till 7 try getting up at 6 sometime, and take a walk around the park.

If you always eat dinner at 6:30 try eating at 6 or 8. If you must have a cocktail before dinner, try something else once.

I like to go out in a storm or very early or very late, because this difference in weather and time makes even familiar places seem different and refreshing.

Keeping the spirit of adventure alive is sometimes rather difficult under modern conditions of living, but by deliberately finding ways to do things differently we can keep ourselves alert and make living much more interesting.

The crowd is not always right. (Sometimes I think it is seldom right.) Try pioneering in new and different ways. It's fun and keeps you young.

If someone had not stepped out and gotten off the beaten path, we would never have progressed — we would more than likely still be monkeys.

S EPTEMBER is the time of ripening, not only of seeds but of all woody growth. The weather may be dry this month, but that is as it should be so that plants are not encouraged to make soft growth that cannot ripen up sufficiently to live thru the cold winter. AFTER the leaves have fallen, which indicates that the plants are dormant for the season, then everything should have a thorough soaking.

❧ Gladiolus should be dug after frost and stacked in shallow boxes with the tops left on until they dry up. They are as easy to store as onions. Cannas should be dug with some earth left around them and kept in a cool, not too moist, spot, like under a greenhouse bench.

❧ Now is a good time to make notes on paper of things that you want to improve another season. When the gardening fever hits you next spring it will probably be too late to move plants. Now is the time to make definite plans for new plants and new arrangements of existing material.

❧ Many perennials should be moved in September. Such rampant growers as Shasta Daisies can be divided now before they crowd out nicer things. Many other perennials have bloomed and may be moved to more appropriate locations. If it becomes necessary to move Peonies, Bleeding Hearts, Rhubarb or Asparagus it should be done in the fall. Some shrubs and evergreens can be moved now if it is necessary and if they are carefully handled. It is much better, however, to wait until they have become dormant. If Tulips, Narcissus and other fall bulbs have been in for several years and need dividing, now is the time to do it. They may be planted right back in their new locations.

❧ New lawns may usually be successfully planted between August 15 and October 15.

❧ Vegetable and perennial tops will soon be dead and may be cut off. Tree leaves will soon begin to fall and lawn clippings will accumulate. Unless full of insects and disease save all these. Use what is necessary to mulch around perennials and shrubs, and pile the surplus in an odd corner for future use. The decomposition of the compost pile will be hastened by keeping it moist, by turning it over every few weeks and by allowing ventilation under the pile thru an old pipe or tile. Proper mulching will do much to correct our two greatest gardening difficulties in the Rocky Mountains: plants drying out in winter, and the lack of humus in our soil.

❧ A little cleaning up now will last all winter. Nothing improves the appearance of a garden more than keeping it neatly raked. Save all leaves and plant tops for the compost heap. A few old dead stems and rubbish look bad, but it is not necessary to keep every single leaf off a lawn or rake everything out of a flower bed. Let the winds scatter and pile a few leaves where they will. Don't forget the few weeds like dandelion, dock, wild lettuce and parsley which have been missed and are now in seed. Digging them out and burning them will prevent a lot of weed seedlings next spring.

❧ The most strenuous work of spading, weeding and watering is now about over. Take time to straighten up your back, look around you and enjoy the results of your season's work. Arrange convenient seats where you can sit and see your garden. Look over the gardens of your friends and neighbors.

T HE KIDS all started to school last month. How about you getting a new book and learning more of the fascinating story of how plants grow?

❧ Sometime this month, the leaves may naturally fall from many of the plants and if necessary they could be moved. For most things, Spring is better, but it is possible to move deciduous plants at any time when they are out of leaf.

❧ Check the Chinese Elm and other trees, evergreens and shrubs for conditions that might cause snow damage if early wet snows should come.

❧ Perennials that are dormant, or almost so, can be moved now, especially if some soil is left around their roots. Peonies, Bleeding Hearts, and such should be moved now, if necessary.

❧ Plant the tulips, narcissus, lilies and other fall bulbs now as soon as they are available. Plant them about 50% deeper than the eastern directions call for.

❧ Don't burn any of the good organic matter that you are now raking up. Compost it all, in an out-of-the-way place. Add a sprinkling of ammonium sulphate to hasten the decomposition.

OCTOBER is clean-up time. Remove the old dead, stems of perennials and annuals, trim the scraggly hedges and edge the lawn around the shrub groups. If gardens are laid out with proper lines and contain a sufficient proportion of the appropriate inanimate features they may be beautiful all the year around, even when no bloom or even green leaves are visible. Neatness is most important when there are no brilliant flowers to catch the eye.

❧ Lawns may be successfully planted any time from the middle of August to the middle of October, in most years. Old lawns may be patched up, also at this time. The days are warm enough to allow the grass to grow, but the nights are cool, making it less difficult to keep the soil moist and weeds are much less of a problem. Prepare the soil thoroughly before seeding and get the best possible seed.

❧ If necessary to mow lawns any more, raise the mower to leave the grass as long as possible, and let the clippings fall whenever possible. This will help to mulch the lawn, tending to keep in the moisture and preventing too sudden changes in soil temperature during our erratic winters. Lawns may need water, several times during the winter, if there are several weeks without much rain or snow.

❧ Heavy frost can be expected at any time now, so bring in the house plants that have been spending the summer out under the shrubs. Trim them or repot them as necessary, and check them for damaging insects.

❧ Another fall job often neglected is the spraying of Dogwood, Snowball and Euonymous just before they drop their leaves. The aphids which do so much damage in the spring are at this time on the surface and easily killed, if you will remember to go after them.

❧ Use the same good judgment in watering now that you have used all summer. A sudden change from watering every other day to no water at all is not good for plants. They should not be stimulated into rank growth by watering late in fall, but after they are dormant they should be checked at least once a month (all winter) to be sure that they have moist soil around their roots. A large percentage of our "winterkill" in the Rocky Mountain area is caused by our hot winter sun drawing moisture from plants which have not sufficient water in the soil to replace the loss. Of course, it is useless to pour water on soil which is already frozen. The time to water THOROUGHLY is before the ground is frozen.

❧ Tender plants may need some shade to prevent winter burn. Wrap or shade the southwest side of small Mountainash, Linden or Oaks. Roses may be left until after Christmas and then use old evergreen boughs to shade them. Small White Fir or White Pine would benefit from a partial shade on the south side. Raspberries will need covering when they are dormant.

❧ Because the leaves and flowers are all gone is no reason to think that there is no beauty left in growing things. Now is when we should enjoy the evergreens, the bright berries which still persist, the plants with bright colored stems and the varied forms of the bare trees and shrubs. Learn to know the different trees from their bare outlines against the sky. It is an interesting game.

G ET things ready for winter now and remember you do not cover to keep things warm, but to keep them cold, and you wrap or shade to keep the hot, dry winter air from drying things out. Tender-barked and newly transplanted trees should be wrapped, perennials mulched and especially tender things shaded.

WHAT IS WINTER KILL?

When a plant is dead or damaged in the spring, we often blame it on "winter kill." The term covers a multitude of things but there is really little damage from just the winter's cold, since many plants which survive in Canada do not survive here.

Here in the Rocky Mountains, we have erratic Falls, when plants are induced to grow vigorously by unseasonably warm weather and abundant moisture. Then suddenly the tender growth is killed by a cold spell. Actually, the greatest amount of kill comes because of frequent sunny days which we often have during the winter. The air is dry, the sun is hot, and there is little rain or snow to supply moisture. This condition evaporates the water from plants at a time when they are unable to replace it.

Some damage happens in the spring after the plant has gone through the difficulties of winter. In February or March, along will come a week of nice warm spring-like weather, the plants, as well as we humans, are fooled into thinking it is time to send out leaves or discard the "longies." Then, before we know it, winter is back in full force. This may happen two or three times before really warm spring weather settles down.

In the early days, many people thought this fickle climatic condition would prevent us from growing a great variety of plants. We now know, however, that we can develop resistance to these conditions and bring in plants from other parts of the world which are accustomed to such environment. If we recognize Mother Nature's idiosyncrasies and prepare for them, we can grow fine things here. And this unpredictable weather simply adds zest to living in this Rocky Mountain country.

THERE is little danger now of inducing soft growth by watering, and it is very important that all plants go into winter with moist soil around their roots. A THOROUGH soaking now may hold them until spring, but if the weather continues open and there is bright sunshine for several weeks, there may be need of additional watering for the more shallow rooted plants. Soak things until the soil is wet to their farthest roots. This may be 8 inches for lawns, 15 inches for perennials, 3 feet for shrubs or 6 feet for trees, depending on soil conditions and variety of plants. The only way that you can be sure that the soil is wet is to prospect in a few places and see.

❧ Any work necessary on trees can be done now. With leaves off it is a little easier to work in trees. Many tree men prefer to leave the work on Maples, Birch and Walnut until they are in leaf, as they may bleed a little when cuts are made during their dormant period.

❧ Irregular stems may be trimmed up on the shrubs, but the bulk of trimming on shrubs should be done just after they bloom so that the blooming wood for the next year is not removed. Hedges should have a final haircut and lawn edges may have a trimming to hold them until spring.

❧ Even though the daily routine of water-cultivate-spray-weed is over, a garden may be kept attractive by just a little neatness.

❧ This "in between" time is just right for those repair jobs that you could never find time for when the routine of garden chores took every spare minute. The fence may need paint, the walk may need leveling, the sunken spot in the lawn may need raising or the gate latch need adjusting. These warm sunny days are just the time to do it.

❧ You have long envied your neighbor's outdoor fireplace, platform or rock garden. You have thought that sometime you would build a trellis against that bare garage wall or fix a little ornamental fountain in the far corner of the garden. Now is the time to do the work on those inanimate things. Look around in the really nice gardens and see how great a part is played by the architectural features. Flowers make a short splurge in summer, leaves decorate the plants for a still longer period, but a garden may be interesting and beautiful all the year thru if the design and inanimate features are well planned.

❧ Then as the occasional "bad" days come along in the fall and winter it is a good time to decide on some phase of gardening that you would like to know more about. Gardening opens up such a vast field of allied arts and sciences. You would like to know more about the associations of plants and insects, more about how fertilizers work, more about the why of plant growth, more about historic gardens or how to lay out a good garden. Select books from those recommended elsewhere in this book and lay out a course of reading that will give you more pleasure in your garden next year.

❧ When the cold weather comes and the snows cover everything remember the birds. Have cornstalk shelters erected for the ground feeders, and shelters and feeding stations in the trees for other birds. The birds will soon find it out if suitable food is regularly available.

December . . . BRING YOUR GARDEN INDOORS

W INTER protection is the keynote of garden work in December. When the cause of most of our winterkill is understood to be our hot winter sun and dry air, it is then apparent that our chief concerns should be to see that the ground around all plants is sufficiently wet before it freezes up and that tender barked trees, tender evergreens or borderline shrubs have some shading from the severe southwest sun.

❧ Check over the stored bulbs once or twice this month. Most of these bulbs will keep best at a temperature around 40-45. Gladiolus need little moisture, Cannas will almost take care of themselves if some soil is left around them, but Dahlias are rather particular as to temperature and moisture. If they show signs of shriveling when inspected, a moist sack thrown over them will help. If they show mould or rot they may be too wet and if they sprout they may be both too moist and too warm.

❧ While you are checking things, look over the house plants again for signs of the start of aphids, spidermites, scale, thrip or mealybug. Again, an ounce of prevention is surely worth many pounds of cure.

❧ Each rose grower has individual methods of protecting his tender roses but the method of hilling up soil around them to a distance of six inches or so seems to give rather universal satisfaction. This should be done between the time that the leaves fall and the ground freezes (which in some seasons is a difficult period to determine).

❧ Shrubs and trees which have low hanging limbs likely to interfere with walks when heavily laden with snow should be taken care of now. This may prevent some breakage to the tree and save someone's temper on a crisp snowy morning. Tall, slim junipers should be checked to see if they might be braced back to a building or another tree to prevent their being bowed down or broken by heavy snow.

❧ One of the most important garden operations of the season may be done while plants are dormant and weather is still fairly warm. This is the dormant spray for the control of scale insects and control of certain other spiders, galls or aphids. Lime-sulphur or miscible oil is commonly used and is a technical job requiring careful mixture and application by adequate equipment if the trees are at all large.

❧ Now that the active growing season is over landscape men are available to do the extensive jobs of removing crowded or dead trees and to do the thorough jobs of trimming and caring for shade trees. It is recommended that Maples, Birch and Walnut trees not be trimmed until they are in leaf again as they are inclined to "bleed" rather badly when trimmed during their dormant period.

❧ When the plants outside in the garden are dormant our attention is directed to the plants that we are able to bring indoors. At the holiday season, these bright spots of green and color are especially appreciated. Success with these plants depends very largely on careful attention to the proper soil to pot them in, to careful watering and regulation of the humidity in the air. If more than the succulents and hardiest plants are attempted it is well to provide additional humidity by having a tea-kettle on a stove register or electric plate a few hours of the day at least.

❧ Last year, as you worked with your plants in the garden did you not often wish that you knew more about the many things concerned with horticulture? Now is the time to look up books and bulletins on the new insecticides, the latest advances in fertilizers, and the new varieties of your favorite plant and the principles of landscape design.

❧ Horticulturists should not have to worry long over their Christmas lists for other gardeners. Bulbs, seeds, tools and books offer unlimited possibilities. And most any good nurseryman will arrange for you to give a Christmas order for those plants which must be moved in spring. Garden magazines are always welcome.

❧ Whenever you have a suitable tree, it is a fine thing to decorate a living tree for Christmas. Many plant a Spruce or Fir in a suitable location for that purpose. A well decorated outdoor Christmas tree gives pleasure to many people going by and helps to prevent the overcutting of forest trees for temporary indoor use.

❧ How about extending the joys of growing things into the winter by planting evergreen window boxes. Small Spruce, Fir, Juniper, Pine, Myrtle, English Ivy and Euonymus are suitable for this. Liven them up with stems of bright berries from shrubs and trees. These can be renewed occasionally.

Index

B

D

Daffodil, 124, 172
Dahlia, 112, *115*, 119, 120, 121,
    126, 127, 148, 153, 222
Daisy, 174, 177
  Blue-eyed, 126
  Painted, 112, 114, 119, 120, 121, 147
  Shasta, *114*, 119, 120, 121
Dandelion, 180, 239, *241*
Daylily, 112, *116*, 119, 120, 121, 144, 151
Delphinium, 112, *115*, 120, 121, 148,
    151, 178, 222
Desert Broom, 152
Desert Candle, *115*, 119, 120, 121
Desert Willow, 152
Design, 51-54
Desmodium, 89, 101, 153
Deutzia, 87, 152
Devils-Walkingstick, 86, 101, 153
Dianthus, 112, *115*, 148, 155, 171
Dicentra, *115*, 119, 120, 121, 144
Dictamnus, 115, 144
Didiscus, 126
Dieffenbachia, 141
Digitalis, 115, 144
Dill, 162
Dimorphotheca, 126
Dirt or Soil, 209
Diseases, *230*, 235
  Lists of, 232
  Of Lawns, 136, 231
  Plants Damaged by 222, 230
Disporum trachycarpum, 179
Dodecatheon radicatum, 172, 180
Dogtooth violet, 179
Dogwood, 102, 143, 148, 152, 165, 222
  Flowering, 151
  Gray, *87*, 101, 153
  Redosier, 150
  Redtwig, 101, 102, 168
  Variegated, 87
  Yellowtwig, 101
Dolgo Crabapple, 79
Dominating Theme, 16
Dormant Sprays, 234
Douglasfir, 65, *66*, 143, 147, 150, 152, 222
Downy Hawthorn, 78
Dracaena, 139
Drainage, 260
Dutch Bulbs, 123
Dutch Elm Disease, 222, *233*
Dwarfindigo Amorpha, 85
Dwarf Ninebark, 91, 101, 168
Dwarf Peashrub, 86, 102
Dwarf Willow, 97, 101

E

Earthworms, 225
Earwigs, 226
Earworm, Corn, 225
Easter Lily, 142
Eating in garden, 36, 50
Echinops, *115*, 119, 120, 121, 147
Elaegnus angustifolia, 79, 88
Elderberry, 101, 102, 143, 148, 164, 165
  American, 97
  Bunchberry, *97*, 150
  Mexican, 152
Elephant Ears, 139
Eley Crabapple, 79
Elm,
  American, *76*, 147, 150, 152, 222
  Augustine Ascending, 76
  Chinese, 78, 147, 150, 152
  English, 77, 153
  Moline, 53
  Siberian (Chinese), *78*, 147, 150, 167
Elm Bark Beetles, 222, *226*
Engelmann Ivy,, 102
Engelmann Spruce, *66*, 150
Engelmann Virginia Creeper, 103, *106*, 147
English Elm, 77, 153
English Hawthorn, 79, 83
English Ivy, 68, 103, *105*, 141, 144, 155
English Oak, 76
Epilobium angustifolium, 178
Epimedium, 171, 172
Eremurus, 115
Erigeron, sp., 171, 177

Erinus alpinus, 171, 172
Eriogonum, 177
  effusium, 177
  umbellatum, 177
Erodium cicutarium, 177
Eryngium, 115, 121
Erysimum asperum, 178
Erythronium parviflorum, 179
Euonymus, 101, 102, 153, 165, 222
  alatus, *88*, 153
  atropurpurea, 88, 143, 167
  europeus, *82*, 88, 167
  fortunei radicans, 68
  fortunei vegetus, 68
  kewensis, 68
  minimus, 68, 104, 144
  Wahoo, *88*, 143
  Winged, *88*, 101, 143, 168
  Wintercreeper, 68, 103, *105*, 144, 155
Eupatorium masculatum, 179
Euphorbia albomarginata, 126, 153, 178
European Alder, 80
European Beech, 80
European Cotoneaster, 101
European Euonymus, 82
European Hornbeam, 80
European Linden, 76
European Mountainash, 80
Eustoma andrewsi, 180
Evening Primrose, *117*, 119, 120, 121
Evergreens, 65
  For Arkansas Valley, 153
  Broadleaf, 68, 144
  For Plains, 146, 147
  For Mountains, 150
  For Shady Places, 143
  For Southwest, 151, 152
  Lists by sizes, 66
Exochorda racemosa, 88

F

Fagus sylvatica, 80
Fairybell, 151, 179
Fairy Ring Fungus, 222
Fairy Trumpet, 178
Fall, Bulbs, 123
Fall Color, 163
Fallugia paradoxa, 88
False Dragonhead, *118*, 119, 120
False Indigo (Amorpha), 85
False Indigo (Baptisia), 112, 120
False Mallow, 177
Falsespirea
  Smooth tree, 97
  Ural, 97
Fences, 186, 193, 195
Fennel, 163
Fernbush, 92
Ferns, 48, 141, 143, 173
  Asparagus, 139
  Bracken, 173
  Care and kinds, 173
  Christmas, 173
  Cinnamon, 173
  Lady, 144, 173
  Maidenhair, 144, 173
  Male, 144, 173
  Ostrich, 144, 173
  Rock, 144, 173, 175
  Wood, 173
Fertilizers, 204, 207, 208, 209
Fibreglass Screens, 189, 197
Ficus, 141
Figs, 141, 152
Filbert, beaked, 87, 150
Fir, 222
  Alpine, 65, *66*, 150
  White, 65, *66*, 143, 150, 152
Fire-blight, 222, *233*
Fireplaces, 184, 196
Firethorn, *68*, 144, 152, 153
Fireweed, 178
  Mexican, 241
Fiveleaf Aralia, 101
Flagstone, 53-55, *182-185*, 192
Flax, Blue, 112, *117*, 119, 120, 147, 177
Fleabeetles, 222, *226*
Fleahoppers, 223, *226*
Flies, 226
Floribunda Roses, 102, 153

What appears to be new is simply a reshuffling of old things and their recombination in a different form. All "new" ideas have been influenced by old ideas from various sources.

My interest in the wonders and workings of Nature, particularly of plant life, have been inspired by a few of those rare souls, the independent and original thinkers; first of all my Mother who helped me identify my first wildflowers, and later such people as M. Walter Pesman, C. F. Leach and Bob Niedrach. No one can have lived without having influenced some one else and have left the world a little better or worse for their having lived. In this way, at least, we are all immortal.

There is no ONE way to design—it grows out of ALL the requirements—ALL the physical conditions—PLUS the creative imagination working with these functional bases.

There is no such thing as "Modern" vs. "Traditional" etc. It is mostly good sense, taste, values, understanding and creative projection; and also DARING to take a step beyond regardless of the political consequences. I have seen as many sickly copies of "Nature" as I have copies of "Modern", "Colonial" etc.

Design is not "copying", "adapting" etc.; it is approaching the problem with humility—an open mind—and trying to break through with a natural and beautiful solution.   DAN KILEY, *Architect and Planner.*

The ever-present mountains and deserts do affect our landscape planning.